D1554158

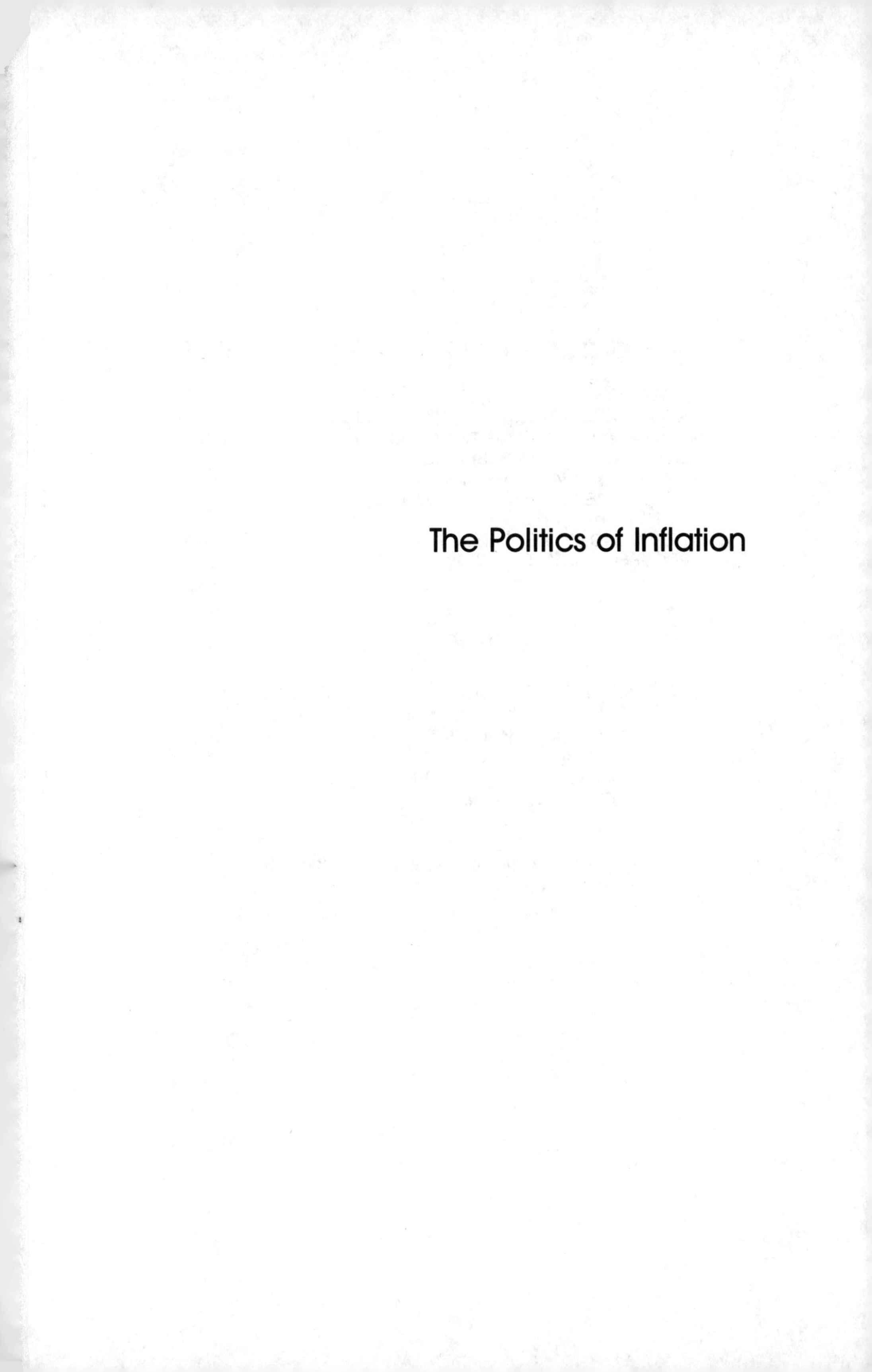

The Politics of Inflation

The Politics of Inflation
A Comparative Analysis

Edited by
Richard Medley

Published in cooperation with the Committee on Atlantic Studies

Pergamon Press
NEW YORK • OXFORD • TORONTO • SYDNEY • PARIS • FRANKFURT

Pergamon Press Offices:

U.S.A.	Pergamon Press Inc., Maxwell House, Fairview Park, Elmsford, New York 10523, U.S.A.
U.K.	Pergamon Press Ltd., Headington Hill Hall, Oxford OX3 0BW, England
CANADA	Pergamon Press Canada Ltd., Suite 104, 150 Consumers Road, Willowdale, Ontario M2J 1P9, Canada
AUSTRALIA	Pergamon Press (Aust.) Pty. Ltd., P.O. Box 544, Potts Point, NSW 2011, Australia
FRANCE	Pergamon Press SARL, 24 rue des Ecoles, 75240 Paris, Cedex 05, France
FEDERAL REPUBLIC OF GERMANY	Pergamon Press GmbH, Hammerweg 6 6242 Kronberg/Taunus, Federal Republic of Germany

Library of Congress Cataloging in Publication Data
Main entry under title:

The Politics of inflation.

(Pergamon policy studies on international politics)
"Based, in part, on the tenth annual conference of the Committee on Atlantic Studies held at the Free University of Berlin, Germany, in September 1978"--Foreword.
Includes index.
Contents: Inflation, recession, and the political process / Leon Lindberg --Economic sectors and inflationary policies / James R. Kurth -- Europe and the United States : the transatlantic aspects of inflation / Susan Strange -- [etc.]
1. Inflation (Finance)--Addresses, essays, lectures. 2. Wage-price policy--Addresses, essays, lectures. 3. Economic policy--Addresses essays, lectures. I. Medley, Richard. II. Committee on Atlantic Studies. III. Series.
HG229.P65 1981 3324'1 81-10719
ISBN 0-08-024625-7 AACR2

Printed in the United States of America

Contents

Foreword

Founded in 1964, the Committee on Atlantic Studies is an international group of approximately 50 scholars from Europe and North America who are dedicated to generating and improving scholarly dialogues on issues of common concern to the Atlantic Nations. The annual colloquia, held alternately in Europe and in North America, are attended by both Committee members and invited guests.

The idea for this volume originated from the Tenth Annual Conference of the Committee on Atlantic Studies held at the Free University of Berlin in September, 1978. About 30 academics from Europe and the United States attended the meeting, and thanks to the efforts of our host, Professor Helmut Wagner of the Otto Suhr Institute of Political Science, the Free University proved to be a stimulating environment.

The coordination of domestic and foreign economic policies by members of the Atlantic world to deal with persistent inflation is an important topic of discussion for both policymakers and scholars, and I hope that this volume will contribute to a constructive, transnational dialogue.

Charles R. Foster
Executive Secretary
Committee on Atlantic Studies

Introduction

Persistent and accelerating, inflation has come to command the attention of academics and policymakers alike during the last decade. It has gone a long way toward eroding faith in Keynesian policies and analytic methods, and it has not responded to the simplistic and politically naive prescriptions of monetarists. In some countries, like Britain, inflation is primarily a problem arising through the economic sector via traditional wage-price spirals. In other countries, inflation has become imbedded through a combination of exogenous commodity shocks and political stalemate. But in all countries we see a gradual movement toward indexation as each individual attempts to secure his economic standing in the future by betting on continued inflation. This volume's emphasis is on both the domestic and international causes leading to each country's level and duration of inflation. It also brings together the political and economic considerations in one place.

It should be clear that the prescriptions of classical or neo-classical economics, whereby the public weal is benefitted through the individual pursuit of private gain, are rendered less compelling when private gain is maximized by actions that fuel inefficient economic responses. Who can blame the worker for demanding wage increases that take feared inflation rates into account, or the capitalist who chooses to invest in short-term commodities speculation rather than long-term plant and machinery purchases when inflation is joined by economic stagnation? Yet in relatively slack economies, like those of the last few years, these cost push elements account for the greatest part of inflation pressures.

*The editor wishes to thank Charles Foster of the Atlantic Committee, for his help in arranging many of these articles. None of the views in this volume necessarily represent the opinion of the U.S. House of Representatives Committee on Banking, Finance and Urban Affairs, or any of its members or staff.

The opening chapter of this volume seeks to place these problems in the framework of a few questions that the other contributions help to illuminate. Professor Lindberg asks three questions central to the problem of dealing with the economic forces of inflation within the parameters of political reality:

1. Why do (or don't) governments help structure institutional characteristics of wage and price setting?
2. Why do (or don't) governments innovate in managing the different sectors and regions within their economies?
3. Why do (or don't) governments intervene forcibly to reduce or moderate the impact of the inequalities of income and wealth?

The chapters in this book deal primarily with these three questions, but with different emphasis on the mix of questions. One point which this volume makes clearly is that inflation is an international commodity. Inflation within each country is affected by what other countries do, and the environment of moderately free trade constrains the set of actions available to one country in dealing with its domestic economic problems.

Professor Kurth's chapter begins to answer some of Lindberg's questions by examining specific theories about the political and economic arrangements within countries that help to explain why some countries have proven susceptible to triple-digit inflation, while others have managed to continue with double or single-digit price rises for decades. His analysis of the various internal political and economic blocs which have an interest in promoting inflation, and those which have an interest in slowing inflation, provide a provocative cross-national study of inflation politics.

Professor Strange addresses the transnational organization of currencies designed to smooth out inflation and speculation-related gyrations of exchange rates since the breakdown of the Bretton Woods agreement. This collection of European currencies, first known as the "snake," then formalized into the European Monetary System, was an attempt to stabilize the participating countries' currencies against the dollar. One curious occurrence is that the German Mark has fallen from the top of the EMS range to the bottom in the two years since EMS was formed. Professor Strange seeks to explain the reasons for forming EMS and the political and economic causes of its less than complete success.

Professor Stallings deals with another international organization of great concern to countries as they battle with recurring inflation. The International Monetary Fund (IMF) has gained a reputation as a great financial help to troubled nations, but the strict and, sometimes draconian, economic policies it requires of a country seeking its help has produced a great deal of anger and controversy in recipient countries. Professor Stallings adds substantially to the debate about the IMF's function by a case analysis of intervention in Britain, Portugal, and Italy. Her conclusions indicate that IMF policy may do nothing to calm inflationary flames – at least in more developed countries with strong left-wing labor organizations. She also presents a clear and compelling analysis of the prevailing economic theory at IMF headquarters, which she terms "eclectic monetarism."

The chapters on specific countries are divided into two sets, with the first three concentrating on major industrial western economies, specifically the United States, England, and Germany. England and the United States have internal, sometimes largely political, developments to blame for the largest share of their inflation problems. Catherine Hill offers a thorough analysis of the political and economic backing and filling which brought England to its economic knees before the advent of Margaret Thatcher, and of the, so far, unfavorable results of Mrs. Thatcher's experiments with monetarism and recession. The chapter on the United States' inflation problems is a solid summary and collection of evidence in favor of the theory of political business cycles, which has received a great deal of attention in the last few years. The evidence presented here indicates the major problems that presidential-type democracies have in forming and carrying out long-range economic plans, as well as the reasonable success presidents have had at manipulating the short-term economic conditions to suit their electoral goals.

Germany has been largely successful in its battle against inflation during the last decade. It is moving, however, toward more serious economic difficulties in the eighties, largely as a result of international pressure from the United States and other major OECD countries. Part of its current balance of payments deficit – highly unusual in post-war Germany – results from the government's decision to stimulate its economy, thus acceding to nearly a decade of OECD pressure to act as the Western world's "locomotive." The theory here is that Germany's strength would provide markets for its weaker sisters, and pull the train of capitalism out of its mid-seventies funk. Other countries did not respond according to theory, and Germany was hit with decreasing exports and increasing import prices creating a balance of payments problem that was exacerbated by the 1979 oil shock. On top of this, the D-Mark's new status as the free world's second largest reserve currency has spawned a heated political and economic struggle as the German Central Bank seeks to keep capital from streaming out of the country in search of higher interest rates, primarily in Britain and the United States. The Bundesbank's primary weapon is to maintain high interest rates, but this tightens liquidity at a time of growing domestic recession that would normally dictate a looser monetary policy.

The final two chapters in this volume present studies of inflation and political problems in two transitional economies of Latin heritage – Argentina and Spain. Both of these countries have had well publicized political and economic difficulties over the last decade, but they are not countries about which much is generally known by non-Latin specialists. The clear recapitulations of events in these chapters gives us a better feel for the universal nature of inflation as an economic and political problem in the modern world.

This volume offers a variety of perspectives on the interrelated problems of inflation and political change. Its purpose is largely expository, seeking to raise questions and provide information about the generation of inflation that takes into account national and international occurrences, presenting them in one forum. The two transnational organizations studied having some specific concern with curbing inflation – or at least with the effects of inflation – give us insight into the problems of simplistic, imposed cures that do not take full account of both these national and international sources of inflation.

Richard Medley
Washington, D.C.

1 Inflation, Recession, and the Political Process: Challenges to Theory and Practice

Leon Lindberg

INTRODUCTION

This chapter explores some aspects of the interplay among economic and political systems and processes as these relate to macroeconomic fluctuations in prices, employment and income, and stabilization policy performance. I am especially interested in the post-1968 period which has seen an acceleration of inflation rates, simultaneous high levels of unemployment, mounting evidence that traditional instruments of fiscal and monetary policy no longer produce anticipated results, and growing concern that economic stability has become unachievable within the framework of a capitalist economy and a democratic political system (Jay, 1977; Brittan, 1977; Buchanan and Wagner, 1977; Hirsch, 1976; Bell, 1976; and many others).

In order to explore political-economic interactions we must go beyond conventional economic analysis which is typically limited to identifying the sources(1) of inflation or unemployment in wage and price determination and monetary and fiscal policies. We must also probe the socio-political environment in which wages are formed, changing institutions and economic structures and the politics of both the expenditure and the revenue sides of the budget. We must also take account of unintended consequences of policies, for example, the conventional deflationary "medicine," rather than lowering expectations may intensify long-term inflationary pressures by increasing union militancy, polarizing groups and eroding government legitimacy, setting off a "politics of compensatory claims" as public expectations of the economy are systematically frustrated, thus institutionalizing "stop-go" economic policies and a tendency toward protracted economic stagnation (Ruggles, 1976; Lindberg and Hammarlund, 1976) and a fiscal crisis (O'Connor, 1973).

I limit my analysis here to the inflation – stabilization process within nations. This does not deny that inflation may often be imported.

Indeed, there is every reason to anticipate that destabilizing shocks from abroad (Lindbeck, 1976; Calmfors, 1977) and from the supply-side (Muller, 1977; Chase, 1975; Lindberg, 1976) generally may become endemic, and that these will greatly complicate stabilization policy. Double-digit (and worse) inflation rates seem to be associated with relative exposure to sudden shocks or to a generalized dependency on the international economy (Maier, 1977). Furthermore, such inflations are much more likely to set in train a competitive process in which groups perceive a need to act decisively to defend their living standards and income shares (Jackson, Turner and Wilkinson, 1972), and have a "much stronger tendency to conserve their momentum (Pazos, 1977).

Thus, the variable capacity of countries to absorb "exogenous" shocks without setting off an internal inflationary cycle will be critical. This is especially the case where changes in the relative prices of fuel, food, and other commodities redistribute income from country to country, or group to group. But it is also true where inflation rates among close trading partners vary rapidly over time. Such shifts no doubt call for great flexibility in the part of government policy as well as in the expectations of mutual understandings of labor and business. Even Sweden, with one of the most enviable records in these dimensions appears to have stumbled badly in the last few years (Calmfors, 1977; Business Week, June 13, 1977).

The facts of international interdependence and the relative weights of different national economies in the global system will limit our ability to explain differences in inflation levels and rates between countries and within countries over time. Some economists argue that most governments have so little autonomous policy control that going into their internal politics of inflation-stabilization does little but add "adventitious detail." Others raise the unit of analysis problem by arguing that the variance of inflation rates among countries is no greater than the variability of inflation rates among regions of any given country.

These criticisms are useful corrections, but surely go too far. There are "homegrown," internally-generated inflations that have little to do with relative exposure to international factors. In some countries, imported inflationary shocks or pressures are dampened, while in others they set off wage-price cycles and ever-accelerating rates of inflation. And clearly, governments seem to vary widely in their ability to manage roughly equivalent imports of inflation and to contain the dynamics of wage and price formation and the "public household" so as to assure a more or less politically acceptable balance among changes in prices, employment, and real income.

ENDOGENIZING POLITICS

It is now widely accepted that macroeconomic fluctuations (inflation, unemployment, stagflation) involve complex socio-political as well as economic forces and processes. The real argument is over how these are to be related in the development of theory and policy. Assar Lindbeck in his paper "Stabilization Policy in Open Economies with Endogenous Politicians" argues that contemporary macroeconomic fluctuations must be seen in the context of "a complicated interaction between market forces and government behavior, i.e., as an interplay between the economic and the political systems." Instabilities and imperfections in the market system render aggregate demand management "insufficient for a successful stabilization policy." The proper functioning of these policy instruments require their supplementation with selective microeconomic intervention on both the demand and supply sides. But this requires institutional changes in the economic system and presupposes reforming and redesigning the political-administrative system as well. "(We) have two interacting systems, the political and the economic, we cannot control one with the other, but we must try to redesign them both to improve the stability of each."

Another argument linking political and economic systems is made by Buchanan and Wagner (1977) (though from a rather different place in the ideological spectrum):

> The criteria for good (economic) theory are necessarily related to the political institutions of the society. . . .This necessary linkage or interdependence between the basic political structure of a society and the economic theory of policy has never been properly recognized by economists, despite its elementary logic and its overwhelming empirical apparency (4-5).
>
> Even if we accept the Keynesian story about the functioning of our economic order, democratic political pressures are likely to generate an assymetrical application of the Keynesian prescriptions. . . .(T)he Keynesian destruction of the balanced budget constraint is likely to produce a bias toward budget deficits, monetary expansion, and public sector growth. Politicians naturally want to spend and avoid taxing. The elimination of the balanced-budget constraint enables politicians to give fuller expression to these quite natural sentiments.
>
> Money creation falsifies the signals that operate within the economy. In consequence, labor and capital move into employments where they cannot be sustained without increasing inflation. The false signals also reduce the informational content of such devices as standard accounting practices, thereby increasing the errors in decision-making that are made by the participants in the economic process (182-83).

Finally, and still on the same general theme, Alfred Kahn (1975) observes that:

> It remains true that there can be no inflation that is not validated by public policy. And that consequently, it is faulty governmental policy that is, in a sense, 'responsible' for all inflation. But if that statement is true, it is also vapid. The

> 'government' is not a deus ex machina, ' exogenous' to the economic procress. It is part of the process, and its decisions are themselves molded by the private economic interest it is supposed to control. . . .The resistance of aggregate government taxes and expenditures to macroeconomic considerations, particularly to the requirements for controlling inflation, is explicable in precisely the same terms as the resistance of private price and wage policies. . . .(When) we attribute inflation to the actions by which private parties with economic power lay claim to the national product – in such a way that the sum total of those claims exceeds the capacity of the economy – we should obviously include among the methods for asserting those claims, not only the administration of wages and prices, but the exertion of influence over government outlays, taxes, tax preferences, and transfers. The government is not external to the process by which private power is exerted to produce inflation. It is part of that process (271-72).

Most neo-classical economists (both Keynesians and monetarists) working in this area and, unfortunately, most political scientists as well, approach the problem of economic-political interactions with overly simplified – even naive – models of both the economy and the polity. In my view, we need to develop models and hypotheses that do much greater justice to the dynamic institutional and cultural contexts which guide and constrain economic and political life. Some progress in the direction of more appropriate economic models can be seen in the work of so-called "post-Keynesian" economists (Eichner, Minsky, Cornwall, Robinson), institutional economists (Peterson, Piore, Dunlop, Solo, Muller), and the Marxists (O'Connor, Kalecki). This chapter seeks to make a modest contribution on the political side. As I see it, the most promising contribution of a political scientist in this area will be to systematically explore the proposition that the nature, rates, and distributional consequences of macroeconomic fluctuations are to a large degree some complex function of the environing political structures and processes, including the established pattern of public-private sector relations. This implies that the interactions among economic agents that produce or amplify inflation, the actions of fiscal and monetary authorities, and the effectiveness of stabilization policy instruments will vary systematically with such factors as interest and class configurations, the cumulative effects of past policies, and the residue of past grievances, coalition alignments, the dynamics of coalition formation, and institutional arrangements in business, labor, and government, and prevailing ideologies and value systems.

Such an inquiry could generate findings of relevance to wide-ranging policy. Laidler and Parkin (1975) note that saying new things about the design of policy awaits an as yet unwritten literature on the "political economy of inflation," which will explain why governments do what they do or don't do what they should do. "(I)f we do not know why governments generate (or permit) inflation, how can we produce arguments that might persuade them to act against it?"(797) I would extend the list of puzzles to include at least:

1. Why governments do or don't, can or can't, act effectively to help structure the institutional characteristics of wage and price setting and the decision priorities of large corporations and trade unions so as to increase the probabilities of achieving restraint and 'improving' the inflation-unemployment tradeoff.
2. Why they do or don't, can or can't, innovate in the area of selective or semi-selective (rather than global) management of different sectors and regions and of such broad components of demand and supply as private consumption, fixed business investment, inventory investment, house-building, etc. (Lindbeck, 1976)
3. Why governments do not, or are not, able to intervene more forcefully to reduce or significantly moderate the impact of the inequalities of income and wealth, access to services and amenities, exposure to economic insecurity and disamenities that feed the inflationary process.

Although we should expect research of this kind to produce findings that bear on leveragable variables and that might generate concrete policy proposals, the main contribution is likely to be in clarifying the political and social costs of various policies and policy configurations and extending our understanding of structural constraints and constants on policy change as these are determined by historical and cultural factors. These are of equal importance for they will help define the longer term consequences of short-term stabilization policy choices and help explain the limitations on the utilization of various policy instruments and the probable distortions they will produce if manipulated or selected. It may also be possible to venture some generalizations as to what kinds of institutional arrangements are most likely to be able to cope with various kinds of inflationary pressures within the constraints prevailing in any particular country, as well as to indicate very generally what kind of "price" will probably be necessary in order to achieve and implement them.

THE INFLATION-STABILIZATION PROCESS

I will take as a starting point the view of the inflation-stabilization process held by various schools of conventional economic analysis. I do not intend to join debates among proponents of demand-pull, cost-push, quantity-theory, or transmission mechanisms as _the_ essence of the inflation process. These debates seem a bit arid, and the competing theories often strike me as tautological. Furthermore, one competing theory can generally be "rationalized" in terms of another (see Hibbs, 1977; also frequent examples in Trevithick and Mulvey, 1976). Consistency with _a priori_ theoretical assumptions, symmetry with desired or preferred policy consequences as these affect particular groups, reducability to a relatively restricted view of "empirical testing," the goal of a "universalistic" theory of inflation, seem to dominate much of the debate. Confrontations with complexity of interacting factors, the pervasive influence of lags and anticipations that make it difficult to separate cause from effect, ambiguities as to which way the causal arrow runs, seem all too often "resolved" by appeals to "theoretical consistency" or the goals of elegance, parsimony, and rigor. The various arguments will thus be taken as a source of hypotheses to explore, to deepen and enrich, and to specify historically and contextually.

I assume that all contemporary inflations have some elements of demand-pull, cost-push, group struggle, excess money-creation, exogenous shocks, etc. The interesting task is not to defend one or another a priori theoretical posture but to learn more about what lies behind the proximate sources of inflation, what are the circumstances and mechanisms of interaction among sources and causes, how and why the relative importance of a factor, or a cycle of interaction, or a cumulative feedback pattern varies from one time period and sociopolitical setting to another. All societies are subject to transmission effects from abroad, but there are factors other than economic ones that determine their relative vulnerability to them. All advanced capitalist societies with democratic regimes have administered prices and wages, but these are more inflationary and disruptive of government macroeconomic policies in some countries than in others. Similarly, all such societies seem to be experiencing a secular increase in the role of the public sector, the size of public expenditures relative to GNP, and the share of transfer payments to earned income or nonmarketed to marketed production. But they differ systematically in the extent to which this phenomenon can be attributed to the greed, cowardice, or idealism of entrepreneurial politicians and their bureaucratic allies, the struggle between the middle class and the working class, the myopicness of voters, the profitability and accumulation requirements of capital, the relative importance of "depression memory," "luxury goods," and concentrated versus general benefits. They also differ widely in the extent to which these changes in the role of government can be financed in noninflationary ways (and in the levels of expenditure that are presumed to be inflationary), and in the impact of expenditure programs on the investment process. All advanced capitalist democracies presumably dispose of the same battery of economic stabilization policy instruments, but they vary widely not only in their preference for one or another instrument, but in their capacities to make use of their chosen instruments in a coherent and coordinated fashion, and in the impact government policy has upon the decision-making behavior of wage-setting, price-setting, and investing economic agents.

Answers to these kinds of questions are also likely to be of greater interest and relevance to the policymaker. The important thing for him or her will not be theoretical consistency or elegance of formulation, or parsimony and generality of formulation, but rather the specific social and historical background, and the institutional contexts and complex internal considerations which influence decisions made by the complex organizations that dominate the labor market and the determination of public policies. (See Dunlop, 1977, and his characterization of U.S. economic research on unemployment and wage inflation, wage and price standards, human capital and manpower programs, and industrial relations, as "almost totally irrelevant to important policy problems confronting decision-makers.") As Peterson (1977) has argued, "to be effective, policy must reckon with the milieu within which it is expected to operate." (See also Lindbeck, 1975, pp. 242-43.) It is not useful to simply argue "that a proposal may be correct, economically, but that it won't work politically." Or that "economically sound advice" might produce "regrettable" political and social consequences!

Figure 1.1 offers a composite flow chart representation of the inflation-stabilization process which enables one to locate, juxtapose, and compare competing "theories." The "model" seeks to relate economic and "non-economic" variables, but the effort is only preliminary. A satisfactory political-economy model would have to find a way of combining and relating flows, decisions (based on threshold or "balance sheet" functions), and structures. It would also have to incorporate and integrate international transmission mechanism (flows, decisions, structures). (For another early effort, see Lindberg and Hammarlund, 1976.) The basic form of the figure (which borrows extensively from Bowen, 1960) follows the main events that make up the Phillips curve or inflation – unemployment dilemma model. These events are identified beginning on the center left of the figure in upper case letters and are sequentially linked by double-shafted arrows. Thus, following the upper-branch first, a wage determination process that produces wage increases more rapidly than can be matched by improvements in labor productivity will put upward pressure on unit labor costs and unit total costs, and these higher costs will be mediated through the price determination process into upward pressure on prices. The increased level of money wages also affects aggregate money incomes (the lower branch) and will increase aggregate demand to the extent that the money supply increases as well. This higher level of aggregate demand helps sustain the upward pressure on prices. Should the supply of money fail to increase, interest rates will rise, forcing a cut back in spending and investment plans. In that case, according to the orthodox model, demand will be insufficient to sustain price increases, and the outcome of the original wage rise will be an increase in unemployment.

This, of course, is where the "monetary and fiscal authorities" (on the right of figure 1.1) come in. They constantly monitor the macroeconomic situation (including pressures on prices, layoffs, level of aggregate demand, money supply, etc.), and "decide" if the trend of events is to culminate in inflation or unemployment. To the extent that price-level stability is a salient goal, they will either refuse to supply additional reserves to the banking system, or take overt measures to contract the supply of money (raise the discount rate, sell government securities in the open market, raise reserve requirements). These actions will reduce output and employment because of their effects on

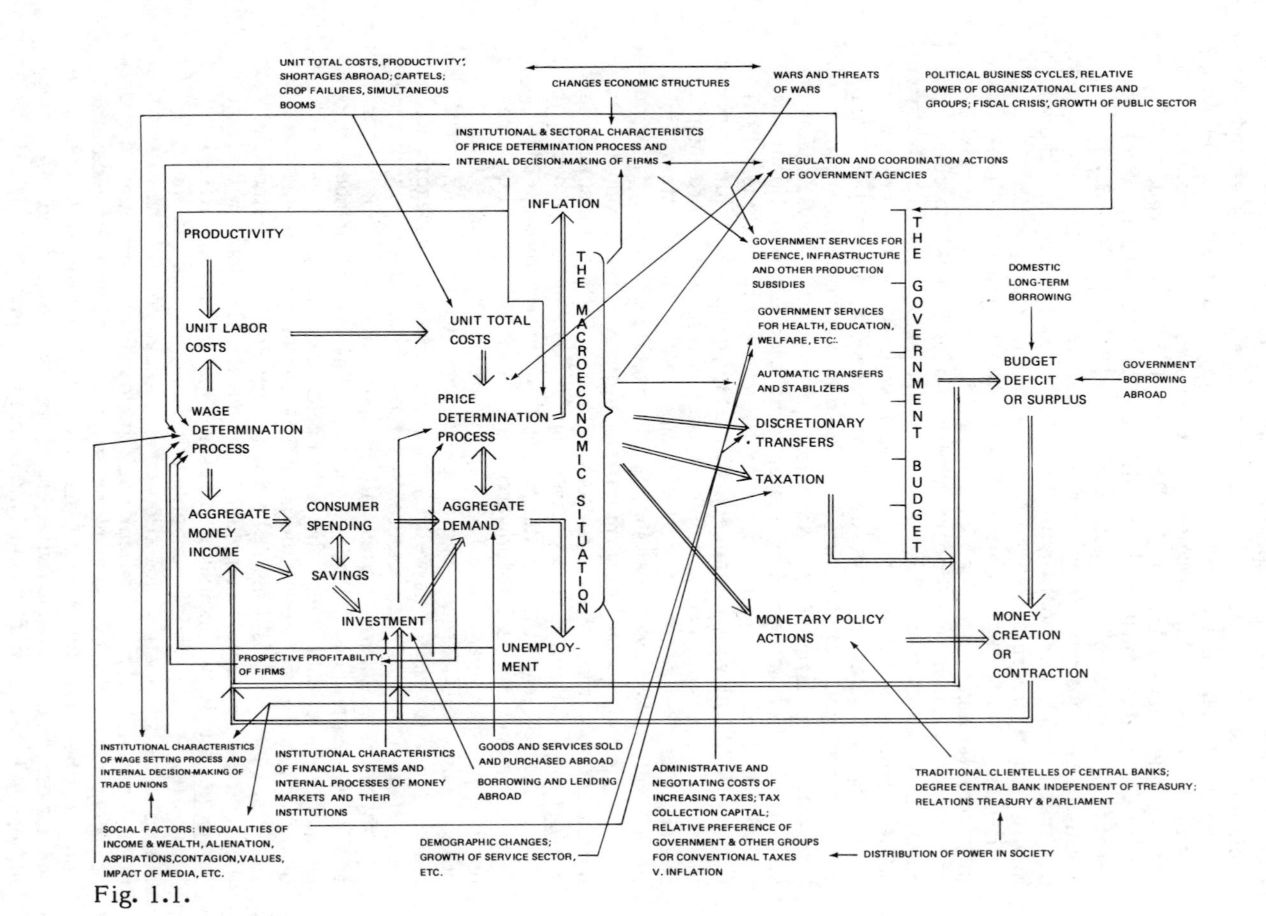

UNIT TOTAL COSTS, PRODUCTIVITY; SHORTAGES ABROAD; CARTELS; CROP FAILURES, SIMULTANEOUS BOOMS
CHANGES ECONOMIC STRUCTURES
WARS AND THREATS OF WARS
POLITICAL BUSINESS CYCLES, RELATIVE POWER OF ORGANIZATIONAL CITIES AND GROUPS; FISCAL CRISIS; GROWTH OF PUBLIC SECTOR
INSTITUTIONAL & SECTORAL CHARACTERISITCS OF PRICE DETERMINATION PROCESS AND INTERNAL DECISION-MAKING OF FIRMS
REGULATION AND COORDINATION ACTIONS OF GOVERNMENT AGENCIES
INFLATION
PRODUCTIVITY
UNIT LABOR COSTS
UNIT TOTAL COSTS
PRICE DETERMINATION PROCESS
WAGE DETERMINATION PROCESS
THE MACROECONOMIC SITUATION
GOVERNMENT SERVICES FOR DEFENCE, INFRASTRUCTURE AND OTHER PRODUCTION SUBSIDIES
GOVERNMENT SERVICES FOR HEALTH, EDUCATION, WELFARE, ETC.
AUTOMATIC TRANSFERS AND STABILIZERS
DISCRETIONARY TRANSFERS
TAXATION
THE GOVERNMENT BUDGET
DOMESTIC LONG-TERM BORROWING
BUDGET DEFICIT OR SURPLUS
GOVERNMENT BORROWING ABROAD
AGGREGATE MONEY INCOME
CONSUMER SPENDING
SAVINGS
AGGREGATE DEMAND
INVESTMENT
UNEMPLOYMENT
PROSPECTIVE PROFITABILITY OF FIRMS
MONETARY POLICY ACTIONS
MONEY CREATION OR CONTRACTION
INSTITUTIONAL CHARACTERISTICS OF WAGE SETTING PROCESS AND INTERNAL DECISION-MAKING OF TRADE UNIONS
INSTITUTIONAL CHARACTERISTICS OF FINANCIAL SYSTEMS AND INTERNAL PROCESSES OF MONEY MARKETS AND THEIR INSTITUTIONS
GOODS AND SERVICES SOLD AND PURCHASED ABROAD
BORROWING AND LENDING ABROAD
ADMINISTRATIVE AND NEGOTIATING COSTS OF INCREASING TAXES; TAX COLLECTION CAPITAL; RELATIVE PREFERENCE OF GOVERNMENT & OTHER GROUPS FOR CONVENTIONAL TAXES V. INFLATION
TRADITIONAL CLIENTELLES OF CENTRAL BANKS; DEGREE CENTRAL BANK INDEPENDENT OF TREASURY; RELATIONS TREASURY & PARLIAMENT
SOCIAL FACTORS: INEQUALITIES OF INCOME & WEALTH, ALIENATION, ASPIRATIONS, CONTAGION, VALUES, IMPACT OF MEDIA, ETC.
DEMOGRAPHIC CHANGES; GROWTH OF SERVICE SECTOR, ETC.
DISTRIBUTION OF POWER IN SOCIETY

Fig. 1.1.

aggregate spending and aggregate demand. The rising level of unemployment will (in combination with other factors) eventually put downward pressure on the size of wage settlements and move the economy closer to price stability. On the other hand, monetary and fiscal authorities may give priority to high levels of employment, or the unemployment "price" required to achieve a desired price stability may prove too costly for political reasons. In either case, "the authorities" will provide the needed increased money supply and/or adopt tax and expenditure programs designed to directly influence money incomes and investment. Inflationary pressures will be revived because the earlier downward pressures exercised on costs and prices by unemployment and lowered money incomes will be relieved, and the size and velocity of the money supply will also rise. The model generally assumes that by manipulating these policy levers in response to changes in the macroeconomic situation, the fiscal and monetary authorities can come close to maintaining their preferred mix of levels and rates of change in employment, price stability, and real income.

Of course, things have rarely worked so smoothly, and there were always economists who challenged this view of the process. The challenges became more numerous with the wage inflations of 1968 and after, and they accelerated to a flood tide after 1973, so that today, very few economists would accept the above simple model. The remaining lines and arrows in figure 1.1 indicate the points at which other factors – some exogenous and some endogenous – are now thought to exert their impact on the process and the ways in which these factors interact with each other. There is little consensus today among economists on these matters, and, therefore, I have tried to make the figure sufficiently eclectic to incorporate the chief factors adduced by the main contending schools of thought. Each emphasizes a particular set of factors as decisive additions to, or amendments of, the general story earlier summarized. Each needs to be evaluated in terms of the "why now" question, i.e., what changes in what variables or linkages accounts for the rapid increase of inflationary pressures, inflation susceptibility, and economic policy performance in the post-1968 period. I have juxtaposed them to suggest how they relate to each other and (out of my own conviction) to show that none of them alone is adequate to the task of explaining inflation or stabilization outcomes at different times and in different nations. Figure 1.1 sets the stage for our effort to distinguish between sources and causes, and for our argument that the processes that generate pressures on prices and employment and that determine the government's policy response to such an evolution are closely interrelated.

Figure 1.1 and the following commentary on it will also introduce my effort to argue that the inflation and stabilization processes may vary systematically with certain critical dimensions of the environing political process and the socio-political structures they reflect. If this turns out to be the case, and if we can demonstrate that political and social factors are not simply "passive vehicles for the transmission of market variables," then we may be able to make some modest contribution to sorting out and specifying competing economic theories.

The "model" can be divided into four sectors or phases: wage determination, costs and price determination, policy response, and the impact of policy on decision-making processes that determine wages, prices, and investment. I have made no effort to provide a full summary of the state of knowledge or the major disputes in each sector. For recent such reviews, see Laidler and Parkin (1975), Trevithick and Mulvey (1975), Means et al. (1975), Fleming (1976), Maynard and van Ryckeghem (1976), Krause and Salant (1977), and R. Gordon and comments by Brunner and Olson (1975). I will only briefly take note of those issues which seem to me to be most central and cite from some of the literature I have found most useful. More detail will be added in later sections of the chapter in which I try to relate specific political and social variables to characteristics of the inflationary process and to the efficacy of stablization policies in different countries.

The organization of the discussion by sectors gives an overall view of the process, but is admittedly arbitrary, and will be difficult to maintain in practice because the interactions among the sectors is so important. Thus wage and price formation processes are mutually interdeterminate, and the two together, and changes in them create new dilemmas for policymakers and put pressure on dominant elites and coalitions and especially on the budget. These may "overload" the system's structural capacity to respond in anything but a short-term, sectoral and stop-go manner. Conventional policy instruments – global fiscal and monetary policies, controls, manpower programs – may be rendered lame or produce unanticipated and undesired results because of conditions created by past policy actions, or because they are based on faulty or outdated assumptions about the structure of wage and price determination.

Wage Determination (Wage Inflation)

What determines the magnitude of wage adjustments? How closely will wages track prices? In particular, under what conditions will wage settlements be able to consistently exceed productivity increases and so push up unit labor costs? The most frequently cited proximate determinants or sources of wage pressure (see fig. 1.1) are the level of excess demand for labor (i.e., the level of unemployment), past or present inflation rates or increases in the cost of living, trade unions, and the structure and behavior of firms. Lying behind and conditioning these variables are the institutional characteristics of the wage and price-setting processes, the level of aggregate demand, the past policies of governments, and such social factors as perceptions of equity, inequalities of income distribution, changing aspirations and social values. The most important theoretical – and policy – controversy has to do with the nature of the relationship between the level of unemployment, presumably reflecting excess demand pressures upon both the supply of labor and wage inflation. Monetarists and growing numbers of neo-Keynesians see that relationship as determinate when "augmented" with "inflationary expectations," i.e., the propensity of workers and unions to build into their wage demands not only the consequences of past inflations, but also their anticipations of future inflations. Barring any change in the distribution of income, this implies that fiscal and monetary policies that seek to reduce the unemployment level below its "natural rate," will produce a permanently high and possibly accelerating rate of inflation without in the end doing much about unemployment. Thus there is no Phillips-Curve tradeoff between inflation and employment.

An alternate view that I find persuasive and that seems to accord with my own observations in different countries, hypothesizes that wage pressures may or may not closely reflect excess demand pressures. It very much depends upon the case. In Sweden, the Netherlands, or West Germany where levels of frictional and structural unemployment have been very much reduced, it may be largely true. But in a country like the United States it seems quite counterintuitive. In either case there are other factors that reinforce or that provide independent pressures upon the wage level. What is important is to understand the ways in which demand factors and other so-called "cost-push" factors may interact and reinforce one another. It is surely not necessary to demonstrate, as advocates of excess demand theories claim, "that the markup which is applied to total costs is arrived at by forces which have nothing to do with prevailing market conditions" (Trevithick & Mulvey, 1975:167). Among these other forces or factors are increased labor market rigidity; traditional differentials, wage-contours, and other bargaining characteristics of the wage formation process; discontent with working conditions, stratification, inequalities; trade union militancy; and the pricing behavior of firms. Some work as autonomous wage inflation pressures, while others exert their influence by effectively indexing wages to price increases. Thus eliminating money illusion in ways not very different from the "expectations" thesis.

The implications of the alternative view are thus not particularly reassuring with regard to inflation, although it does suggest that in a country like the United States much more could be done to reduce unemployment levels and to stimulate the economy without that putting pressure on prices by way of wage inflation. Other upward pressures on wages seem likely to continue to mount, however, and these reflect a number of deep-seated features of the political economy of capitalist democracies that cannot be eradicated or controlled by increasing the unemployment rate, but which may respond to other policy strategies.

Increased labor-market rigidity

Gösta Rehn (1976) argues that there is a fundamental long-term trend leading in a "rigid security direction." "This appears as the immediate (short-term) self-interest of the overwhelming majority of both employers and employees" and Rehn sees it as an important future complication for economic management. It is a reponse to social demands for employment security, the diffusion of white-collar and middle-class traditions of job security and "fairness" and reflects higher levels of affluence, the influence of unemployment insurance, and other automatic stabilizers. This trend is characteristic of the more well-established categories of workers, i.e., those who have the decisive influence over economic developments and wage-profits spirals. Deflations have to be quite severe before they are substantially affected.

Wage contours, differentials, and other bargaining characteristics of the wage formation process

(Piore, Eichner, Dunlop) operate as sources of wage distortion and produce wage spirals, especially in a rapidly changing economy, and as relative prices change, a process of internal readjustments is generated and all shifts are upwards.

Discontents and inequalities

Piore, Hirsch, Goldthorpe, Bronfenbrenner, and others foresee a growing discontent with the quality of work, with advancement opportunities and stratification constraints. They see a more or less anomic (or alienated) pressing of wage demands, wage bargaining as an outlet for aggression, a low readiness to be "reasonable," higher absenteeism, and lowered rates of productivity increase. Perhaps advanced capitalist societies have used up what Albert Hirschman has called their "tunnel vision" capital, i.e., their tolerance for income inequalities (see also Crozier, Wiles).

Trade union militancy

To some extent trade unions only channel and focus the above forces, suggesting, of course, that their importance may vary according to trade union militancy and organizational strength. But, Hibbs (1977) has found that in the United States, United Kingdom, Italy, and France trade union militancy has had a significant autonomous influence on the rate of change of wages quite independently of price movements and unemployment. Only in the United States did wages not fully keep up (or run ahead) of price increases. Trade unions will play an important role in inflation – and especially in any inflation control policy. While union mobilization or organization rates have not changed in the last decade, union militancy (as measured by strike activity, etc.) has reached high levels (especially in Italy and France). We know relatively little about trends in union militancy, wage structures, "orderly" bargaining, and the internal politics of unions (Olson) as these might affect wage inflation rates. There is no consistent theory that explains the behavior of trade unions, e.g., their response to unemployment. We need to know more about the relationship between militancy and trade union organization. Are decentralized or centralized unions more "pushfull"?

Pricing behavior of firms

Economists have long recognized that firms with unilateral wage-setting power may not resist wage pressures, especially if there is little price competition but nonprice competition sufficient to sustain a relatively high rate of production. But most economists have not accepted the argument that oligopoly and monopoly pricing could be a continuous source of increases in unit wage costs. Kahn's argument in this regard seems worthy of exploration. He sees a complicated relationship over time between the exercise of market power and wage costs – but also including managerial salaries and other prerequisites(2) in which a tendency to inflation of the profit rate gets transmuted and imbedded in chronically increasing unit costs, with realized profit margins relatively unchanged in percentage terms, floating on top of a secularly increasing unit cost base. What he envisages is a complex interaction process in which high profits and decision-making flexibility (cost slackness) gets built into the behavior of oligarchical and monopoly firms so that they become the cause of rises in their own costs (see also Eichner, 1976).

The chief implication I derived from the above cited literature is not that rising wages are the cause of inflation, though they may be an important contributing <u>source</u>, but that "wage lag" and "money illusion" are unlikely to operate, except where trade unions are very weak and traditional constraints on mobility and life style aspirations are relatively strong. Labor can no longer be counted upon to be the main "stress-bearing" part of the economy. Wages will follow prices and profits very closely, and will run ahead of them where emerging demands for greater equality and fairness are frustrated.

Hirsch argues that the inflationary crisis of the mid-1970s has to be seen as, in part, "a result of the surfacing of political and economic pressures by the poor to get what they saw as their fair share." The diffusion of middle-class modes and aspirations, long regarded as the ultimate safeguard of bourgeois capitalism is becoming a prime cause of economic and political instability because asymmetries in the structure of occupations in the modern division of labor impede realization of these goals. Excess demand of middle-class life styles reinforces the underlying inflationary thrust. Hirsch concludes such growth as a substitute for redistribution of resources worked only in a transitional period. The distributional struggle "will intensify unless means are found to specifically legitimize the distribution of benefits in society." For similar views, see Eichner (1976), and Balogh (1977).

We need a systematic and comparative sociopolitical treatment of the dynamics of labor markets, the institutions that govern them, and the underlying societal conditions and transformations that make inequalities of condition more or less acceptable. What accounts for the ebb and flow of "tunnel vision"? What forces may intensify resentment at the "advancement of others"? What determines the vulnerability of a country to "wage push" pressures: poor industrial relations, accumulated working-class hostility, the existence or non-existence of corporatist institutions cutting across the labor market, cultural aversions to rational bargaining, the adamant resistance of land-owners, rentiers, and capitalist groups, etc.? How and why do countries differ in these regards, and what has been the outcome of various policy efforts to deal with them?

Price determination

How shall we understand the pricing behavior of firms? Figure 1.1 indicates the variables that have been adduced. There are two major contending interpretations. Prices vary:

1. As a response to changes in unit total costs (primarily labor costs, but also rising factor costs, energy and materials) and capital costs (due to changes in capital costs per unit output because of technological innovations), tempered to some degree by fluctuations in demand (which varies from sector to sector and from concentrated to non-concentrated industries);
2. As a response to the internal goals and objectives of firms who are able to set prices for long periods of time quite independently of short-term fluctuations in demand, and with a relationship to unit-cost increases that is tempered by the possibility that the firm owns or controls, the source of inputs supplied or systematically supports the prices of such inputs.

Which patterns of behavior most affects macroeconomic fluctuations and the efficacy of monetary and fiscal policy instruments depends on the relative importance of these two modes of pricing. I find it difficult to avoid the conclusion that the second mode probably predominates and is becoming more and more important. Once again, it is not necessary to assert that oligopolistic or monopolistic firms can cause inflation without the help of an accommodating monetary and fiscal policy or some relationship to anticipated or actual demand. It is only necessary to show that their activities are based on other goals which may or may not be market determined in the short or medium term, and that their activities can create new dilemmas for policy-makers by loosening the connection between monetary and fiscal policies and price/investment decisions.

The most interesting variant of this "market-power" argument (Kahn, 1975; Eichner, 1976) is one which stresses the capacities and motivations of large corporate enterprises for what we might call "counter-cyclical pricing." Prices are stabilized relative to the movement of direct costs over time and relative to the planning goals of the firm – including investment decisions (see Eichner, 1976; Nell, 1977). The goals and motivations include:

- it is often administratively costly to change prices frequently and more convenient to hold and change only periodically;
- customers also prefer stable prices;

- firms are uncertain how price increases will affect sales, customers, and competitiors (competitive entry is easier if prices and profits are rising);
- firms with market power take a longer view of pricing which inclines them toward cyclical stabilizaton or target returns on an annual or longer basis (Blair, 1976; Wachtel, 1976);
- firms avoid cutting prices where demand falls for competitors will do the same and all will lose profits;
- firms prefer to stabilize the wages they pay, they resist cutting wages in slack periods in order to preserve good will of workers and prevent departure of skilled employees;
- in vertically integrated firms, the raw materials prices you cut on the downward side of a cycle are your own;
- firms may as a matter of policy stablize prices of labor and materials;
- pricing decisions may also be made according to the firm's need for internally generated funds in order to finance a desired rate of capital expansion;
- pricing decisions are increasingly made (according to Business Week) on the basis of anticipations of future inflation and expectations of future government expenditure policies.

The existence of a capacity for counter-cyclical pricing seems to me to be quite evident. Corporations are complex organizations with a variety of goals and elaborate long-range planning processes. Less clear is the nature and degree of impact upon the inflationary process and upon the efficacy of government stabilization policies. This would seem likely to vary with the nature of historical relationships between state agencies and business; the ideological attitudes of businessmen toward government (Vogel, 1976); the importance of trade associations in the decision-making processes of firms and the degree to which the business sector is centralized or fragmented (Olson, 1976; Vogel, 1976); the existence of quasi-corporativist planning institutions that coordinate inter-firm and government and union decisions, especially investment decisions; the regulatory authority of the state vis-à-vis the activities of firms; the extent to which the business community perceives a "public vocation" or responsibility for macroeconomic stabilization.

Policy response

Why do governments actively or passively permit or pursue inflationary policies? How could they "be persuaded" to lengthen their time horizon and bring monetary expansion under control? How might we reform the political system so that politicians might be made to accept the commandment "thou shalt not inflate"? Under what conditions will "cowardly politicians" prefer the "inflationary tax" to "biting the bullet"? What determines the "reaction function" of politicians to macroeconomic fluctuations? How do "entrepreneurial" politicians competing in the political market for popular support impart an inflationary bias to the expenditure/revenue ratio? Why has the budget become such an "inelastic tool" for dealing with excess demand and how might we separate the budget of the national government from discretionary fiscal policies? Why does a meddling and inefficient government actively pursue regulatory policies (e.g., Federal Mediation and Conciliation Service, CAB, Department of Agriculture, Department of Labor and Commerce in support of maximum wages and tariffs, etc.) that raise wages and prices above what the "free market would allow"?

These examples taken at random from the economics literature illustrate the puzzlement of economists about the "political economy of inflation." They also illustrate the persistent tendency noted earlier to conceive of the political system as exogenous to the economic system, and preview the argument to be made later in the paper that economists have a naive and limited concept of "the government" or the political process. One promising strategy for cutting through the confusions and simplifications that abound about the relationships between the economy and the polity as they relate to the inflation-stabilization process is to ask what functions or tasks the government – or, as I would prefer, the state – performs relative to the economy and the processes of economic growth and development. This is the strategy adopted by Hirschman (1977) in his discussion of the "entrepreneurial" and "reformist" function. My own treatment relies on the essays gathered together in Lindberg et. al. (1975) and on the review article by Caldwell and Woolley in Hammarlund and Lindberg (1976).

The "state" in capitalist societies is composed of a set of structural relationships between political-administrative agencies and the economy. The state is both an apparatus for decisionmaking and a locus of conflicts (Poulantzas, 1973). It is not a mere instrument of business and other economic elites or pressure groups. The business community, or the dominant elite, are often deeply divided on particular issues and are often "incapable of transforming their specific interests into political interest. Left to themselves, the classes and fractions are not only exhausted by internal conflicts, but . . . founder in contradictions which make them incapable of governing." There are also other groups making demands – citizen's organizations, labor representatives, local governments – and these may establish tacit or formal alliances with parts of the state. The state is itself divided into competing bureaucracies and institutions, each with its own organizational interest and its own set of external clients or constituencies. A divided and complex economy makes it necessary for the state to play an active role and to constantly assume new activities. One classification of such functions or roles is to distinguish among the needs to rationalize the economy, to assure accumulation, and to insure legitimation.(3)

Rationalization refers to the efforts of the state to create a framework for economic activity, to smooth out economic fluctuations, to maintain peak capacity, and to improve economic efficiency. These activities have characterized capitalist development from the very beginning. The market economy was not, as Polanyi (1957) reminds us "the result of the gradual and spontaneous emancipation of the economic sphere from political control." It was rather "the outcome of a conscious and often violent intervention on the part of government which imposed the market organization on society for noneconomic ends." The state's initiating role in industrialization was also critical in other countries (Moore, 1966; Kindleberger, 1964; etc.). This role has become deeper and more explicit in the post-World War II period: responsibility for demand-management, economic planning, the reduction of structural and regional disequilibria, the nationalization of industries that were in decline or had become unprofitable, industrial policies, training in "production skills" and in business and administration, etc. (Beer, 1969; Shonfield, 1969; Winch, 1969; Holland, 1972; OECD, 1975).

The accumulation function refers to the activities of the state that assures profitable capital accumulation will take place, and that increasingly involves the "socialization" of many production costs: R & D, direct subsidies, tax subsidies, long-term contractual relationships as in the military procurement area, infrastructure developments, loan guarantees, etc. Legitimation involves satisfying the need for support of or acquiescence in the overall system from the groups that carry the major costs of economic growth, or who have been neglected or squeezed, and those elites or groups who champion their cause, including often particular state agencies. These needs have become more acute and the growth of welfare state expenditures is the principal response. These expenditures, like those for defense, are "nonproductive," and thus the legitimation function may come into conflict with the rationalization and the accumulation functions. O'Connor (1973) argues that satisfying these "contradictory" functions will bring about a persistent structural gap between expenditures and revenues. This so-called "fiscal crisis" will be further exacerbated by the redundancy, overlap, and fragmentation that characterize the pluralist state. Data on expenditures and receipts for OECD countries between 1955 and 1969 tend to confirm this general view.

> (S)tate expenditure growth has tended to outpace receipts. Expenditures have increasingly reflected concern for the negative externalities created by advanced capitalism while the tax burden has been shifted away from corporations. The largest single area of increases in revenues has been in social security taxes, which at least in many cases, are regressive. Thus, one can perceive the general outlines of the tendency of the state to move toward fiscal crisis in the process of regulating capitalism (Caldwell and Woolley, 1976: 137).

Whether or not we adopt this terminology to the analysis of the dilemmas of the "the public household," the same general argument has been made by Bell (1976) and it goes at least as far back as Schumpeter and the "fiscal sociology" of the 1920s. We must adopt a more sophisticated approach to an understanding of the dynamics of the public budget (especially any persistent and structural deficit) and the behavior of "monetary authorities" and "regulatory and coordinating" authorities than is typically employed in analyses of the inflation-stabilization process. We should bring such a framework to bear on the conventional breakdown of the budget and upon the arguments favored by macroeconomists and "rational choice" economists in accounting for the fiscal or monetary or regulatory behavior of the state. The right-hand portion of figure 1.1 illustrates one way in which this might be done.

In order to understand why the budget shows a tendency toward persistent deficits, we must, first, analyze why different types of expenditures show a tendency to rise. And this means more than looking at discretionary expenditures (or tax changes) that are an explicit response to changing macroeconomic conditions. It also requires analysis that goes deeper than "excessive expectations," the perversities of misguided egalitarians or left-wingers, the costs and benefits and information costs of specific as against general programs, politicians' "need for novelty" in policy fads, that presumably push up the welfare bill and get us stuck with "inefficient" automatic stabilizers. It will surely look at production subsidies, military expenditures, the pattern of R & D supports, etc.

And we should not neglect taxation – the revenue side of the budget. Whether or not the Treasury or Finance Ministry must issue securities, borrow abroad, or from the central bank to increase the money supply in order to cover a given level of expenditures depends (see Gordon, 1975; Maier, 1977) on "the relative preference" of the government and other groups for conventional taxes as against the inflationary tax, the available "tax collection capital" (extractive capacity of tax collection agencies, their efficiency and honesty, the willingness of taxpayers to file), and the "administrative and negotiating costs" of increasing taxes (time spent debating changes, political power of various groups in the population). Thus it may not be that "people" aren't willing to vote the taxes needed to pay for the services "they demand" from the state, but that 'some' people are unwilling to be taxed in the interests of 'legitimation' or greater equality of income and services and have the capacity to resist and/or collude with the state in so doing. Thus, a paper on the Italian economic crisis (Basevi, Onofri, and Tantazzi, 1977) argues that the inflationary consequences of the budgetary increases that were forced through following the 'hot autumn' of 1969 was due as much to the composition of receipts as to the size of the deficit.

> The social and economic changes between the fifties and the sixties had been managed mainly with a view to preserve a social consensus for the ruling classes. The burden of public services had been distributed through indirect taxation and social contributions instead of income taxes. Both types of tax collection influence price formation and give origin to distortions of relative prices between sectors. . . .Moreover, when the weight of indirect taxes and social contributions becomes larger with

> respect to income tax, their inflationary impact is such as to bring about higher overall tax incidence on low personal incomes. . . .This structural bias of the composition of government receipts, is an inheritance from the past, but it will be the main feature through the seventies, until nowadays, when the full implementation of the new indexation scheme and the opposition of trade unions to excluding from indexation indirect tax increases, at last froze that easy tool of fiscal policy.
>
> Given those basic conditions of the government budget, and the political constraints to a use of the whole spectrum of tools of fiscal policy, the social claims for an enlargement of welfare policy mainly with regard to old people and to health assistance were fulfilled without any increase of fiscal pressure but simply increasing the current-account deficit.(24)

Undoubtedly, some societies may be reaching some real limiting threshold of taxation – this is said to be the case in Scandinavia (Cerny, 1977) – and the circumstances and politics of "welfare backlash" (Bell, 1976; Wilensky, 1975) will need to be studied closely. Nevertheless, societies clearly vary greatly in the percent of total income taken in taxes, in the nominal and real incidence of taxation upon various population groups, in the relationship between direct and indirect taxes (which are usually passed on), in the willingness to tolerate great inequalities and a high incidence of misery and poverty in their midst, and in permissive relationships between owners of wealth and the political process. These factors are as important in determining whether a society can "live within its means" as is the dynamics of expenditure. Social conservatives who decry "excessive expectations" and call for a "truce in the income struggle" or who decry letting "economic allegiances become unified" (Bell, 1976), are vulnerable to a charge of objecting only that such allegiances, and a capacity to act on them, has now extended beyond the minority of capitalist entrepreneurs, renters, and landowners.

Besides these issues of the political economy of the government budget, attention should also be given to the stabilization policy process *per se*, that is, the pattern of monetary, fiscal, price and wage, and labor-market policy responses of the state to macroeconomic fluctuations. Here, the weakness of most economic approaches is most evident. "The political authority" is typically seen as a singular central actor, plus a central bank, and *maybe* political parties. This popularly-elected authority has an undifferentiated Downsian constituency and is entirely dependent on reaching economic targets for re-election, which is its primary goal. It can perfectly control economic tools, predict exogenous changes in the economy, and knows the degree to which its instruments affect its targets and the lags involved.

A more useful approach – and one consonant with what political scientists have learned over the past 30 years – would disaggregate formal government, look at ideologies, constituencies, particular tools of policy and the sub-governments that control them. Sub-governments not only determine whether or not a tool can be used, or coordinated with other tools or instruments, but also the conditions of effectiveness of the instruments.

Finally, there is the problem of public opinion and inflation. A number of different themes come together here to focus on the question, "what are the mass political bases of deflationary as against expansionary macroeconomic policies in different countries and what is their relationship to electoral and policy outcomes?" How do publics in various countries perceive inflation – or, more precisely, the relative impact on the country and on their own interests, of variations in prices, employment, and income? Will we find the same incoherence between real interests and perceived impact in other countries as Peretz (1977) found in the U.S.? What are their preferred policy instruments for dealing with inflation, e.g., willingness to accept incomes policies, higher taxation, etc. How valid or useful are the economists' *a priori* notions about the impact of macroeconomic fluctuations, and citizen attitudes and perceptions and their relationship to party support and subsequent voting? How do attitudes toward inflation-unemployment vary across income and occupational groups and across countries with different kinds of party systems? How can we account for differential "inflation-aversion" or "taxation acceptance"? How do attitudes vary toward the basic "justice" of the distribution of economic opportunities and outcomes? Are feelings of relative deprivation waxing or waning? Do these have anything to do with attitudes toward or pressure for inflation? (For some interesting British data, see Daniel, 1975.)

The Effects of Policy on Wages, Prices, and Investment

This sector obviously joins the categories of wage and price formation, for here the stress is on how changes in the structure of labor, product, and financial markets have complicated the tasks of economic stabilization. Comparative analyses of the experiences of several countries may help pin down specific circumstances under which standard policy instruments have been found to be inadequate, as well as cast light on policy innovations that appear to be appropriate within the changing institutional framework of advanced capitalist economies. This will pose the question – to which we will turn in the final sections of the paper. What are the political preconditions for adapting fiscal, monetary, and regulatory-coordination policies to more stringent political, social, and economic conditions?

Wage formation

According to the conventional view, wage formation processes are indirectly affected by fiscal and monetary policies *via* the influence of these policies on aggregate money income, aggregate demand, unemployment, and the prospective profitabililty of firms (see fig. 1.1). However, the materials reviewed earlier (and the performance of most economies in the 74-77 period) suggest that the capacity of these global fiscal and monetary policies to affect wage-setting behavior has been much attenuated – the results are much less predictable, the lags are longer, the unemployment "costs" are heavier and heavier. The flow of consumer expenditure is more independent of the current flow of income, 'built-in stabilizers' cushion the effects of deflationary policies, unemployment is concentrated in low-status groups or those with the loosest relation to the labor market. Wages rise – leading the way or closely tracking price increases – and following dynamics that are not affected by standard policies, except at very high rates of unemployment and excess capacity. By this time standard policy "medicine" is worse than the disease it purports to cure. Any attempted application exacerbates the conflicts and resentments that escalate union militancy, fuels aggressive wage and competitive behavior, and applies pressure to the government budget as growth rates sag and compensation is given to marginal groups who are hurt. Carried to the extreme, these "cures" are likely to undermine political stability.

At least four alternative lines of policy seem to be available: controls and incomes policies, manpower and selective labor-market policies, policies that bring about a greater equality of condition or equal access to what Hirsch calls "positional goods," and policies that promote industrial democracy, worker participation, profit and asset sharing.

Under what institutional and political conditions can they become effective instruments for dampening "received" inflation or the "struggle for income shares"? What impedes their implementation? Are there alternatives to the quasi-corporatist arrangements that seem so effective in Austria, West Germany, Sweden, and the Netherlands? How might such forms be approximated in countries with very different traditions, ideologies, and state-business relationships? To what extent can wage stabilization be achieved short of according trade unions a greater voice in determining the macroeconomic target variables which not only govern the profit margins of firms, but most directly affect the growth of real income and the tradeoff between the rate of growth in aggregate output and real incomes. And will this be possible short of the participation of trade union-based parties in the government? (Headey, 1970; Hibbs, 1977).

Finally, can a stabilization of the income struggle be achieved without substantially increasing the scope of government services and transfers and, hence, very high levels of public expenditures as a proportion of GNP. Balogh (1977) writes:

> A clash between the actual distribution of economic power and the distribution of income and wealth has arisen, and must be resolved. This imbalance impairs the working of the mixed large-scale industrial system and must undermine the cohesion of society. Resistance against wage increases has been weakened.

> The law of the market, that is the law of the strong based on sheer bargaining power, can only lead to a bitter confrontation and common ruin. The attainment of a balance without mass unemployment depends, in my view, on making effective a sense of individual and group responsibility about policies for production, income distribution, and management and expansion of the public sector, especially of social services. (41-42)

Price formation and the behavior of firms

As with wage formation, evidence (and experience) seems to be accumulating to indicate that global stabilization policies increase unemployment and curtail output without having much of an impact on the level of prices. The wage-price spiral is translated into a political trade cycle and into a trend toward stop-go and stagnation. The policy alternatives most discussed are: "selective demand management" (Lindbeck) or "differential targeting" of monetary and fiscal policies (Müller) on the one hand, and some kind of "indicative planning," on the other. Thus says Eichner (1976: 285):

> The necessary new social mechanism is a series of industrial planning panels, with government officials and representatives of the consuming public joining with company executives and labor leaders to decide what type of investment program, including R & D, is going to be required if each industry is to meet the long range goal set by the social and economic council. The investment program decided upon by the panel would be regarded as a socially optimum one, and that part of the government charged with coordinating economic policy would then see to it, both through the margin above costs allowed firms in the industry and through the credit extended by the government's own specialized lending agencies, that this amount of investment was financed.

In this context, and in view of the emerging new great debate on planning in the U.S., it will be interesting to review and update the experiences of different countries with selective intervention and formal or informal variants of indicative planning and, in particular, to inquire as to the political preconditions that seem to determine their success or viability. It may also be worth asking if (and why!) "indicative planning" in a country such as France hasn't been inflationary rather than a stabilizing force.

Public expenditures, monetary policies, and the investment process

Two streams of literature (and flows in fig. 1) converge on the relationship between capital formation and inflation. One builds upon Keynes' theses about the enduring instability of the capitalist financial system and argues that the system that has emerged since the 1960s has strong inflationary and destabilizing tendencies that outstrip the regulatory capacities of most central banks (see especially Minsky, 1975 and 1977; de Cecco, 1975). Transformations of the banking system and the impact of international monetary flows appear to be especially important in eroding the capacity of conventional monetary policies to control the money supply.

The second link between inflation and the investment process is the purported impact of the growth of public expenditures and taxation (and their impact on profits and the ratio between marketed and non-marketed goods and services) upon the savings-investment process and, hence, the rate of economic growth. Maynard and van Ryckeghem (1976) conclude that the capitalist system is not likely to succumb to an insufficiency of demand, but to a failure to generate sufficient savings to finance the investment necessary for a rate of economic growth that satisfies real consumption expenditures. "Inflation is the result, not the cause; but it no longer as it once did, forces savings to match investment." This same theme constitutes the main argument in Bacon and Eltis' (1976) influential Britain's Economic Problem: Too Few Producers. They see the problem as particularly acute in Britain, but as one which is likely to become so in other countries as well. They see only two viable solutions. One is "pro-market solution" that keeps public expenditures (including defense as well as welfare) at a relatively low fraction of output and provides sufficient inequalities of reward to fuel the investment process. The alternative is a "left solution" which accepts and approves of the profit squeeze that results from high levels of expenditure and taxation and a very large public sector, but in which the state uses its powers to ensure that the productive investment needed to provide jobs is also undertaken. Countries that fail to choose between these or that vacillate from one to the other are likely to suffer chronic inflation, balance of payments crises, and dependence on outside loans, etc.

> The Left and pro-market sector policies are distinct, but in practice it is likely that governments will not consistently pursue either. Governments which have pro-market sector intentions may fail to cut public expenditures significantly through inefficiency or concessions to pressure groups. They will then have to pursue Left policies if they want a viable economy, even if they are nominally Conservative. They will have to choose import controls, draconian incomes policies and the control of property development, or face a collapse of private investment and the balance of payments. In times of crisis the Left and Right positions can become so mixed up that it is difficult to tell which is which. (114-115)

> (C)ompanies will not invest without profits, and the personal savings will have to be lent to the government (for who would wish to lend directly to unprofitable companies?), which will then have to find a way of passing it on to the company sector. This would again involve Left policies, so these are inevitable if

> saving is predominantly personal, and companies are unprofitable.

Bacon and Eltis criticize economists who "believe that the government should continue to take extra resources from the market sector and raise taxation to finance this, because that is the direction in which a civilized community should progress," but who simultaneously oppose "dirigiste Left policies."

> If growing public expenditure and accompanying taxation are allowed to reduce profits to the point where a market economy cannot function effectively, only Left policies can prevent chaos. So these economists, and they are numerous, must choose. They can support the allocation of investment resources through the market, or they can support Left policies of higher public spending, but they cannot have both. (115-116)

The problems signalled by Bacon and Eltis are real, but it is unclear what exactly they mean by "Left policies." Their favored example of a "pragmatic" Left strategy is Sweden and its evolution to something resembling what Keynes called "the socialization of investment." They seem to think that only Left governments can pursue such policies because only such countries "have the machinery to bargain about the social wage at the national level and trade union leadership that can commit the rank and file." The critical issue is under what conditions will workers acquiesce in reduced private consumption to pay for public expenditures and to support the investment process.

"If workers are frustrated by rising taxation, either inflation will accelerate (if the money supply is allowed to expand), or unemployment will rise (if the money supply is controlled)." Government ranges of options will deteriorate to either more inflation, more unemployment, or strongly sanctioned income policies, and they are likely to end up with endemic stagflation.

But other countries, notably West Germany, have managed to combine high levels of public expenditure with stable prices and relatively high growth rates. Perhaps the answer lies in the composition of public expenditures, in the nature of the tax system, or in some informal forms of 'guidance' or coordination or subsidization of investment (see also the examples of France and Japan). In other words "Left policies" seem to be pursued by governments of very different political complexion – and not necessarily as a last resort.

It is hard to evade the conclusion that the investment process is closely interrelated with the inflation-unemployment nexus and with basic underlying stakes of power in society. Investors, rentiers, and businessmen have an implicit power to lead or hold back the recovery process – remember hints in the press at a "capital strike" in the U.S. because of a "lack of confidence" in Carter's economic policies, and note the common problem of "capital flights" from countries experiencing or anticipating shifts of political power toward Left parties.

CONCEPTUALIZING THE POLITICAL PROCESS

Most economists in thinking about economic policymaking appear to adhere to a rather naive and undifferentiated individualist-pluralist model of the political process. This model not only fails to give an adequate representation of the nature of policymaking in this arena in any known country; I think it also may lead to a theoretical misspecification of the dynamics of the political-economic inflationary process, and to an incomplete and ultimately faulty analysis of policy alternatives.

Against the pluralist model (or models, for there are more than one), can be arrayed a number of alternatives which may be labeled "elitist" and "class." Some of the major differences among these models (or sets of models) are summarized in Table 1.1 which is based on Alford (1975). These models are probably most usefully seen (especially when analyzing liberal, democratic politics with capitalist economic systems) not as alternative characterizations of the overall political process in any polity, but as hierarchically organized, overlapping and interpenetrating "levels" of the political process or "types of politics." The policy process may combine varying elements of these types of politics from one issue-arena to another, from one point in time to another, from one country to another. (For an application of this kind of approach see Lindberg, 1977 and 1977a.) Relationships among pluralist, elitist, and class politics are fluid; there are incoherencies, lapses of control, and contradictions. Pluralist and elitist politics can sometimes penetrate the domains of class politics depending upon the activities of "power brokers" or perhaps political parties based in active mobilization of working-class and middle-class clienteles (Lindberg, 1977; Alford, 1976; Martin, 1975).

Nevertheless, some policy arenas are more decisive or important than others, and characterizing the prevailing policy process in such an arena may come close to a depiction of the policy process as a whole. I have made this argument for macroeconomic policy and for energy policy stressing that these arenas are not only critical to the general capacity of advanced capitalist societies to adapt to rapidly changing economic and political circumstances, but that they will also tell us a great deal about the relative resources of different organized groups and the preference and powers of decisive dominant coalitions. (Lindberg, 1976; Lindberg, 1977). Peretz (1977) makes the same point:

> Macro-economic policy is clearly one of the most important kinds of policy both for its direct and indirect effects. Directly its effects in terms of the scope and salience of the results to the public is clearly very great with only decisions on peace or war being more important. Indirectly its results have strong effects on what is possible in other policy areas, both because it largely determines the resources available for division and because different outcomes can have strong effects on particular areas as for example with unemployment and civil rights. (426-427)

Table 1.1. Possible Political Process Models

	Pluralist	Elitist	Class
a. What social forces shape the state and legitimize its actions	Individuals and groups	Bureaucratic organizations	Social classes
b. From what context of action is the explanatory power of the model drawn?	Situations in which individuals and groups choose to mobilize to influence political decisions.	Organizational contexts in which bureaucracies deploy their resources	Societal contexts where social classes shape institutions that reinforce their rule.
c. What is the core function of the state?	To achieve consensus and social order through continuous exchange of demands and responses by social groups and government and a continuous sequence of bargaining.	The maintenance of domination by existing elites.	The reproduction and management of existing class relationships by means of formal and informal processes.

Table 1.1. (Cont.)

	Pluralist	Elitist	Class
d. What is the strategic focus of the paradigm and the definition of power?	The conditions of the mobilization of particular groups and individuals for political action and the strategies of influence and the outcomes of action in particular situations. Power = the winner in a pluralistic combat between potentially equal opponents.	Stable coalitions of resources in organizations managed by elites and emphasizing limited ranges of decisions. Power the long range capacity to deploy organizational resources.	Basic institutions of property and objective class relations arising from these institutions. Power = is held by those who continuously benefit from the functioning of these institutions regardless of particular forms or who makes decisions within them.
e. What does each neglect?	Origins and preferences that lead individuals to form groups. Sources of inequalities in basic resources or the capabilities of groups. Institutional and resource barriers to participation. Extent to which the state creates and controls group activity.	The concrete social and economic interests actually served by bureaucratic organizations. Differences in power of different bureaucratic organizations. Origins of bureaucracies in past critical decisions.	Extent of social and cultural diversity within classes. Persistence of authority relations and requirements of hierarchical organizations under high-technology industrialization. The problem of providing stable representation of diverse group needs.

Clearly, any claim to generality on the part of pluralist, elitist, or class models will depend critically on their ability to describe activity in this area of policy.

Peretz (1977) has undertaken an analysis of macroeconomic policymaking in the United States which explicitly tests alternative pluralist, elitist, and Marxist (class) models. His specification of pluralist models closely resembles the view of the macroeconomic policy process held by most economists or, at least, used by them in their efforts to relate the economic and the political process. According to Peretz, the pluralist model assumes a state structure of which parties and interest groups are a part and which makes macroeconomic policy. This policy embodies an expected tradeoff point between inflation and other economic variables, principally growth and unemployment. When these policies are executed some changes take place which may affect the tradeoff point; these policies then impact the economic system and work their way through into characteristic rates of inflation, unemployment, and growth. Changes in these variables produce changes in the real incomes of wage and salary earners, the self-employed, profit-receivers, those on fixed incomes; and these effects are then perceived by individual members of these groups who decide whether they have been affected favorably or unfavorably. If the effects are positive, they will support the policies causing the change, if negative they will demand appropriate policy changes. These demands are made to interest groups and parties that represent them to obtain the policies demanded by their constituents. Parties and interest groups act as if they were in a competitive market and must be responsive to constitutent demands, and they work to obtain the policies demanded by their constituents. Government structures and critical decision points are seen as "free floating resources" and parties and interest groups representing pro and anti-inflation positions work to acquire a preponderance of these resources through persuasion and through the formation of coalitions. Entrepreneurial, vote-maximizing politicians will react to these pressures so as to improve their chances of re-election.

There are admittedly a number of imperfections or what Breton calls "frictions" in the translation of citizen preferences to political outcomes. Barriers to entry inhibit the emergence of new parties and interest groups. High information costs and a divergence between individual and group rationality hamper the emergence of anti-inflation "consumer" groups. Nonmajoritarian rules for decision-making, the length of time between elections, and the fact that voters have only a single vote for a multiplicity of interests do give politicians leeway to ignore citizens. Nonetheless, the pluralist model sees these "frictions" or imperfections chiefly as lags that eventually produce social movements forcing accommodation and a return to a political equilibrium. Ultimately, government responses to political actions by citizens aren't influenced by who they are, but by calculations of votes won or lost. Democracies are relatively efficient mechanisms for accommodating all expressed interests subject only to the constraints of uncertainty and the costs of participation. Thus the image of the neutral state whose actions respond to pluralist pressures toward consensus.

The elitist model asserts that: pressure groups facilitate elite control by making it seem as if policy is influenced by mass demands and preventing more effective influence mechanisms; income receivers other than profit earners are unlikely to strongly perceive their relative interests in inflation, employment, and real income and even less likely to translate needs into political demands; parties are socialization mechanisms for coopting the more active individuals among the masses and for mediating inter-elite conflicts. Thus the major impact from the rate of inflation comes through effects on profits and on the political stability of the bureaucratic elite. The Marxist model sees the main influence on policy from profit receivers, with wage and salary earners in political roles insofar as they develop class consciousness. The "new inflation" might be seen as a "tool" employed by capitalists to prevent workers from increasing their share of the GNP during booms now that unionization (and political support for high levels of employment) has made other methods of control less effective.

To document my assertion that the pluralist model generally characterizes most economists' analyses of the macroeconomic policy process, let me note more or less at random some representative items from the recent literature.

1. Robert Gordon in "The Demand and Supply for Inflation" argues that accelerations in money and prices are not caused by capricious governments, but rather represent vote-getting responses of governments to political pressures exerted by potential beneficiaries of inflation. Governments respond as they expect their constituents might vote. Hence, "demands for inflation" come from taxpayers who resist tax increases required by expenditures and the beneficiaries of government programs. The "supply of inflation," i.e., the monetary expansion supplied, will be calculated in terms of weighting the electoral losses that can be expected from accommodation as against those from resistance taking "voter myopicness" and "decaying memories" into acount. It also depends on the degree to which party lines coincide with the division in society between relative gainers and losers from inflation.

2. William Nordhaus, "The Political Business Cycle." Sees political parties that know voter preferences and are only interested in winning elections. The incumbent party always chooses an economic policy which will maximize its plurality in the next election. Voters are myopic and have decaying memories. The outcome is a political business cycle in which immediately after an election the winner raises unemployement to fight inflation, and as elections approach pushes up economic activity to stimulate employment, knowing inflation will lag behind. It is interesting to note that although Nordhaus acknowledges Kalecki (1943) as the only prior serious theorist of the political business cycle, Kalecki's elite-class version is implicitly rejected as inappropriate for a "representative system." Kalecki's version of the cycle saw a process in which rentier interests and business leaders collude to

sabotage the Keynesian revolution. Full employment lets workers get out of hand and they must be taught a lesson from time to time; inflation disadvantages rentiers who eventually get "boom tired."

3. Assar Lindbeck's version in "Stabilization Policies in Open Economies with Endogenuous Politicians" follows much the same lines as Nordhaus, except that he assumes a partly "idealistic" and a partly "entrepreneurial" target preference function of governments.

4. John Fleming concludes his little book Inflation (1976) by acknowledging that he has offered "the economic half of a possible explanation." The political half takes only a few paragraphs.

> In a time of price stability workers' and consumers' price expectations become sluggish; politicians learn that expansionary policies reduce unemployment and raise output. Even if they know that they are storing up trouble for later this option is attractive to a politician nearing an honorable retirement whose interests do not extend beyond the next election. The process of inflating before elections can be repeated several times if expectations are sluggish enough; but there are reasons for doubting whether it can be repeated indefinately.
>
> On the assumption that voters' expectations are also rational, in the weak sense, they will eventually learn that inflation follows the pre-election boom. When this lesson is learned they are in a position to impose their time preference on politicians. . .(T)he electorate's learning about the relationship between boom and inflation is facilitated by the fact that the sensitization of their price expectations reduces the lag between causes and effects.
>
> By the time it ceases to be easy to fool the electorate inflation will be endemic. The politicians may also learn only from experience that their old tricks no longer work. If they thus try two or three electoral booms after the public wakes up both rapid inflation and political disenchantment set in.
>
> Popular demand for the reduction of the established rate of inflation leads to a political contest as to who can best slow it down. The difficulty of fulfilling the commitments politicians make in their process is liable to lead to further disenchantment, which may make some approaches to the task harder. However, despite these problems the existence of a fairly reliable, if unpleasant, method means that relative stability will probably be re-established in the end. In this case expectations will eventually become sufficiently sluggish for it to be politically attractive to start the whole process over again – assuming that democracy survives the disenchantment.(131-132)

5. For essentially congruent images of the policy process but not always its product, see also Brunner (1976), Buchanan and Wagner (1977), Peter Jay (1977), and the literature cited in the two review essays by Amacher and Tollison (1976, 1976a).

On the basis of a close analysis of the macroeconomic policy process in the United States, Peretz concluded that the pluralist, elitist, and class models were each consistent with some of the observations in the area, but that the elitist and class models gave better descriptions of the overall process. The primary defect of the pluralist-democratic model "is the assumption that interests are accurately perceived and represented." There seemed to be "little similarity between the real long term interests of the public and their views on the importance of inflation," and "little correspondence between those groups which inflation affected most adversely. . .and the degree to which those groups opposed inflation." Nor was there "correspondence between the strength of the desire to stop inflation and the efficacy of the means chosen to halt it." Finally, many population groups "had virtually no representation" in the process.

On the other hand, the Marxist model "helps explain the fact that the tradeoff between inflation and unemployment in the U.S. . . .has placed heavier stress on inflation than is the case in other developed countries with more developed labor movements. It is consistent with the fact that workers do not seem to be aware of the effects that inflation has on their income, the tradeoff between inflation and unemployment, or the best means of solving inflation, and with the lesser ignorance among profit receivers and those with higher incomes. . .the high priority placed on controlling inflation by the lumpen-proletariat also fits the model."(421)

The elitist model also does better than the pluralist-democratic model, as well as explaining some inconsistencies in the Marxist account (e.g., the strong independent role that is played by technocrats, bureaucrats, and academics). "It contains a plausible alternative to the short versus long-term explanation of why inflation is generally feared so much more than the facts seem to justify, namely that people's opinions are manipulated by the dominant elite who seize on current inflation and project evil effects on the population." The model also fits "inconsistencies between reality and opinion and between perceived harm and proposed remedies," and "disparities. . .between the views of pressure group leaders and their followers. This kind of result we would expect from a combination of elite manipulation of media and willingness to co-opt group leaders."

The critique of the pluralist-democratic model – at least for U.S. data – seems farily persuasive to me. But I was also impressed that none of the models was really very satisfactory. This recalls our earlier discussion of the possibilities of overlap and interpenetration among pluralist, elitist, and class models and the likelihood of important variations over time and from one country to another. What I know of the stabilization policy process in other advanced capitalist democracies, especially in Western Europe and Japan, persuades me that each differs from the U.S. and from one another. Each process represents a different, possibly shifting mixture of pluralist, class, and elitist politics. And these different mixtures seem to be associated not only with different outcomes – with different rates of inflation, unemployment, and growth – but also with the dynamics of the inflation-producing process. But to begin to disentangle the relationships among inflation, policy process, and outcomes requires that we move beyond the simple trichotomy of policy processes.

Peretz did not link his analysis of the stabilization policy process with an analysis of the economic-political system interactions that produce the inflationary process itself, such as was called for in the previous sections of this paper. But the data he adduces and the conclusions he reached have some interesting implications for that process and converge in two ways with the political business-cycle literature, at least with its "liberal" variants, as represented by Nordhaus and Lindbeck.

Nordhaus and Lindbeck both argue for two main remedies for the tendency toward a political business cycle. On the one hand, they would improve information about the costs and benefits of inflation and make it available to voters. Voters should pay more critical attention to the promises of politicians, and they must also temper their expectations and not spend beyond their willingness to be taxed. More information would make it harder for entrepeneurial politicians to compete with each other in promises costing more than available national income. The second proposed remedy is to broaden the base of policy making. Nordhaus cites French "indicative planning" as one possible model (shades of Andrew Shonfield!), because it forces entrepreneurial government officials and political parties to negotiate policy with the opposition, with labor and management, and with other groups rather than getting locked into "myopic competition." Lindbeck would accomplish the same end by replacing single-party or small coalition governments with broader "grand" coalitions.(4)

It thus seems that information – in the sense of accurate perceptions by various groups in the population of their interests – and group participation – or non-exclusion of major interests from decisive decisions – are two dimensions upon which we might build in our effort to work toward a more adequate way of conceptualizing policy processes. It is along these dimensions that the U.S. policy process most diverged from the pluralist model, according to Peretz. And perhaps, the political business cycle of Nordhaus and Lindbeck works according to a Kalecki dynamic rather than a representative democracy logic. In that case, the informational and representational defects they hint at could be seen as reflections of oligarchical control, manipulated information, class hegemony, and a skewed distribution of power. In other words, as divergences from the postulated pluralist model which might also constrain the political reforms Nordhaus and Lindbeck call for.

But we will want to enlarge the concepts of information and participation to take into account elitist and class critiques of individualist pluralist theory. Whose information and about what? How easy or hard is it to obtain information? Is the system somehow structured to conceal it? What is the direction of the flow of information? Is information separable from an organizational capacity to act? Does participation mean only electoral participation? Can the opportunity to participate in political contests and alternate in political power, balance off concentrations of economic power? What is the relationship between representation and the exercise of the power of the state? In what follows, I propose a first cut at a specification of these two dimensions as the basis of a taxonomy of macroeconomic policy processes.(5)

A TAXONOMY OF POLICY PROCESS

Each of the two dimensions upon which this taxonomy is to be based will be conceived of as a continuous variable and each is itself some complex function of other variables reflecting historical, sociocultural, and political factors. The presentation will be divided into three parts: definition, determinants, and presumed behavioral consequences.

Information (INFO)

(a) definition: The extent to which there is among members of all major groupings whose relative income shares are at stake a symmetrically distributed capacity to perceive how variations in prices, employment, and real income affect their interests (and those of others?), and to organize to articulate demands based on these interests. A society with a high score of this dimension would approximate what Schmitter has called "associational saturation" in which everyone has available "an alert, resourceful, independent, and influential organization to defend his interests." It would be a "symmetrically organized" society in Mancur Olson's terms; a condition he implies is desirable, but not attainable.

(b) determinants: (INFO) = f(a,b,c,...n) position along this continuum might be determined by:

- The degree to which groups are subject to formal and informal controls on leadership selection or to which they agree to respect regime-defined limits on their articulation demands.
- The degree to which political parties and other elites and interest groups actively mobilize their membership and clientelles.
- Past government actions to provide organizational incentives or disincentives for group formation.
- The system of interest intermediation from fragmented to "encompassing" (see Olson).
- Extent to which groups have autonomous research, intelligence, and informational networks.
- The extent of class ideological hegemony, false consciousness, traditional deference to authority, etc.
- Levels of literacy, education, media exposure, etc.
- The 'symbolism' of government policies and key group positions (e.g., as to tradeoff possibilities and constraints).
- Etc.

(c) behavioral consequences:
High scores would be related to:

- Low levels of "myopia" and more slowly "decaying memories."
- Low levels of "money illusion."
- Greater flexibility in "adjusting inflationary expectations" (learning curve, error adjustment, lag correction).
- Reduced effects from increasing complexity and uncertainty.
- Increased chances of distinguishing between cyclical and secular fluctuations and acting "correctly."
- Low deference to "traditional" political leaders calling for sacrifices in the name of their definition of what is societally optimal.
- Strong pressure for income redistribution policies.
- Etc.

Group Participation

(a) definition: The extent to which common interest groupings, with the power to press (successfully?) for a larger nominal share of the incremental social surplus, symmetrically and continuously participate in the decision-processes that determine macroeconomic target variables and instrumental variables. What is the size of 'winning coalitions' (assuming more than electoral arenas) from 'oligarchical control' to minimum winning coalitions, (as in the form of alternations in power by pro-labor and pro-business parties), to 'grand coalitions' or quasi-comprehensive and encompassing 'elite cartels.' Should be distinguished from the power of trade unions in wage bargaining, though that may be reason for extending participation.

(b) determinants: (GP PART = f(a',b',c',...n'). Positions along this continuum might reflect such things as:

- Systems of interest intermediation – are groups themselves fragmented or encompassing.
- Skewness in the distribution of power.
- Institutional centralization or decentralization of decision sites.
- The structure of group cleavages and record of past grievances.
- Historical relationships between the state and dominant elites.
- Prevailing ideologies – e.g., as to role of the state in the economy.
- Cultural tradition, norms, values.

(c) behavioral consequences:

- A 'high' position would indicate that the potentiality for group divergence (in Peretz' sense) which is implicit in macroeconomic choices is dampened by bargaining and cooptation, or by adequately compensating 'losers'.
- A low score indicates important groups are excluded and suggests high potential for group divergence.
- In a polity with formal democratic representative institutions, the only way to sustain effective oligarchial control of an important policy arena might be to limit the scope of government (e.g., insulate monetary policy) or to decentralize policy arenás.

- High positions might provide mechanisms for constant negotiation and updating of expectations and calculations among groups. They might facilitate development of mutually satisfactory "technical means for determining the econometric relations between instrumental and target variables" (Eichner).
- High scores might increase the sense that social product is 'fairly' distributed and be associated with higher probabilities of symmetrical perceptions among "social partners."

We can now generate the two-dimensional space depicted in figure 1.2. I have labelled each quadrant (borrowing from Peretz again) and provided a general description of four types of policy process. These best describe an area from the center of each quadrant to the intersect. Because each dimension is a continuum we should ideally provide different labels for different sectors of each quadrant for they will have distinctive properties.

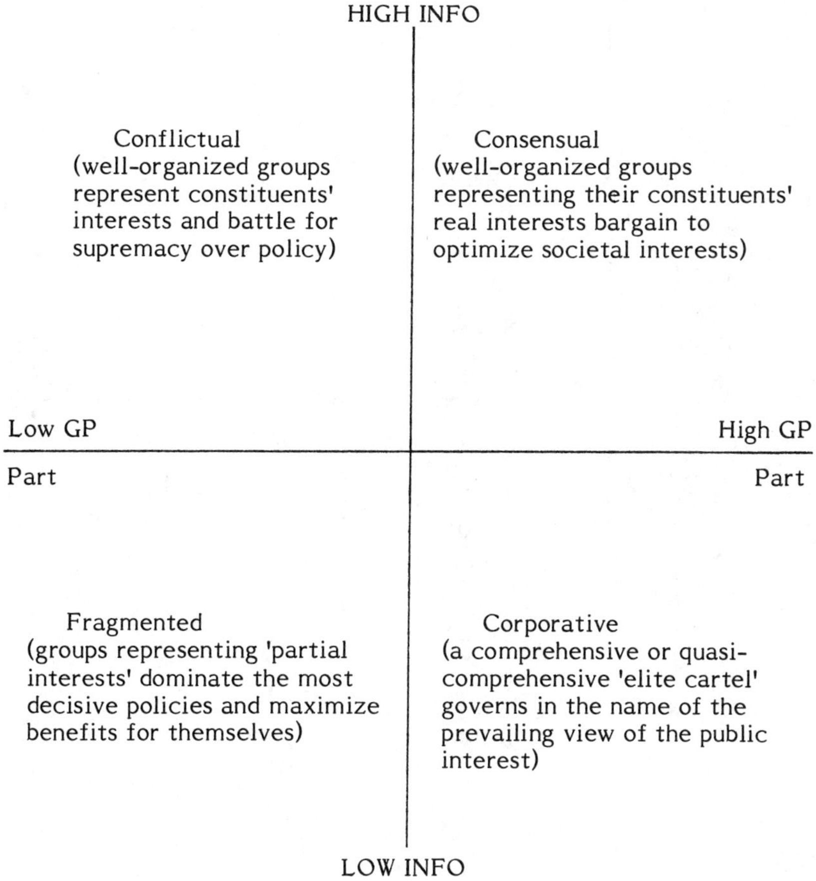

HIGH INFO

Conflictual
(well-organized groups represent constituents' interests and battle for supremacy over policy)

Consensual
(well-organized groups representing their constituents' real interests bargain to optimize societal interests)

Low GP

Part

High GP

Part

Fragmented
(groups representing 'partial interests' dominate the most decisive policies and maximize benefits for themselves)

Corporative
(a comprehensive or quasi-comprehensive 'elite cartel' governs in the name of the prevailing view of the public interest)

LOW INFO

Fig. 1.2

If the device is to turn out to be a useful heuristic, it should be possible to locate both countries and characteristic inflation-stabilization configurations at various places in each quadrant. I make a very preliminary impressionistic effort to do this in figures 1.3 and 1.4. A full-scale effort would imply that we take into account economic endowments and vulnerabilities, and that we specify how variations in information and group participation affect processes of wage determination, price determination, the politics of the budget and of stabilization policy response, and the impact that government, fiscal and monetary, policy decisions have on private economic agents. I don't have the time or the data to do that here. Let me only list a few initial and tentative hypotheses:

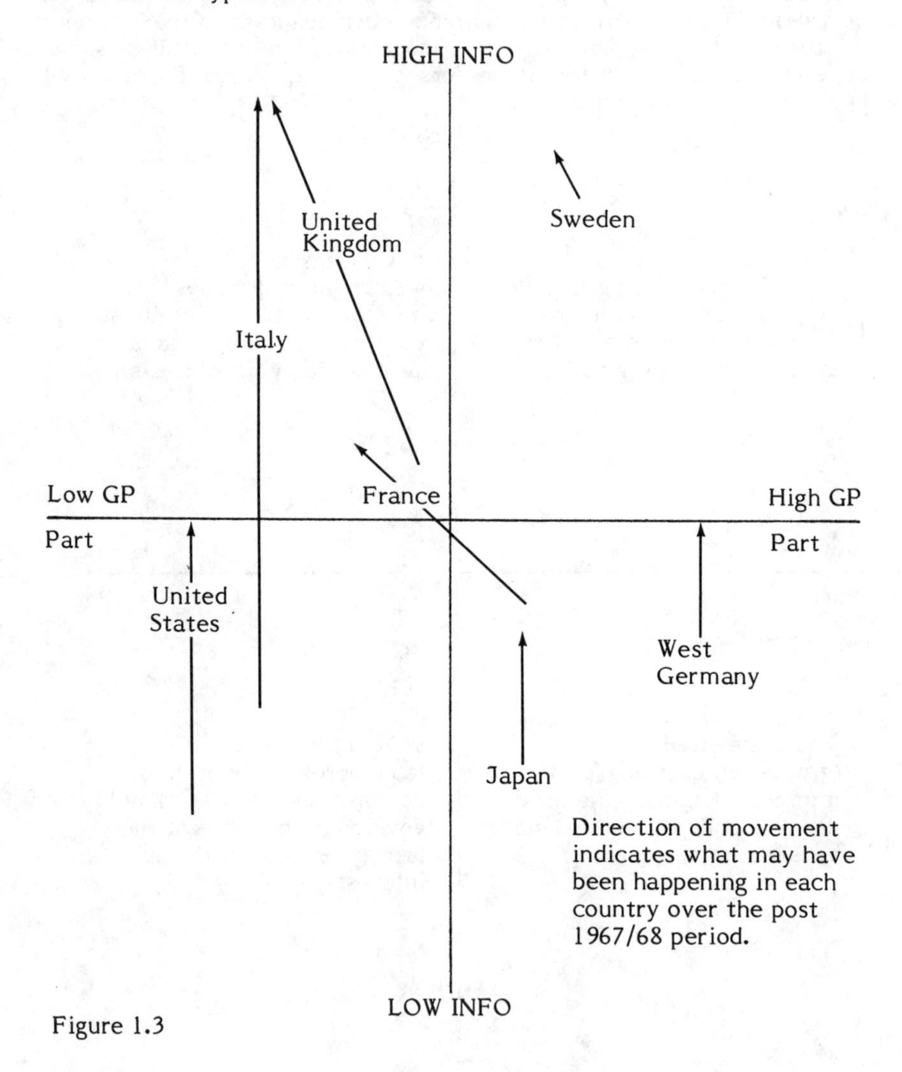

Figure 1.3

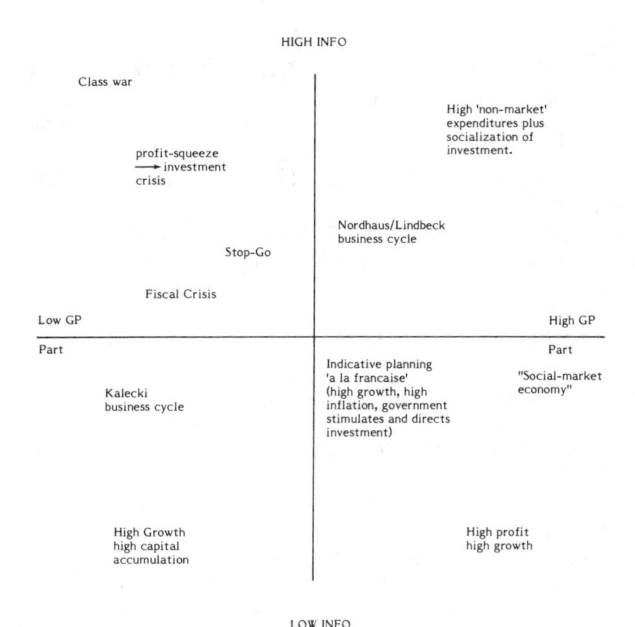

Figure 1.4

(a) wage determination

- Prices chase wages as you move up the information scale, especially in conflictual systems.
- Wages chase prices in fragmented systems.
- Structural unemployment is highest in fragmented systems.
- Wage differentials, wage-wage spirals and wage contours will be more of a constraint on stabilization policy in fragmented and conflictual systems.

(b) price determination

- The ability of firms with oligopolistic power to set prices on the basis of 'cost-plus' or in view of future investment needs will be most inflationary in fragmented systems and least so in consensual and corporative systems.

(c) policy response

- Fragmented policy systems will characteristically produce 'incoherent policy' with different groups and clienteles in control of different sub-policies; a low capacity for the cordination of fiscal, monetary, and regulatory instruments.
- Reliance on monetary policy is especially characteristic of fragmented systems.
- Both fragmented and conflictual systems avoid reliance on extensive regulatory instruments, e.g., manpower and labor-market policies.
- The politics of the budgetary process are more inflationary in fragmented and conflictual systems.
- Fragmented and conflictual systems will periodically resort to wage/price controls but only as stop-gaps.

(d) policy feedback

- Monetary policy will be relatively less effective as a stabilization instrument in fragmented systems.
- Wage and price controls will be least effective in conflictual and fragmented systems.
- Conflictual systems will be least able to absorb inflationary shocks from abroad.
- 'Counter-cyclical planning' by the corporate sector will frustrate government fiscal policies in fragmented systems.

EXPLANATIONS AND POLICY IMPLICATIONS

The present position each country occupies on the information and participation dimensions can be interpreted as the product of particular historical or developmental circumstances. Indeed, there is a symmetry between these two dimensions and the factors emphasized by many theorists of political development (e.g., Lipset, Rokkan, Eckstein, Almond, etc.). The direction in which any country may be moving today reflects changes in the 'loads' they have to cope with (e.g., increased frequency of 'exogenous shocks') and autonomous socio-political developments which increase the 'pushfulness' of groups, enhance their capacity to organize so as to recognize and articulate demands, or induce previously dominant elites to coopt or incorporate new groups into key policy decisions. The implication is that in each case policymakers face constraints that are the product of history, culture, and political structure, but that they also have policy options along the participation and information dimensions if they are prepared to pay the 'costs.' We can get some idea of what those constraints, options, and costs are by further exploration of the matrix.

All I have space for are some random observations:

1. It seems to be much easier to move E in the matrix (toward higher participation) when information levels are relatively low. The policy and power 'costs' to dominant elites are doubtless lower. Thus, Sweden and West Germany with a late pattern of industrialization both have followed a characteristic _↑ or SW → SE → NE path.

2. If information levels are high – or rapidly increasing – and group participation has been low – it is much more difficult and costly to successfully incorporate previously excluded groups and to evolve some set of shared evaluations and expectations.

3. It is difficult to move toward the SE, i.e., when information levels are high, 'corporativist' agreement on targets and instruments will generally not be acceptable. Perhaps this is why Britain failed in efforts to adopt "indicative planning."

4. We need to learn much more about the problems and politics of moving to the E, especially under conditions of high or increasing information and an increasingly volatile economic environment. Countries in SW and NW will experience stop-go, stalemate, in addition to high rates of inflation (esp. in NW) and low growth rates.

5. Where labor and business are themselves characterized by a decentralized rather than an 'encompassing' organizational pattern, what strategies are available to public authorities to encourage organizational change or to induce collaboration in inflation-stabilization decisions?(Schmitter, Olson).

NOTES

(1) Much of economics looks at sources – the immediate occasions for an increase in prices or the supply of money, or in productivity, and to neglect causes. "Sources. . .have the same relationship to causes. . .as the small streams and lakes that are 'sources' for a river have to the meteorological and geological phenomena that explain why a given watershed has the location, shape, and flow of water that it has."(Olson, 1976).

(2) I am puzzled at the neglect of managerial salaries, emoluments, etc., as part of wage push processes. Similarly with professionals, civil servants, and technocrats. Statistics on factor shares of income lump together wages and salaries (including self-employed). My own very rough calculations show that the incidence of the earnings of managers, administrators, professionals, technicians, and high-paid salesworkers is surprisingly high compared with craftsmen, operatives, laborers, and clerical workers.

(3) We might also distinguish a fourth function, which could be called "houskeeping" (following Solo, 1975). This includes providing national defense, internal security, protecting liberties, including private property, and providing a number of residual services. Some analysts would include these tasks under rationalization and accumulation.

(4) Both also propose various mechanisms implying a depoliticization of macroeconomic policymaking, e.g., longer time between elections, an insulated monetary authority, more executive discretion, incomes policies, etc. Such proposals seem to me to either depend for their viability upon the prior existence of grand coalitions or a planning process that resembles the theory of French planning, or they are fudamentally inconsistent with the principle of broadening representation in policymaking. They are more in tune with the proposals of these for whom the problem is too much information or too much democracy. (Brittan, Jay, Schumpeter, Buchanan and Wagner).

(5) I have built upon the useful first steps taken by Peretz in his effort to generalize his findings to a model of the policy process. The dimensions differ, however, as does the placement of cases within it.

REFERENCES

Ackley, Gardner, 1975-Comment on Perry. Brookings Papers on Economic Activity 2:1975

Alford, Robert, 1975-"Paradigms of Relations Between State and Society," in Lindberg, et. al.

______, 1976-Participation and Public Policy: Paradigms of Power," paper delivered at the 1976 Annual Meeting of the American Political Science Association, Chicago, Ill.

Amacher, Ryan C. and Robert D. Tollison, 1976-"Inflation and Democracy: A Review of the Public Choice Literature on the Inflationary Biases in Political Processes" (March).

______, 1976-"Economic Variables and Voting Behavior: An Interpretive Essay."

Bach, G.L., The New Inflation.

Bacon, Robert and Walter Eltis, 1976-Britain's Economic Problem: Too Few Producers (London: MacMillan, 1976).

Balogh, Thomas, 1977-"Monetarism and the Threat of a World Financial Crisis," Challenge (May/June, 1977).

Basevi, Giorgio and Paolo Onofri and Angelo Tantazzi, 1977-"Italian Stabilization Policies Under Social Constraints and International Shocks: 1972-76." Preliminary ms prepared for Brookings conference on National Stabilization Policies in Industrial Countries, Rome, May 30-June 3, 1977.

Beer, Samuel, 1969-British Politics in the Collectivist Age (New York: Random House, 1969).

Bell, Daniel, 1976-The Cultural Contradictions of Capitalism (New York: Basic Books, 1976).

Bowen, W.G., 1960-The Wage Price Issue: A Theoretical Analysis (Princeton, N.J.: Princeton University Press, 1960).

Breton, A., 1974-The Economic Theory of Representative Government (London: MacMillan, 1974).

Britton, Samuel, 1975-"The Economic Contradictions of Democracy," British Journal of Political Science.

Bronfenbrenner, M. and F.D. Holzman, 1963-"A Survey of Inflation Theory," American Economic Review (4).

Brunner, Karl, 1975-"Comment" on R. Gordon, The Journal of Law and Economics (December).

Buchanan, James M. and Richard E. Wagner, 1977-Democracy in Deficit: The Political Legacy of Lord Keynes (New York: Academic Press, 1977).

Business Week, 1977-"Prices Rise in Spite of Spare Capacity" (March 21, 1977).

Caldwell, Martha and John T. Woolley, 1976-"Energy Policy and The Capitalist State," in Hammarlund and Lindberg (eds.).

Calmfors, Lars, 1977-"Swedish Stabilization Policy Experiences 1971-76: A Case Study of the International Dependence of a Small Open Economy" (April, 1977). Preliminary ms prepared for Brookings Conference on National Stabilization Policies in Industrial Countries., Rome, May 30-June 3, 1977.

Cerny, Karl H. (ed.), 1977-Scandinavia at the Polls: Recent Political Trends in Denmark, Norway and Sweden (Wash., D.C.: The American Enterprise Institute).

Crozier, M., 1975-"Western Europe," in Crozier, Michel S. Huntington and J. Watanucki, The Crisis of Democracy (New York: New York Press, 1975).

Daniel, W.W., 1975-The PEP Survey on Inflation (London: Political and Economic Planning, 1975).

de Cecco, Marcello, 1976-"International Financial Markets and U.S. Domestic Policy Since 1945," International Affairs (July, 1976).

Dunlop, John T., 1977-"Industrial Relations, Labor Economics, and Policy Decisions," Challenge (May/June, 1977).

Eichner, Alfred S., 1976-The Megacorp and Oligopoly: Micro Foundation of Macro Dynamics (Cambridge: Cambridge University Press, 1976).

Fleming, John, 1976-Inflation (Oxford: Oxford University Press, 1976).

Goldthorpe, John H., 1974-"Social Inequality and Social Integration in Modern Britain," in D. Wedderburn (ed.), Poverty, Inequality and Class Structure (Cambridge: Cambridge University Press, 1974).

Gordon, Robert, 1975-"The Demand for and Supply of Inflation," The Journal of Law and Economics (3).

______, 1976-"Recent Developments in the Theory of Inflation and Unemployment," Journal of Monetary Economics (2).

Hammarlund, Jeffrey R. and Leon N. Lindberg, 1976-The Political Economy of Energy Policy: A Projection for Capitalist Society, (Institute for Environmental Studies, University of Wisconsin, Madison, Wisc.)

Heady, Bruce, 1970-"Trade Claims and National Wages Policies," Journal of Politics.

Hibbs, Douglas A., Jr., 1977-"Trade Union Power, Labor Militancy and Wage Inflation: A Comparative Analysis," Center for International Studies, M.I.T. (April).

Hirsch, Fred, 1976-Social Limits to Growth (Cambridge, Mass.: Harvard University Press, 1976).

Holland, Stuart, 1972-The State as Entrepreneur (London: Weidenfeld and Nicholson, 1972).

Hollis, Martin and Edward Nell, 1975-Rational Economic Man: A Philosophical Critique of Neo-Classical Economics (Cambridge, Mass.: Cambridge University Press, 1975).

Jay, Peter, 1977-"England's Sickness," The Washington Post (May 15, 1977).

Kahn, Alfred E., 1975-"Market Power Inflation: A Conceptual Overview," in Means, et. al.

Kalecki, M., 1943-"Political Aspects of Full Employment," Political Quarterly (October/December, 1943).

Kindleberger, Charles P., 1964-Economic Growth in France and Britain (Cambridge, Mass.: Harvard University Press, 1964).

Krause, Lawrence B. and Walter S. Salant, 1977-Worldwide Inflation: Theory and Recent Experience (Wash., D.C.: Brookings Institution, 1977).

Laidler, David and Michael Parkin, 1975-"Inflation: A Survey," The Economic Journal (December, 1975).

Lindbeck, Assar, 1975-Swedish Economic Policy (London: MacMillan, 1975).

______, 1976-"Stabilization Policy in Open Economics with Endogenous Politicians," American Economic Review (May, 1976).

Lindberg, et. al., 1975-Stress and Contradiction in Modern Capitalism: Public Policy and the Theory of the State (Lexington, Mass.: Lexington Books, 1975).

Lindberg, Leon N. and T. Hammarlund, 1976a-"Introduction: The Persistent Stagflation Model," in Hammarlund & Lindberg.

Lindberg, Leon, 1977-The Energy Syndrome (Lexington, Mass.: Lexington Books).

______. 1977-"Energy Policy and the Polities of Economic Development," Comparative Political Studies (forthcoming).

Lockwood, William, 1968-The Economic Development of Japan (Princeton: Princeton University Press, 1968).

Maier, Charles S., 1977-"The Politics of Inflation in the Twentieth Century." Paper prepared for Warwick Conference on Political Economy of Inflation, May 26, 1976.

Martin, Andrew, 1975-"Is Democratic Control of Capitalism Possible?" in Lindberg, et. al.

Maynard, Geoffrey and W. van Ryckeghem, 1976-A World of Inflation (London: B.T. Batsford, Ltd., 1976).

Means, Gardiner C., et. al., 1975-The Roots of Inflation (New York: Burt Franklin and Company, 1975).

Minsky, Hyman P., 1975-John Maynard Keynes (New York: Columbia University Press, 1975).

______, 1977-"The Financial Instability Hypothesis," Challenge.

Moore, Barrington, 1966-The Origins of Dictatorship and Democracy (New Haven: Yale University Press, 1966).

Müller, Ronald, 1977-"National Economic Growth and Stabilization Policy in an Age of Multinational Corporations: The Challenge of Our Post-Market Economy." Prepared for the Joint Economic Committee of the U.S. Congress.

Nell, Edward J., 1977-"Inflation, Market Power and Monetary Restraint," Challenge (May/June 1977).

Nordhaus, William D., 1975-"The Political Business Cycle," Review of Economic Studies (April, 1975).

O'Connor, James, 1973-The Fiscal Crisis of the State (New York: St. Martin's Press, 1973).

OECD, 1975-The Aims and Instruments of Industrial Policy. Organization for Economic Cooperation and Development, Paris.

Olson, Mancur, 1975-"Comment," on R. Gordon, The Journal of Law and Economics (December, 1975).

______, 1976-"The Political Economy of Comparative Growth Rates." U.S. Economic Growth from 1976-1986: Prospects, Problems, and Patterns, Vol. 2, The Factors and Processes Shaping Long-Run Economic Growth, Joint Economic Committee, U.S. Congress (November 10, 1976).

Peretz, Paul, 1977-The Political Economy of Inflation. Unpublished Ph.D. Dissertation, University of Chicago.

Perry, George L., 1975-"Determinants of Wage Inflation Around the World," Brookings Papers on Economic Activity 2:1975.

Peterson, Wallace C., 1977-"Institutionalism, Keynes and the Real World," Challenge (May/June, 1977).

Piore, Michael, 1976- "Memorandum on Economic Policy."

Polanyi, Karl, 1957-The Great Transformation: The Political and Economic Origins of Our Time (Boston: Boston Press, 1957).

Poulautzas, Nicos, 1973- Political Power and Social Classes (London: New Left Books, 1973).

Rehn, Gösta, 1976- "Recent Trends in Western Economies: Needs and Methods for Further Development of Manpower Policy," in Reexamining European Manpower Policies (Wash., D.C.: National Commission for Manpower Policy, August, 1976).

Robinson, Joan, 1971- Economic Heresies; Some Old-Fashioned Questions in Economic Theory (New York: Basic Books, 1971).

Ruggles, Richard, 1976-"Economic Growth in the Short Run: Its Behavior and Measurement," U.S. Economic Growth from 1976-1986: Prospects, Problems, and Patterns, Vol. 2, The Factors and Processes Shaping Long-Run Economic Growth. Joint Economic Committee, U.S. Congress (November 10, 1976).

Shonfield, Andrew, 1969-Modern Capitalism (London: Oxford University Press).

Solo, Robert, 1975- "The Economist and the Economic Roles of the Political Authority in Advanced Industrial Societies," in Lindberg, et. al.

Steinbrunner, John, 1974-The Cybernetic Theory of Decisions (Princeton: Princeton University Press, 1974).

Trevithick, James A. and Charles Mulvey, 1976- The Economics of Inflation (London: Martin Robertson and Company, 1976).

Vogel, David, 1976- "Why Businessmen Mistrust Their State: The Political Consciousness of American Corporate Executives." Prepared for delivery at the 1976 Annual Meeting of the American Political Science Association, Chicago.

Ward, Benjamin, 1972- What's Wrong With Economics? (New York: MacMillan, 1972).

Wilensky, Harold, 1975- The Welfare State and Equality (Berkeley: U. of California Press, 1975).

Wiles, P., 1973- "Cost Inflation and the State of Economic Theory," Economic Journal (June, 1973).

Winch, Ronald, 1969- Economics and Policy (New York: Walker and Co., 1969).

2 Economic Sectors and Inflationary Policies: The Politics of Inflation in Historical Perspective

James R. Kurth

THE COMPARATIVE ANALYSIS OF INFLATION: ECONOMIC ACTORS AND POLITICAL CONFLICTS

Why do some countries have high (double-digit) inflation rates, others have lower (single-digit) ones, and still others have virtually no inflation at all? Why have some countries had high inflation at some time, low inflation at another, and no inflation at still another? And what are the consequences of different inflation rates for a country's politics? These questions about variations in inflation across countries and over time have become especially important in the last decade, a period when most OECD nations have experienced their most severe inflation since the years immediately after World War II.

The existing answers to such questions have not been very satisfactory. Economic theorists have developed abstract models which point to the central role of government spending, but these tell us very little about why public officials make the fiscal and monetary choices they do, or why these choices vary from one to another country or from one to another time. Conversely, economic historians have given us extensive accounts of particular inflations in particular countries, but these too do not comprehend variations over space and time.(1)

One historian, Charles Maier, has gone a good deal beyond the abstract economic theories or the _ad hoc_ economic histories, however. Maier has compared inflations and stabilizations in a large number of European and Latin American countries for the period since World War I, and he distinguishes between three kinds or degrees of inflation; creeping inflation (less than 10 percent per year); "Latin" inflation (from 10 percent to 100 percent per year); and hyper-inflation (from 100 percent to 1000 percent per year). He argues that the particular path different countries have taken at different times is the result of political conflicts and coalitions between a variety of economic groups and actors (Maier, 1978).

The approach of the present essay is similar. It attempts a comparative analysis of inflation and deflation in Europe, the United States, and Latin America since the beginnings of industrialization. In particular, we will seek to compare different countries at different stages of economic development. We will also compare different stages of development within the same country. The essay follows Maier in focusing on political conflicts and coalitions between economic actors as an explanation of variations in inflation. The major economic actors discussed will be: (1) financial institutions, in particular, commercial banks and investment banks; (2) industrial producers, in particular, consumer-goods industries and capital-goods industries; (3) agricultural producers; (4) middle-class groups, in particular, small shopkeepers and salaried employers; and (5) working-class organizations.

In general and, not surprisingly, the commercial banks and the salaried employees have been the most consistent supporters of noninflation or even deflation. The other economic actors have been more variable. Industrial and agricultural producers, normally debtors, have generally supported inflation. This has been especially true of producers with high capital investments (who have heavy debts) and of those with crucial export markets (who support devaluation). However, once a period of high inflation or excessive inflation has in effect abolished the debts of the producers, they then see substantial benefits in the restoration of economic predictability and, relatedly, political order; at this point, they are ready to form a political coalition for monetary stabilization, especially a stabilization that imposes its main burden on the working class rather than on themselves.

These monetary tendencies of different economic actors are logical enough and, as we shall see, they are largely reflected in the historical record. They are not inevitable, however (Maier, 1978). For example, in recent years, various measures in some countries, be it indexing middle-class salaries, or lagging the indexing of working-class wages behind the rise in prices, have altered the calculations of certain actors. And as we shall suggest at the conclusion of this essay, this may result in some new and interesting patterns in the future.

AS THE TWIG IS BENT: VARIETIES OF ECONOMIC DEVELOPMENT IN THE AGE OF DEFLATION

If different inflation rates are a product of different political coalitions and conflicts between economic actors, then the relative weights of these actors become important. These in turn derive from differences in the kinds and stages of economic development. In particular, it is the argument of this essay that the countries which industrialized early (Britain, France, and the United States) developed a particular kind of banking sector – commercial banks with substantial international interests and with strong political power – which in the nineteenth century operated to bring about a general deflation in the world economy and which in the twentieth century operated for many years to keep British,

French, and American inflation rates lower than those in other countries. Countries which industrialized later (Germany, Austria-Hungary, and the countries of Latin Europe – Italy, Spain, and Portugal) developed a different kind of banking sector – investment or industrial banks with few international interests – which by the eve of World War I had interests almost identical to the industries themselves and which would pose no impediment to inflation after the war. Still other countries remained efficient producers of primary commodities for the world market (the countries of Latin America). They thus industrialized still later, in most cases not until they were compelled to do so by the disruption of international trade during World War I, the Great Depression, and World War II. For many years, these countries had no strong national banking sector at all. Further, their producers of primary commodities, being in a world market for their products which was supply-inelastic and demand-elastic, often had an interest in devaluation. Latin American countries thus entered into relatively high inflation rates even before World War I and would continue in that tradition down to the present day.

EARLY DEVELOPERS, CONSUMER-GOODS INDUSTRIES, COMMERCIAL BANKS, AND DEFLATIONARY FORCES

On the eve of the industrial revolution, Britain was already the leading commercial power and London the leading financial center in the world. France also was a major commercial power and Paris a major financial center. By itself, this early, pre-industrial development of a strong financial sector, centered on commercial operations and with extensive international interests, would have given the political economies of Britain and France a special character in later years. In fact, the commercial and international orientation of banking institutions in London and Paris, we well as their political power was reinorced by the particular nature of British and French industrial development. Britain and France were "early developers,"(2) and their industrial development was centered first on light consumer goods, especially textiles, and later on railroads. Both countries established a strong competitive position in the world market for particular products. And in the case of low-price cotton textiles, Britain completely dominated the world market for more than a century.

Let us first consider the development of light-consumer-goods industries. The first stage of industrial development in almost all countries has been the creation of such industries especially the textile industry. The development of light-consumer-goods industries has required mobilization of relatively modest amounts of capital. The required capital was modest both in relation to the amount of capital already available in the country as a result of pre-industrial enterprises and in relation to the amount of capital required by the creation of later industries, such as steel, railroads, chemicals, electrical goods, and automobiles. Consequently, the light-consumer-goods industries of Europe, the United States, and Latin America were created for the most part by family firms, and the industries grew through reinvestment of their earnings. In contrast with later industries, the capital accumulation for consumer-goods industrialization could be accomplished largely without dependence upon financing from banks, the state, or foreign investors (Gerschenkron, 1962; Hobsbaum, 1962).

The lack of dependence upon financing from banks had important consequences for the development of financial institutions. The financial agencies that grew up around the consumer-goods industries were clearing houses and commercial banks engaged in short-term credits to merchants. They were not investment houses and industrial banks engaged in long-term credits to industry. Those banks that did engage in long-term credits at the time did so with loans to governments, not to industries. Thus, a commercial banking sector and a consumer-goods manufacturing sector both grew up but with no direct interest, in the form of equity investment, between them, (Kemp, 1978).

This pattern was especially pronounced in the "early developers" – Britain, France, and also the United States – where for several decades in the early nineteenth century the consumer-goods industries and the commercial banks were the only major industries and banks undergoing development. In contrast, and as we will see in the next section, there was a more complicated pattern in the "late developers" – such as Germany, Austria-Hungary, and Italy. In those countries consumer-goods industries and commercial banks developed nearly side by side with certain capital-goods industries and investment and industrial banks.

The British textile industry, in part because it was the first such industry, was highly competitive in the world market, especially in low-price cotton goods. This success of British textiles in the world market led to the reinforcement of the British banking system of clearing houses, commercial banks, short-term credits, and insurance companies and eventually to its expansion into the world arena. This kind of banking system, with its peculiar combination of short time horizons and world-wide space horizons and its center in the City of London close to the seat of political power, had a major impact upon British government policies, including its fiscal and monetary policies. It became a consistent and successful force for maintaining a stable or rising value for the pound sterling, for noninflation or even deflation. Indeed, its impact would only diminish in the 1970s, with the diminishment of the role of the pound as an international reserve currency.(3)

Portions of the French textile industry were also competitive in the world market, especially in high-price woolen and silk goods. As in Britain, but on a smaller scale, this led to reinforcement of the French banking system in its commercial and international orientation. The French commercial and international banks, like the British, were also a force for deflation. But just as the power of these French banks was less than that of their British counterparts in the world capital market, so too the power of French banks in French national politics was less than the power of British banks in British national politics. From the 1830s to the 1930s, the French commercial and international banks suffered three or four serious, although temporary, political defeats, and France underwent a brief period of inflation.

A strong banking sector with commercial and international orientations also grew up in the third early developer, the United States. In some ways, the American pattern resembled the British. The enormous success of American raw cotton in the world market led to the creation of an American banking system centered in New York and something of a miniature British system composed of clearing houses, commercial banks, and short-term credits with international interests. But, unlike the London banks and even unlike those in Paris, New York banks took several decades to establish a strong influence over the national government's fiscal and monetary policies. From the 1870s to the 1930s, however, they were a generally consistent and successful force for deflation.

Thus, in the early decades of the industrial revolution, Britain, France, and the United States achieved great success in the world market each dominating one segment of the textile industry; low price cotton goods, high-price woolen and silk goods, and raw cotton, respectively. Each country then developed or reinforced a strong commercial and international banking sector which exercised great political influence and served as a generally consistent and successful force for deflation for a century or more.

Indeed the three great financial centers of Paris, New York, and especially London, played a large role in making most of the nineteenth century a time of world-wide deflation (Polanyi, 1957). But already in the nineteenth century, the late developers and the capital-goods industries were generating new patterns of political economy which would, in the twentieth century, come to fulfillment and would transform the age of deflation into an age of inflation.

LATE DEVELOPERS, CAPITAL-GOODS INDUSTRIES, INDUSTRIAL BANKS, AND INFLATIONARY FORCES

The second stage in the industrialization of a country normally has been the creation of capital-goods industries, especially the steel industry, and the related creation of those industries which are the final consumers of steel – railroads and shipbuilding. The creation of a steel industry, and its crucial consumer in the nineteenth century, the railroads, required far more capital than was required to create the consumer-goods industries. This distinction between the capital required for consumer-goods industrialization and that required for steel and railroad industrialization is one aspect of the distinction that Alexander Gerschenkron drew between early industrialization and late industrialization. Gerschenkron argued that the late developers' need to mobilize large amounts of capital led to the need for financing by large investment banks or even by the state. If financing occurred primarily through private capital, investment banks organized industrial cartels to prevent competition between the recipients of their investments. The resulting complex of cartelized industry and industrial banks was well-positioned to shape state policies. When the state itself undertook the financing of industrialization, it led to authoritarian measures. In Gerschenkron's view it was no accident that the late developers, in particular Germany, Austria-Hungary, Italy, and Russia were, or eventually became, authoritarian states (Gerschenkron, 1962). And, as we shall see below, the particular character of industry and banks in the late developers also eventually made these countries more prone to inflationary policies than were the early developers.

In the early developers, mobilization of capital for the second stage of industrialization occurred without any great change in financial institutions. In Britain, and to a lesser extent in France and the United States, the world market success of their textile operations (be it cotton goods, woolen and silk goods, or raw cotton) generated large profits and large amounts of capital for investment in the new enterprises of iron, steel, and railroads. This made it easier to do without new kinds of investment and industrial banks.(4)

In addition, the special features of railroads reinforced the established banking systems in their existing orientations. The banks financed railroads by the sale of long-term bonds. The banks' reliance on this kind of financial instrument was quite rational, given the nature of railroads, with their high initial investment or "start-up" costs followed by a long-term period of relatively steady return. But this reliance on long-term bonds, rather than on equity or even on short-term loans, meant that the banks would not make a transition from being commercial and brokerage institutions to being investment or industrial banks. In addition, British and French banks soon began selling foreign railroad bonds, reinforcing their international orientation (Henderson, 1972; Cameron, 1961).

The path to steel and railroad industrialization in Germany was very different from that in the early developers. At the time Prussia and then Germany undertook this second stage of industrialization (1860s-1870s), they had achieved no world market dominance for any product of the first stage, that of textiles. Accordingly, there was an absence of large profits from foreign trade and thus of large amounts of capital to be invested in iron, steel, and railroads. So, new kinds of financial institutions were needed – specifically industrial investment banks (Gerschenkron, 1962; Borchardt, 1973). The weakness of German textile firms and commercial banks created a relatively open space in the German financial system for these new institutions to develop and, indeed, to reach a dominant economic and political position. The strength of the industrial banks, in turn, made it easier for Germany to mobilize capital for the third stage of new capital-goods industries, that is, chemicals and electrical goods. Finally, the success of these new industries reinforced the strength of the industrial banks (Henderson, 1975).

Within the alliance of capital-goods industries and industrial banks, the banks, at first, were generally the more powerful partner. But by the beginning of the twentieth century, the balance had shifted to the industries, or the banks had come to define their own interests as virtually the same as the industrial ones (Borchardt, 1973). This was to have important monetary implications after World War I.

A somewhat different pattern characterized the still-later developers of Austria-Hungary, Italy, Spain, Portugal, and Latin America. In these countries, the nexus between steel and railroad industrialization was severed, with the building of the railroads occurring several decades before the development of the iron and steel industry. The railroads were partially financed by bonds sold to British, French, and German investors, delaying the development of a local banking sector (Cameron, 1961). This foreign debt created a foreign exchange problem for the governments of these later developers and encouraged them to devalue the national currency to increase exports and decrease imports, with inflation a result. This was especially the case with Italy in the 1860s-1870s and with the more developed parts of Latin America for much of the period after the 1870s (Kemp, 1969; Chapter 6).

When Austria-Hungary and Italy developed capital-goods industries at the turn of the century, they also relied on the aid of industrial banks, including German ones (Kemp, 1969; Gross, 1973; Webster, 1975). Thus, on the eve of World War I, they were like Germany in having a commercial banking sector that was economically and politically weak and an industrial banking sector that was economically and politically strong.

In several Latin American countries at the end of the nineteenth century, the continuing dominance of the economy by agricultural exporters produced national inflations even in an age of general deflation. Agricultural exporters were characterized by high indebtedness, high fixed costs, supply-inelasticity, and demand-elasticity. These features led them to favor devaluation of the national currency. In addition, they were strong supporters of free trade. But free trade in commodities led to free trade in capital, and this meant the development of Latin American commercial banking institutions was delayed for many years. Thus, in several countries of Latin America the pressure for inflation was especially strong and the pressure against it was especially weak (Furtado, 1976).

On the eve of World War I, the course of the industrial revolution over the preceeding century had resulted in combinations of economic actors that seemed to correspond to the different timings and different stages of economic development of countries throughout the world. These different combinations, in turn, had different potentials for inflation once the old world economic order, centered in London, broke down. The deflationary potential was greatest in the early, and now advanced, developers of Britain, France, and the United States. The inflationary potential was greatest in the late, and now advanced developer, of Germany and in the still-later and less-advanced developers of Austria-Hungary, Italy, Spain, and Portugal. And inflation was already a practice in the still-later and least-advanced developers of Latin America.

THE FIRST GREAT INFLATION: INFLATION AND STABILIZATION IN THE AFTERMATH OF WORLD WAR I

World War I was a great divide in monetary history. The war disrupted international trade, forced the belligerents into massive deficit financing and into currency non-convertibility, destroyed productive assets, and greatly increased the political mobilization of the working class. It was inevitable that there would be a period of double-digit inflation for several years. However, the countries we have discussed varied greatly in regard to the rates of inflation that they experienced and to the ways in which stabilization was eventually achieved.

The lowest, single-digit inflation rates were experienced by the United States and Britain. Double-digit inflation rates were experienced by most of the other countries that we have discussed: France, Italy, Spain, Portugal, and the more developed countries of Latin America. And triple-digit inflation rates, culminating in hyper-inflation experienced by Germany, Austria, and Hungary (Aldcroft, 1977, Chapter 6).

When stabilization came about, it was done under democratic governments in the United States, Britain, France, Germany, and Austria. Stabilization was imposed by new authoritarian regimes in Italy, Spain, Portugal, and Hungary; and stabilization never really was achieved in the more developed countries of Latin America.

What explains these variations in rates of inflation and ways of stabilization? The United States and Britain, of course, had suffered no direct physical damage from the war; this meant that they had no large reconstruction costs to be financed by deficit spending so they could quickly renew their export markets, and with them their earnings of foreign exchange. The United States and Britain also had relatively moderate labor political organizations. Finally, they had the two strongest commercial and international banking establishments in the world, and these had a clear interest in stopping inflation of their national currencies. Many factors, then, operated to keep U.S. and British inflation rates low (Aldcroft, Chapters 2-7; Hobsbaum, 1968, vol. II).

The double-digit cases were more problematic. France had suffered extensive destruction of productive assets during the war and also repudiation of its Russian loans after the Bolshevik Revolution. These factors temporarily weakened and threw off balance the French commercial and international banking sector. Accordingly, and in contrast to its Anglo-Saxon counterparts, it could not bring to bear enough power to contain the inflationary actors at critical points in the first years after the war. Conversely, the French working class was more radical and militant than its Anglo-Saxon counterparts. And it was more organized than the numerous but diffuse French middle class of small proprietors and salaried employees.

As a consequnce, the three major economic actors with an interest in encouraging inflation (industrialists, agriculturalists, and organized labor) would get their way for a while. But it was also the case that there were strong potential limits to inflation. First, as the banking sector regained its economic strength, it would regain its political strength and would become a force for stabilization. Second, as the middle class identified its interest against inflation, it would eventually be able to organize and translate that economic interest into political strength, thus becoming another force for stabilization. This is what occurred by 1926 when a conservative majority in parliament under the leadership of Poincaré stabilized the value of the currency (the "Franc Poincaré") (Maier, 1978; Maier, 1975; Schuker, 1976).

The countries of Latin Europe (Italy, Spain, and Portugal) provide an illustrative contrast. Although Italy and Portugal were active belligerents in the war (Spain was neutral), they did not experience extensive physical destruction like France. Yet the inflation rates of these three countries were more intense than the French and their stabilization methods were more authoritarian. On the other hand, their rates did not reach the triple-digit or hyper-inflation of German, Austria and Hungary.

As we have noted above, the late developers, including these Latin-European countries, did not have a banking sector with commercial and international orientations and with economic and political power. Accordingly, when the war produced the initial pressures for inflation, there was no organized and established economic actor with the political power to contain them, as happened in the United States and Britain alsmost immediately, and in France after several years. Therefore, in the Latin-European countries inflation accelerated more rapidly and a stabilization coalition formed only after higher rates had been reached than was the case in France.

Yet the Latin-European countries did not go on to triple-digit or hyper-inflation. The main actors in the inflationary coalition were industrialists, agriculturalists, and organized labor. Of these, the owners of industrial and agricultural productive assets had an interest in stopping inflation short of hyper-inflation levels, with its accompanying economic unpredictability and political instability. This was especially so in the aftermath of the Bolshevik Revolution and the "Great Fear" it had spread over Europe.

After several years of double-digit inflation had eliminated their indebtedness, some owners of productive assets could benefit from stabilization, which normally rewards the holders of physical assets and "real estate."

Stabilization after inflation invariably imposes costs upon the working class, however, and some forms of stabilization impose almost all the costs upon the working class. When the elite stabilization coalition (industry, agriculture, the weak banking sector), was finally formed in the Latin American countries it excluded the chief victims – organized labor – from political power to achieve the stabilization goal. This might have been done through the democratic political process if there had existed a middle class of small proprietors and salaried employees large enough to provide an electoral majority for stabilization, as in France. But in the 1920s, the countries of Latin Europe had not reached the level of economic development normally associated with such a large middle class. And since the democratic electoral process could not produce a political formula for stabilization and the exclusion of labor, an authoritarian regime had to do the job, either in the form of a fascist party (Italy 1922) or in the form of military rule (Spain 1923 and Portugal 1926) (Ricossa, 1976; Maier, 1975).

With the exclusion of organized labor, a coalition of industrialists, agriculturalists, and weak banks remained. The strong members of this coalition do not necessarily have an interest in deflation or noninflation. Rather, the preferred outcome for industrialists and agriculturalists is usually single-digit ("creeping") or double-digit ("Latin") inflation, which work to reduce their continually renewed indebtedness while not immediately producing unpredictability and instability which cannot be managed. Thus, in the Latin-European countries, these forms of inflation continued for a number of years after the advent of the authoritarian regimes.

The monetary policy of Fascist Italy, however, suggests a useful distinction between industries in regard to the import-content of their product. For several years after the Fascists came to power in 1922, the government followed policies of industrial development which resulted in continuing inflation. In 1927, however, Mussolini imposed a drastic stabilization policy and revaluation of the lira (from 32 lira to the dollar to 19 lira to the dollar) which resulted in severe deflation and, indeed, recession. Most historians have explained Mussolini's deflationary policy as the consequence of his rather frivolous disregard of economic realities and his obsession with political prestige; however, another industrial element was present. The dominant Italian industries at the time produced capital-goods for the Italian market behind high tariffs already granted by the Fascist government. They had no expectation of producing for foreign markets (which would have led them to push for devaluation and inflation), but their products did have a high import-content (e.g., iron ore for the steel industry). At this point, therefore, revaluation and deflation suited their interests best (Ricossa, 1976).

It was the late developers of Central Europe, Germany, and the recently severed countries of Austria and Hungary that moved quickly into triple-digit and then hyper-inflation. To some extent, this can be explained by the fact that these nations had been defeated in the war, and that their old political systems had collapsed to be followed by a revolutionary interlude. However, even after these factors are taken into account, the extravagance of German inflation poses something of a puzzle since the country suffered virtually no physical destruction in the war. By 1914, the peculiar nature of German economic development had produced a political economy which was almost a perfect recipe for uncontrolled inflation, once the state had to resort to deficit financing. Each of the major economic actors would benefit by inflationary policies.

First, the weakness of the German commercial and international banking sector meant that, as in other late developers, there was no strong elite economic actor working to inhibit inflation. Second, the

German industrial sector was dominated by capital-goods industries which had high fixed-costs. This meant that these industries would tend to keep production going by giving in to the wage demands of organized labor, rather than to fight labor by waiting out a strike.

The chemical and electrical industries, in particular, saw their foreign markets as crucial and, therefore, supported devaluations. Third, the Junker agricultural producers were economically inefficient, heavily indebted, yet politically influential even after the Revolution of November 1918. They supported inflation to reduce their debts and devaluation to increase the domestic prices of grain produced by their foreign competitors. Fourth, because of the collapse of the old authoritarian regime and the course of the revolution, the political power of the Social Democratic Party and of organized labor was especially, although temporarily, great. Fifth and, conversely, because of the authoritarian nature of the old regime, middle-class groups were not, at first, well organized for preserving their interests in a political process defined by democratic elections and parliamentary bargaining (Maier, 1978 and 1975; Feldman, 1977).

The inflationary coalition of industrialists, agriculturalists, and organized labor in Germany was thus even more powerful and more in favor of inflation and against stabilization than the inflationary coalition in Latin Europe. For several years there would be no brake whatever on the inflationary process. But when total economic collapse was near in 1923, an elite coalition formed for stabilization in Germany as it did elsewhere. Since Germany's high level of economic development provided it with a large middle class, elites could produce a democratic and parliamentary majority to support stabilization, and organized labor could be excluded from political power, for a while, by non-authoritarian means (Aldcroft, 1977).

Austria in the early 1920s had a structure of economic actors similar to Germany, and it experienced a similar hyper-inflation, albeit a less surreal one. The economic development of Austria was less than that of Germany, but because Vienna had been the bureaucratic center of a great empire, the salaried middle class was very large. Accordingly, the stabilization coalition in Austria was able to get its way in 1922 without destroying the new democratic and parliamentary system.

Finally, the more developed countries of Latin America largely continued in the way of steady inflation already established before World War I. The old producers of agricultural commodities with an interest in inflation and in periodic devaluations were now reinforced by new producers of domestic consumer-goods who had grown up when trade with Europe and the United States had been disrupted by the war. These new consumer-goods industries also had an interest in inflation, which would reduce their indebtedness, and in devaluation, which would serve as the functional equivalent of a tariff barrier to protect them from the renewed flow of foreign textiles. Since both the agricultural exporters and the consumer-goods industries had an interest in devaluation, and since only the second had an interest in tariff barriers while the first had an interest in opposing them, it was natural that a coalition could form around a policy of devaluation and therefore inflation, while maintaining the principles of free trade. And this was to be the pattern in the more developed countries of Latin America for much of the inter-war period (Furtado, 1976).

With the Great Depression of the 1930s, the world economy experienced a last and intense recapitulation of the nineteenth century age of deflation. Some countries attempted to compensate for the systemic deflation with inflationary government policies; the most successful, for a while, were the policies of Nazi Germany. Even the commercial banking countries of France and the United States made inflationary efforts, although without evident and sustained success. But Britain, the very model of a country dominated by a commercial and international banking sector and the financial center of the world economy, consistently followed a path of noninflation or even deflation. This was especially true after the runs on the pound in "the terrible year" of 1931 which made the City of London extraordinarily sensitive to any inflationary sign that might trigger a new flight from the pound (Shay, 1977; Hobsbaum, 1968; Chapter 12). The consequences for British industry and labor were continuous depression until the eve of World War II.

THE SECOND GREAT INFLATION: INFLATION AND STABILIZATION IN THE AFTERMATH OF WORLD WAR II

Like World War I, World War II disrupted international trade, forced the belligerents into massive deficit financing and currency nonconvertibility, destroyed productive assets on a far greater scale than in the first war, and greatly increased the political mobilization of the working class. In addition, the overturn of political regimes was far more extensive and pervasive at the end of the second war than at the end of the first. Every country that had been occupied by the Nazis underwent a political revolution of some sort. In France and Italy, the Communist parties, who had been leading actors in the Resistance, became powerful members of the governing coalitions. In Germany and Austria, they became influential political actors under the aegis of the Soviet army which occupied a part of each country (Milward, 1977).

These tremendous political upheavals readily explain the double-digit and even triple-digit inflation rates which were experienced by many countries in the mid-1940s, including France, Italy, Germany, and Austria. The absence of such upheavals in the United States and Britain helps to explain the largely single-digit inflation rates in these two fortunate countries.

As after World War I, however, there were some significant variations between different countries of Continental Europe in regard to their eventual stabilizations. The exclusion of organized labor and particularly the Communist party from political power seems to have been a necessary condition for stabilization (Maier, 1978:58), but the ways in which this was done varied.

Italy provided an almost ideal-typical case of stabilization politics in a democratic system. There, under the impact of the Cold War, organized labor was divided into three competing union movements (Catholic and Socialist as well as Communist), the Communist party was excluded from the governing coalition in 1947, and the hegemony of the Christian Democratic Party was confirmed in the election of 1948. The government imposed a severe stabilization plan which was almost immediately effective in stopping inflation. (The Italian inflation rate was 96% in 1945, 18% in 1946, 63% in 1947, 6% in 1948, 2% in 1949, and 2-3% for several years thereafter) (Maier, 1978:45).

The strength of the Catholic Church was an important factor in the Christian Democratic electoral success. But Italy in the 1940s was also a more developed country than it had been in the 1920s and indeed was now rather comparable to the France of the 1920s. There thus existed a large middle class to provide a mass electoral basis for stabilization, and it could now be achieved and maintained by democratic rather than by authoritarian means. Italian inflation rates remained below the average of that of fourteen developed countries (for the most part those in the OECD) for a decade and a half. This was so until "the opening to the Left," which brought the Socialist Party into the governing coalition with the Christian Democrats in 1963. Even then, Italian inflation rates did not exceed the average for developed countries by more than one percentage point throughout the next decade.

As for France, the War, the Occupation, and the Liberation together destroyed the economic foundations and political power of the old French commercial and international banking sector. With liberation, the Bank of France, major commercial banks, and major insurance companies were nationalized. The classical actor in the battle against inflation vanished from the scene, and France in this respect became like the other countries of Continental Europe. In France as in Italy, however, organized labor became divided into three competing union movements, and the Communist party was excluded from the governing coalition in 1947. But in contrast to Italy, the Socialists remained in the French governing coalition, the Catholic party was far weaker, and a large center-right party, the Gaullists, was excluded from the government. The center of gravity of French cabinets in the Fourth Republic was thus to the left of that of Italian cabinets. The French government did impose a stabilization, but it was less severe, less immediate, and less effective than the Italian one (the French inflation rate was 37% in 1945, 71% in 1946, 62% in 1947, 59% in 1948, 9% in 1949, 14% in 1950, 17% in 1951, 9% in 1952, and 4-6% for several years thereafter) (Maier, 1978:45). Clearly, part of the explanation for the return to double-digit inflation in the early 1950s lies in the expenditures on the war in Indochina. But the composition of the governing coalition helps also to explain the generally more relaxed quality of stabilization, in comparison to that of Italy.

In Germany, stabilization was imposed in 1948 by the American and British occupation authorities and was implemented and maintained by the Christian Democratic party. The power of the occupation authorities, the electoral strength of the Christian Democrats, and the issuance of a new currency resulted in an immediate and effective stabilization reducing inflation from triple-digit rates to almost nothing in a few months.

In Austria, in contrast, Soviet and Western occupation authorities continued to operate within the same political system, and the Socialist party continued to govern. Accordingly, the Austrian inflation rate remained at 10-15 percent until about 1954.

Among the smaller, developed countries of Europe, inflation rates which were slightly higher than the average for the fourteen developed countries were experienced by Sweden, Denmark, Norway, and the Netherlands in the 1950s and 1960s. This slight variation above the norm seems to be explained by the continuous political power of organized labor and moderate Social Democratic parties in these countries (Hibbs, 1977 and 1976; Blair, 1975).

The less-developed countries of Spain and Portugal provide an illustrative contrast both with the developed countries and with each other. These countries were neutral in the war and remained authoritarian in their politics, and post-war stabilization accordingly was imposed with relative east. But in the two decades thereafter, their monetary paths greatly diverged.

In Spain from 1949 to 1969, the inflation rate generally was between 5 percent and 7 percent. At any given point, especially after the mid-1950s, the Spanish inflation rate was higher than that of almost every developed country in Europe. But so was the Spanish rate of real economic growth. Spain was beginning its first great expansion in the capital-goods industries and even in the consumer-durables industries. It also retained a politically-powerful agricultural sector. The structure of economic actors dominated by agricultural elites and capital-goods industries had much in common with Fascist Italy in the 1920s and had a strong proclivity toward moderate inflation. But Spain's growing export-oriented and consumer-durable industries assured that there was no government-imposed revaluation and deflation, such as occurred in Italy after 1927.

Conversely, in Portugal from 1949 until the mid-1960s, the inflation rate generally was less than 2 percent. At any given point, the Portuguese inflation rate was lower than that of almost every developed country in Europe. But so was the Portuguese rate of real economic growth. Portugal, being smaller and less developed than Spain, was further from entering its capital-goods stage of industrialization. Even more important was the role played by the Portuguese colonial empire. After the 1940s, the ratio of the size of the colonial economy to the size of the metropolitan economy was greater for Portugal than for any of the other colonial, and now decolonizing, powers. The Portuguese colonial empire was just entering the first stage of economic development, and it provided the base for the economic expansion and political strength of a Portuguese commercial and overseas banking sector, such as the international trade and colonial empires of Britain and France had done for those countries a century or more before. And this Portuguese commercial banking sector also had a strong interest in no inflation.

This conjunction of limited metropolitan economic growth, substantial colonial economic growth, powerful commercial banking, and no inflation rate was an unstable equilibrium, however. By the late 1960s, metropolitan Portugal was undergoing rather rapid economic development. Even more important, the colonies in Africa now demanded increasing military expenditures to contain the guerrilla wars. Under these conditions, increasing inflation became inevitable, and by 1970 the Portuguese inflation rate was above 7 percent.

Finally, the most developed countries of Latin America (Argentina, Uruguay, Chile, and Brazil) experienced continuous double-digit inflation in the quarter-century after World War II. We have already noted that these countries developed their consumer-goods industries when international trade was disrupted first in World War I, then in the Great Depression, and then again in World War II. The growth of these industries strengthened the old inflationary coalition of agricultural exporters and protectionist manufacturers. And they added to it a third member, the "popular sector," composed of the new labor force at work in these industries and other new urban workers. The four countries each entered into a period of "national populism" before the end of the second war (Argentina under Peron in 1943, Uruguay under the Colorado party even in the 1920s, Chile under the Popular Front in 1938, and Brazil under Vargas in the 1930s). Despite their conflicts over other issues, the three dominant economic actors in these countries united around the pursuit of inflationary policies; continuous double-digit inflation was the result (Furtado, 1976; Maynard and van Ryckeghem, 1975; Maier, 1978:45).

Even with double-digit inflation, however, there are important differences between what might be called "low" double-digit inflation (a rate less than 50%) and "high" double-digit inflation (more than 50%). During most of the quarter-century after World War II, the inflation rates of the four countries were less than 50 percent, and this seemed to be within the acceptable bounds of predictability and stability from the perspective of agricultural exporters and industrial elites.

Over the years, however, continuing economic development produced a growing working class. In the democratic systems of Chile and Uruguay and the periodically democratic systems of Argentina and Brazil, this, in turn, produced an ever-growing political power for organized labor. The more developed Latin American countries were recapitulating – in the 1950s and 1960s – the experiences of Latin European countries in the 1900s and 1910s. As the political power of organized labor increased, so did inflation rates.

In Brazil, organized labor reached its greatest power in the Goulart government of 1961-1964. The Brazilian inflation rate was 24 percent in 1960, 43 percent in 1961, 56 percent in 1962, 86 percent in 1963, and was continuing to accelerate in early 1964 (Maier, 1978:45). But in March 1964, the military stepped in, overthrew Goulart, established an authoritarian regime, excluded labor from political power, and brought the inflation rate down to 46 percent in 1965, 41 percent in 1966, 24 percent in 1967, and kept it below 25 percent, but above 12 percent until the great oil price rise of 1974. As we shall see in the next chapter, in the 1970s this "Brazilian model" would be in the minds of the military in Argentina, Chile, and Uruguay as these countries moved into accelerating double-digit inflation (Kaufman, 1979).

THE THIRD GREAT INFLATION: THE EXPANSION OF THE POWER OF ORGANIZED LABOR IN THE 1970s

The 1970s brought a third era of high inflation, less dramatic than the first two, but more pervasive and sustained. For a time, the conventional explanation of this new inflation focused on a conjunction of ad hoc factors, such as the oil price revolution of 1973-1974. But inflation accelerated significantly before 1973. Further, the continuation of these higher inflation rates into the 1980s and their likely continuation in the future, under existing economic conditions, also casts doubt on the oil price explanation.

Another possible explanation seems to lie in the expansion of the power of organized labor in a number of countries in the 1960s and 1970s. The form this expansion took was somewhat different in developed than in developing countries. In a number of developing ones, such as Spain, Portugal, Chile, and Argentina, it took the familiar form of a rather rapid or even sudden increase in the political power of the organized blue-collar, wage-earning working class. In a number of developed countries, however, it took the form of a slow but steady penetration of union organizations into portions of the middle class, in particular, salaried employees in the civil services.

Since other essays in the volume focus upon contemporary inflation in developed countries, our main emphasis here will be on the developing countries in Latin Europe and Latin America which we have already discussed.

In the last years of the Franco regime in Spain and the Salazar-Caetano regime in Portugal, the dominant economic actors were agricultural and industrial elites, typical members of an elite inflationary coalition. In Spain, these included elites in capital-goods and consumer-goods industries which were now very substantial. Given our earlier analysis of Germany and Austria after World War I, and of these two countries plus France and Italy after World War II, one might have expected that, after the 1974 Revolution in Portugal and the 1976 democratization in Spain, there would have been a period of sharply increased inflation rates, as the elite members of the inflationary coalition were joined by a new mass member – in the form of organized labor and the Communist and Socialist parties. Furthermore, there should be some suspicion that the pressures for inflation would be compounded in Portugal, since the Revolution resulted in the nationalization of the commercial banks. This, of course, has been the result, as these two countries experienced inflation rates between 20 percent and 40 percent since their respective changes in political regimes.

Some observers have thought that these conditions in Portugal and Spain could result in continual accelerated inflation in the future, until the military once again stepped in and established a new authoritarian and labor-repressive regime. In fact, however, Portugal has followed a pattern similar to that of Italy and France in the 1940s and that of France in the 1920s. Organized labor was divided into two union movements (Socialist and Communist), and the Communist party was excluded from political power in 1975. The large Portuguese middle class of small proprietors and salaried employees provided a mass base for two political parties, the Social Democrats and the Center Democrats. This large middle class was a factor, as was pressure from Portugal's creditors (such as the United States, West Germany, and the IMF), causing the Socialist Party leader, Mario Soares, to impose rather severe austerity measures during his tenure as Premier from 1976 to the summer of 1978.

Since the economic development of Portugal over the past two decades produced a large middle class comparable to that in Italy during the 1940s and in France during the 1920s, the Socialist party lost votes in the next parliamentary eleactions, while the Social Democratic and Center Democratic parties gained votes. The two non-labor parties then formed a governing coalition and carried out an even more severe stabilization program than that already in effect. The result was organized labor being excluded from political power in yet another country, without an authoritarian regime.

In Spain, the transition from authoritarian regime to democratic politics has not yet passed through an interlude of labor power at the cabinet level. Spain is now at a level of economic development roughly comparable to that of Italy in the 1940s and France in the 1920s – but more comparable to that of France in the 1940s. Here, too, there is a large middle class of small proprietors and salaried employees to provide a mass base for non-labor political parties, and eventually for stabilization policies. The loose Democratic Center coalition led by Premier Adolfo Suarez from 1976 to 1981 may become one of these parties. If not, some other political party may have to be organized to play the role. But in Spain there is also a good chance that organized labor will be excluded from political power by nonauthoritarian means.

The experience of the more developed countries of Latin America in the 1970s, however, shows that there is a more somber possibility. In Chile, Argentina, and Uruguay, as in Brazil in the 1960s, the exclusion of organized labor from political power was carried out by unusually violent and repressive means.

Chile in the early 1970s recapitulated Brazil in the early 1960s. Organized labor reached its greatest political power in Chile in the Allende or Popular Unity government of 1970-1973. Not surprisingly, the Chilean inflation rate was 27 percent in 1969, 35 percent in 1970, 20 percent in 1971, 78 percent in 1972, and 320 percent in 1973 (Maier, 1978:45). In September 1973, the Chilean military overthrew Allende with a coup more violent than Brazil's, to be followed by a singularly repressive regime. In part, because the post coup era were years of simultaneously depressed copper prices (in part because of the end of American fighting in the Indochinese War) and quadrupled oil prices, the Chilean junta was not able to substantially reduce inflation in the medium term. The Chilean inflation rate was 586 percent in 1974, 380 percent in 1975, and 230 percent in 1976.

Similarly, in Argentina, organized labor reached its greatest political power in the Campora-Peron governments of 1973-1976. The Argentina inflation rate was 59 percent in 1972, 63 percent in 1973, only 23 percent in 1974, but then 171 percent in 1975, and was accelerating in early 1976 (Maier, 1978:45). Here, too, the military provoked a coup, imposed a severe authoritarian regime, and carried out labor-repressive policies. These, and other austerity actions, have not yet brought the inflation rate down to traditional Argentinian levels, accepted by agricultural and industrial elites – that is, to levels of 25 to 50 percent. Finally, in Uruguay, a comparable sequence occurred in the early 1970s, with an authoritarian regime being established in 1973.

Let us conclude by briefly speculating upon the future political consequences of inflation in the most developed Western countries. As Charles Maier has observed, "the concept of growth as a surrogate for redistribution appears, in retrospect, as the great conservative idea of the last generation" (Maier, 1978:70). But now, in the developed countries of the West, economic growth has largely come to an end. Double-digit inflation combined with no economic growth – stagflation – is de facto redistribution from the middle class to the working class (and to agricultural and industrial property owners).

When confronted with such redistribution, the middle class historically has turned to one or another of three solutions.

The first was that adopted in countries which had not developed economically to the point that they had a middle class large enough to compose a parliamentary majority (Latin Europe in the 1920s, Latin America in the 1960s-1970s), that is, the authoritarian regime. The second was that adopted in countries whose economic development had produced a middle class large enough to compose a parliamentary majority (France, Germany, and Austria in the 1920s; these countries plus Italy in the 1940s, Spain and Portugal in the 1970s). A third solution, adopted in recent years in some developed countries, has been to convert a substantial portion of the middle class into aligning their interests with double-digit inflation, e.g., by indexing the salaries of middle-class employees like the wages of working class ones.

But after this third solution has worked its way, who then will be left among the major economic actors in the developed countries to oppose a double-digit world? Not, if our historical review is any indication, will it be the agricultural or industrial elites who have long tolerated double-digit inflation rates in other countries. Nor will it be the commercial and international banking elites, because in most countries they will be overshadowed by the other interests. So double-digit inflation will continue.

However, this "Latinization" of inflation rates in the developed countries would probably lead to a Latinization of their political processes. Indexing requires government action, and every indexing decision or nondecision would become politicized. The political system would become overloaded and stalemated, producing a high-level political stagnation analogous to the "high-level economic stagnation" of the Great Depression of the 1930s.

From "low" double-digit inflation and high-level political stagnation, a gradual spread of indexing and an upward movement of the inflation rate would result. More and more people would be indexed at higher and higher rates. But as low double-digit rates become high double-digit ones, the agricultural and industrial elites would begin to find difficulty in obtaining new long-term credits, and in predicting the personal consequences of their investment and production decisions. The elites would then abandon the coalition for inflation and would seek to construct an alternative stabilization coalition. But because of mass indexing, there would be no mass base for stabilization policies. At this point, the elites of our most developed economies may turn to the most simple of political methods. The one step forward from the stage of a stability-oriented middle-class to that of an inflation-oriented middle-class could become two steps backward to the stage of an authoritarian regime.

NOTES

(1) An extensive compendium of conventional economic analyses is Lawrence B. Krause and Walter S. Salant, editors, Worldwide Inflation: Theory and Recent Experience (Washington, D.C.: The Brookings Institution, 1977). A critique of some conventional approaches is given by Fred Hirsch and John H. Goldthorpe in the prologue to their edited volume, The Political Economy of Inflation (Cambridge: Harvard University Press, 1978), especially pp. 1-2.

(2) The concept of early versus late development was central in the analysis of Alexander Gerschenkron, Economic Backwardness in Historical Perspective (Cambridge: Harvard University Press, 1962). I have applied the concept in my "The Political Consequences of the Product Cycle: Industrial History and Political Outcomes," International Organization, volume 33, number 1 (Winter 1979), pp. 1-34; and in my "Industrial Change and Political Change: A European Perspective," in David Collier, editor, The New Authoritarianism in Latin America (Princeton: Princeton University Press, 1979), pp. 319-362.

(3) Frank Longstreth, "The City, Industry, and the State, in Colin Crouch, editor, State and Economy in Contemporary Capitalism (London: St. Martins Press, 1979), pp. 160-173; Susan Strange, Sterling and British Policy: A Political Study of an International Currency in Decline (London: Oxford University Press, 1971); Stephen Blank, "Britain: The Politics of Foreign Economic Policy, the Domestic Economy, and the Problem of Pluralistic Stagnation," in Peter J. Katzenstein, editor, Between Power and Plenty: Foreign Economic Policies of Advanced Industrial States (Madison, Wisconsin: University Press, 1978), pp. 89-137 (also published as a special issue of International Organization, volume 31, number 4 (Autumn 1977).

(4) Although as Gerschenkron observes, France did develop investment banks (e.g., the Credit Mobilier of the Pereire brothers in the 1850s). But this investment banking sector soon became subordinated to the commercial banking one.

REFERENCES

Aldroft, Derek H. From Versailles to Wall Street, 1919-1929. (Berkeley: University of California Press, 1977).

Blair, John M. ed., The Roots of Inflation: The International Crisis. (New York: Burt Franklin, 1975).

Borchardt, Knut. "The Industrial Revolution in Germany, 1700-1914," in Carlo M. Cipolla, ed. The Emergence of Industrial Societies. (London: Collins, Fontana Books, 1973), pp. 76-156.

Cameron, Rondo E. France and the Economic Development of Europe, 1800-1914. (Princeton University Press: Princeton, N.J., 1961).

Feldman, Gerald D. Iron and Steel in the German Inflation. (Princeton: Princeton University Press, 1977).

Furtado, Celso. Economic Development of Latin America, second edition. (Cambridge: Cambridge University Press, 1976).

Gerschenkron, Alexander. Economic Backwardness in Historical Perspective. (Cambridge: Harvard University Press, 1962).

Gross, N.J. "The Industrial Revolution in the Habsburg Monarchy, 1750-1914," in Carlo M. Cipolla, ed. The Emergence of Industrial Societies. (London: Collins, Fontana Books, 1973), pp. 228-276.

Henderson, W.O. Britain and Industrial Europe: 1750-1870: Studies in British Influence on the Industrial Revolution in Western Europe, third edition. (London: Leicester University Press, 1972).

______. The Rise of German Industrial Power, 1834-1914. (Berkeley: University of California Press, 1975).

Hibbs, Douglas A., Jr. "Industrial Conflict in Advanced Industrial Societies," The American Political Science Review. volume LXX, number 4 (December, 1976), pp. 1033-1058.

______. "Political Parties and Macroeconomic Policy," The American Political Science Review. volume LXXI, number 4 (December 1977), pp. 1467-1487.

Hobsbam, E.J. The Age of Revolution: Europe 1789-1848. (London Weidenfeld and Nicolson, 1962), chapter 2.

______. Industry and Empire: The Making of Modern Society, Vol. II, 1759 to the Present Day. (New York: Pantheon, 1968), chapters 11-12.

Kaufman, Robert R. "Industrial Change and Authoritarian Rule in Latin America: A Concrete Review of the Bureaucratic-Authoritarian Model," in David Collier, ed. The New Authoritarianism in Latin America. (Princeton: Princeton University Press, 1979), pp. 319-362.

Kemp, Tom. Industrialization in Nineteenth-Century Europe. (London: Longman, 1969), chapter 6.

______. Historical Patterns of Industrialization (New York: Congman, 1978), chapter 6.

Maier, Charles S. Recasting Bourgeois Europe: Stabilization in France, Germany and Italy in the Decade after World War I (Princeton: Princeton University Press, 1975).

______. "The Politics of Inflation in the Twentieth Century" in Fred Hirsch and John H. Goldthorpe, eds. The Political Economy of Inflation (Cambridge: Harvard University Press, 1978), pp. 37-72.

Maynard, Geoffrey, and W. van Ryckeghem. A World of Inflation. (New York: Barnes and Noble, 1975), chapter 9.

Milward, Alan S. War, Economy and Society, 1939-1945. (Berkeley: University of California Press, 1977).

Polanyi, Karl. The Great Transformation (Boston: Beacon Press, 1957), chapter 1.

Ricossa, Sergio. "Italy, 1920-1970," in Carlo M. Cipolla, ed. Contemporary Economies (London: Collins, Fontana Books, 1976) pp. 266-274.

Shay, Robert Paul, Jr. British Rearmament in the Thirties: Politics and Profits (Princeton: Princeton University Press, 1977).

Shuker, Stephen A. The End of French Predominance in Europe: The Financial Crisis of 1924 and the Adoption of the Dawes Plan. (Chapel Hill: University of North Carolina Press, 1976).

Webster, Richard. Italian Industrial Imperialism (Berkeley: University of California Press, 1975).

3 Europe and the United States: The Transatlantic Aspects of Inflation

Susan Strange

The domestic aspects of inflation – those political and social pressures originating within each national economy – are fully explored elsewhere in this volume. Many of the pressures are common to industrialized and developing countries, and governments have had differing measures of success in coping with them. It is with the second aspect, the international and transnational aspect – with the inflationary effects on domestic rates of inflation of changes coming from outside – that this chapter will be more particularly concerned. For inflation may also be generated, or exacerbated, by developments in the international monetary system itself, by an increase in global liquidity, by the lavish creation of transnational credit, and by the communication, via foreign exchange and capital markets of inflationary pressures from dominant economies to dependent ones.

In this context, it will be argued that the arrangements for a European Monetary System (EMS) negotiated by the European Community in 1978 and implemented in 1979 were a direct response to these transnational inflationary forces, forces either liberated or directed by the United States. They were an instinctive gesture of protest at the disorder of the international monetary system, revealing deep disagreement with conventional American views of the causes and consequences of the stagflation of the 1970s. Many Americans – or so it seems in Europe – appear to accept unquestioningly the assumptions of the McCracken Report and to regard the monetary disorders of recent times as a passing phase, the result of some unfortunate coincidences whose disruptive effects will soon be overcome.

But many Europeans are much more pessimistic, far less sanguine about the prospects for good management of the world economy. The EMS, therefore, reflected an implicit (though seldom articulated) disillusion with the regime of dirty (or managed) floating exchange rates which succeeded the Bretton Woods system. Not only had this failed to be the magical solution to the troubles of the international monetary system that neoclassical economists once argued it would be, it had also proved little help to governments in their efforts to maintain jobs and incomes. The gesture of protest made at Bremen in July 1978 was no less real for being largely unconscious and unpremeditated and, indeed, for conflating two quite distinct purposes in its single declared aim of creating a 'zone of monetary stability.' For what the Europeans wanted to do was, first, to stabilize the intra-European pattern of exchange rates and, second, to bring down European inflation rates. This duality of purpose was never made explicit and was obscured by the predominance at the time of immediate German and French interests in putting the scheme forward. As things have turned out since, the Europeans, assisted by the Americans, have more or less succeeded in achieving the final objective – relative exchange rate stability within the Community – but have signally failed to achieve the second objective of insulating Europe from the inflationary credit-creation of the transnational Eurocurrency banking system and from the inflationary repercussions of the United States deficit financing.

For there is a continuing paradox in Euro-American relations that goes back to the early days of the Cold War and is still unresolved as President Reagan plans a $47 billion increase in U.S. defense spending while urging the NATO allies (in vain) to do likewise. It is now more than thirty years ago that the United States first embarked on a long and largely unsuccessful diplomatic campaign to persuade its European allies to make a bigger contribution – military and monetary – to the common cause of the defense of Europe. The Europeans, the members of NATO as well as the nonmembers, mostly delayed and prevaricated. The main defense burden stayed with the United States. But paradoxically, as the 1960s gave way to the 1970s, the Europeans found themselves holding more and more American promises-to-pay. And those who in effect had refused to implement the principle of direct taxation for common defense found themselves being indirectly taxed as the American promises-to-pay lost more and more of their real value. The frustrated tax gatherer was exacting an ironical revenge against the free-riders through the mechanisms of the international monetary system.

The argument that the outline proposals for EMS put forward by the French and German heads of state at Copenhagen in April 1978 were engendered in some sense by the weakness of the dollar has first to deal with the fact that earlier proposals for European monetary union were made some time before the breakdown of the Bretton Woods system and before the first devaluation of the dollar was achieved in the Smithsonian Agreement of December 1971. The answer to this apparent paradox is that the earlier proposals – the Barre Plan of 1969 and the Werner Report of 1970/71, blue-printing the plans for the famous 'snake in the tunnel' – were essentially inward-looking. They aimed simply at consolidating the Community, at protecting its one signal achievement, the Common Agricultural Policy, and at taking one more significant step towards greater economic union among the members. This was the time when the earlier concept – that liberal concept expressed in the Roma

Treaty of the Community as a common market in which all fiscal and monetary restraints on free trade and free movement of factors of production within the union would have disappeared making political unity that much more natural – still had given way to a belief in the need to pass from what John Pinder called 'negative integration' (the removal of barriers) to 'positive integration' (the adoption of common policies, internally and externally). The coordination of European currencies so that exchange rates between them stayed within the limits of the snake was one such step of positive integration. The only argument at that time was between monetarists and economists as to whether monetary coordination would assist the integration of national economic policies or whether the economies had first to be coordinated through parallel management policies so that monetary systems stayed fairly naturally in step with each other. In the late 1960s and early 1970s, therefore, the differences in European rates of inflation and of economic growth were almost universally ascribed mainly to domestic causes and to good or bad national management. Monetary order was a matter – especially in Germany – for self-congratulation; monetary disorder revealed a need for self-criticism. At times, certainly, national governments had to cope not only with domestic sources of inflation but with foreign ones. There were international mechanisms by which inflation could be spread, like a foreign virus infection, from one country to another. But having identified the source of the trouble, alert national authorities could take defensive or remedial action. The international monetary system itself was not generally perceived as playing a decisive role.

But by 1978, after five years' experience of floating exchange rates, perceptions had changed. What Roy Jenkins, President of the European Commission, described as 'this rickety structure' seemed to be creating many more problems for national monetary authorities than it solved. It was the external environmental factor from which Europe would need to shield itself, if it was to continue to enjoy a measure of monetary order.

It is important at this stage of the argument to stress the point that the general resort to floating rates in 1973 was not a deliberate act of policymaking. It was an apparently unavoidable capitulation to the forces of the market by national monetary authorities who found themselves quite unable to keep up with – and still less able to defeat – the volatile behavior of foreign exchange dealers. These market forces had grown so immensely powerful in determining the external values of currencies because for a decade governments permitted, even encouraged, the development of an international (or rather transnational) banking business on a hitherto undreamed of scale. This operated by and through a series of Eurocurrency markets in short and medium-term credit which allowed the highly profitable use of funds beyond the jurisdiction of national banking laws or exchange controls, and which facilitated the conversion of deposits and liabilities in one currency into deposits and liabilities in another.

For whatever reasons it occurred, the resort to floating rates, was welcomed as a reform of the international monetary system. For there was a widespread belief that it would restore both equilibrium to the international system and autonomy to national monetary management. On the one hand, Americans believed that it would allow the dollar to depreciate without diplomatic conflict and confrontation, thus, enabling the U.S. to preserve the trade surplus so keenly sought by export interests, both agricultural and industrial. On the other, Germans believed that floating would restore their lost but valued monetary autonomy by relieving the Bundesbank of the embarrassing inflows of foreign funds into Germany, flows which diluted and polluted the German money supply and infected it with inflation. Both thought the market, left to itself (more or less and for most of the time), would produce a miraculous balancing of monetary accounts and currency values.

Only after five years experience of the so-called reform did it begin to become clear that it was achieving neither, that it was impossible to leave the market to take care of exchange rates by itself, and that monetary autonomy was as elusive as ever. As Robert Triffin pointed out at the end of 1978,

> The most striking feature of the last six to eight years of floating rates is that they hardly changed the broad pattern of previous disequilibria among the major trading countries. The countries which experienced the largest surpluses before the increase of oil prices have about doubled these surpluses, in spite of the strong appreciation of their currencies, and the countries then in deficit already, saw their deficits more than triple in the following years, in spite of the sharp depreciation of their currencies.(1)

The fact that the system did not collapse under the strains of such surpluses and deficits is undoubtedly due to the resort – on a global level as on the domestic – to inflation as a substitute for redistribution. The oil-producing states reacting to the inflationary price rises of the early 1970s exploited the market trends to exact a fourfold increase in oil prices, effectively seeking a redistribution of real resources in their favor. To the extent they succeeded in getting paid more for their oil but did not at once spend it, the results were deflationary and set off a recession in world demand. But to the extent that they failed to achieve any real redistribution – because the 'haves' in the world economy created additional credit to allow those of them in deficit to carry on consuming imports more or less as before – the result was inflationary. The additional demands of the OPEC new-rich were added to the undiminished demands of the industrialized countries, and to the only-marginally-diminished demands of the non-oil developing countries. The first lot of demands were largely met through the creation of credit by governments, the third through the unrestrained creation of credit by the banking system. As Triffin further points out, the world total of national reserves redoubled between 1973 and 1977, having already doubled between 1969 and 1972. This increase occurred despite the claim that under a floating regime reserves would be more or less superfluous because adjustment would be achieved through the exchange rate. Half that increase of reserves in the mid-1970s was accounted for by the financing of U.S., British, and Italian deficits. Add together the German, Swiss, and Japanese surpluses of those years accumulated in unspent dollars and thus 'lent,' as it were, to the United States, and the increase in British and Italian reserves due to borrowing, and this represents about half the overall increase in world reserves between the end of 1975 and the end of 1978. Under what Triffin calls the paper-dollar standard (under which dollar reserves cannot be converted into gold), the United States has a new kind of 'exorbitant privilege.' Under the gold exchange standard it could pay its external accounts with dollars-convertible-into-gold, but which in practice piled up as with other countries' reserves. Under this paper dollar standard system the United States has been able to pay its external accounts with inconvertible paper dollars accumulating as U.S. Treasury securities in the surplus countries' reserves and with credit created by U.S. banks abroad on the strength of foreigners' deposits of dollars with them.

And as everyone now understands, the LDCs dependent on imported oil were able to meet their resulting deficits by going into debt to the banks, both directly through private loans and credits and indirectly by borrowing on the mushrooming Eurocurrency markets. Their total public debts increased from $80 billion in 1973 to $180 billion in 1976. And their salvation came not from governments but from the avidity of profit-making banks for eager borrowers. Foreign lending by the banks reporting to the Bank for International Settlements in Basle (which though probably by far the most substantial are not the only ones in the game) rose by $600 billion between 1972 and September 1978. This fact alone would explain the inflationary pressures emanating from the international monetary system.

What is less easy to explain is why the German government, having lived with this anarchistic monetary disorder for most of the decade of the 1970s, should have suddenly decided in the spring of 1978 to resuscitate the seemingly moribund idea of a European monetary union. That is the first question to be answered. And the second is linked to it. It is what political significance should be attached to EMS. Is there any sign that after the thirty years of dependence on the United States and obedience to the wishes of Washington, the Federal Republic is making, at last, its own declaration of independence?

Two kinds of explanations have been given and the weight attached to each is a matter of subjective judgment. One can be described as the monetary explanation, the other as the commercial and industrial one.

The clues to the monetary explanation are to be found in an exposé of German monetary policies, domestic and foreign, over the last 20 years or so, made in 1977 by Dr. Otmar Emminger, President of the Bundesbank. This was published as Princeton Essay in International Finance. For historical and ideological reasons, German governments were passionately concerned to maintain the internal stability of the currency. For strategic and commercial reasons, they were also concerned to maintain external stability, a balance of payments that would keep the value of the deutschmark reasonably steady in relation to the dollar and to the other major trading currencies. For most of the first half of its independent existence, the Federal Republic managed successfully to pursue its domestic and its external goals of currency stability. But in the second half, from about 1965 or 1967, the coincidence between Germany's domestic goals and the 'milieu goals' of the United States disappeared; Germany was obliged to resort to various defensive strategies to fend off the destabilizing influences from outside. It went through one bad patch in 1957 before the 1958 devaluation of the franc and another in 1960/61 when the Kennedy Administration unthinkingly "unhorsed" the Bundesbank's careful strategies of credit control aimed at keeping out foreign funds from inundating the domestic money supply. The Federal Reserve cut American discount rates just as the Bundesbank had raised German rates. However, once the revaluation of the deutschmark had been managed in 1961, the pressures eased and did not reappear until after 1968. Then, as Emminger relates, German domestic monetary strategies found themselves once again at the mercy of external ups and downs. These emanated, in the terminal stages of the fixed rate regime from the foreign exchange markets, but were often set off by sudden switches in American interest rates reflecting the changing political priorities which U.S. Administrations gave to fighting price increases or to reviving employment.

Then, with the resort to floating, although the pressures from the foreign exchange markets made it hard for the weaker European currencies so that the European snake, as originally conceived, soon expired, a group of lesser European countries remained linked to the deutschmark in a de facto deutschmark zone. This group managed for quite a while to maintain a fairly stable rate with the U.S. dollar. This was partly made possible by the fact that in 1974 so many of the OPEC oil funds found their way into (or stayed in) dollars. But as the petrodollars dispersed through the system and the dollar weakened, so the costs to Germany of maintaining the dollar-deutschmark axis rose, more so when the United States did not see its own interest in keeping up its end of the relationship. And as the markets' confidence in U.S. monetary policies altered, the effectiveness of such intervention also declined. Early in 1978, for instance, the Bundesbank spent DM 1.7 billion in one month trying in vain to arrest a falling dollar. In March 1978, the swap arrangement with the Federal Reserve was doubled to a limit of $4 billion. But to no avail, the dollar remained weak. Turning away in despair from its partnership with the United States, Germany looked once again to its European neighbors and, especially, to France.

The commercial and industrial explanation for this change of direction rests on the assumption that German governments, like those of other industrialized countries, cannot survive high rates of unemployment. Workers without jobs, even managers of shops and factories without customers, won't vote for them. When the post-OPEC recession in the world economy began in 1974/5, many people hoped it would be short-lived and that growth rates would soon pick up again as the system adjusted. These hopes faded as 1977 ended with numbers in employment in every industrialized country except the United States and Germany falling well below 1975 levels. Although both Germany and Switzerland have eased the unemployment problem to some extent by sending home their Gastarbeiter to Turkey, Italy, and points south, the political dangers of any further cutbacks in industrial orderbooks were only too clear.

But German industry had, by then, become more dependent on export markets than any other industrialized country, save Britain. Foreign trade accounted, by 1978, for nearly 23 percent of German GNP compared with less than 7 percent for the United States. In 1960, this trade dependence was equal to only 18 percent of GNP. Moreover, the important export markets for Germany lay close at hand in Europe. Half of German exports were going to other countries in the European Community, 65 percent to Europe as a whole. Only 5 percent went to the United States, 6 percent to the Eastern bloc countries. One job in five in the Federal Republic depended on maintaining export orders, with the proportion much higher in certain politically sensitive capital goods sectors.

Faced with continued world depression, a growing trend in all the industrialized countries toward protectionism in commercial policy, and the clear possibility that further appreciation of the currency would, finally, price German exports out of their European markets, the decision to try once more to stabilize exchange rates in the Community made political as well as economic sense.

Moreover, broader political considerations reinforced Chancellor Schmidt's will to try again. The Bonn Summit with President Carter in March/April 1978 had been disappointing, despite its bland communiqué. The United States was more concerned with its relations with China and the Soviet Union than with Europe, and was still suggesting on the basics of a rather dubious 'locomotive theory' that it was up to Japan and Germany to spend the world economy out of recession. The clumsiness of its handling of Brazil's order for a West German nuclear power plant still rankled. The assurances given by Carter to the Soviets on the neutron bomb seemed to show that the United States was quite prepared to buy detente with the USSR at the expense of Europe's security. The failure to make any headway in Congress with an energy policy to reduce U.S. dependence on imported oil had depressing implications for the longterm strength of the dollar. On all these points, President Giscard's reactions were most probably much the same as the Chancellor's. The French government, too, was convinced of the importance for domestic economic management of keeping up the external value of the franc. Prime Minister Raymond Barre was making a determined bid to check inflation while dismantling a great many obsolete price controls. Confidence in the future and the prospect of renewed growth in the economy were vital to the success of these domestic policies. The French planners, moreover, were well aware that demographic trends were going to make it necessary to find nine million new jobs in the course of the next decade, 1965-75. Tying the franc to the German D-mark carried risks – but not so great as the political risks of sluggish economic growth. Schmidt's offer looked like an invitation to leave the second rank of European economies and join the first class.

The basic proposition which the two heads of state put to the other members of the Community at Copenhagen, therefore, was for a stronger and more impressive snake. The European central banks would intervene to keep the cross rates between their currencies within close limits and stable in relation to a European currency unit, or ECU. The participants would increase their mutual credit commitments and would consider pooling 20 percent of their national reserves of gold and dollars to form a fund for coordinated intervention in the foreign exchange markets. By this means the Community would try to create, as indicated earlier, a 'zone of monetary stability' in Europe which would be both resistant, through the discipline exerted on the weak-currency countries, to inflation and immune to international monetary disorders. The key question was, and is, whether it could do so, and what were the necessary and sufficient conditions for success in achieving either objective.

Looking back, it is surely clear that all the intricate points so fiercely debated in the early days of EMS, in 1978/79, were largely irrelevant to this question. It is not therefore necessary here to go into the arguments over the valuation of the ECU and thus over the trigger indicators which would require central bank intervention to support or suppress a currency's market value; the controversy between the grid method and the basket; the British objections and hesitations; the special rules worked out for Italy and for Ireland, nor even the last-minute French attempt to bargain a better deal for French agriculture out of the common anxiety to get EMS into action.

Indeed, the crucial variable deciding whether the Europeans could or could not achieve greater stability in intra-EC exchange rates had already been identified by the Community's own Monetary Committee.

In an Annexe to their 1977 Annual Report, they had pointed, clearly and firmly, to the instability of the dollar. 'Both because of the dollar's general importance as a vehicle and reserve currency, and because of its different weight in member countries' external transactions, it will be difficult to achievce a reasonable degree of stability between snake and non-snake member currencies (<u>and even to avoid tensions within the snake</u>) without concerted endeavours to keep exchange rate movements between the snake and the dollar within reasonable bounds.' Less bureaucratically, M. van Ypersele, the Belgian chairman explained why this was so:

> When people move out of the dollar because there is a lack of confidence, they do not more equally into all the European currencies. They move specifically into one currency in Western Europe, the mark. This pushed the mark up and it widens the

> relationship between the mark and the French franc or sterling. So one can say that sharp fluctuations in the dollar have also in a certain way contributed to too sharp fluctuations between European currencies. And when I say 'too sharp' fluctuations, what I mean is fluctuations much in excess of what would be allowed by differential rates of inflation between European currencies (Ypersele, 1977).

The implication of this – and the conclusion to be drawn from observation of the behavioral patterns of foreign exchange markets in the course of 1976 and 1977 – was clear. It was that EMS would succeed in keeping European cross rates reasonably stable if the dollar held its value in terms of marks (or even, Japanese yen, since some of the flight from dollars into yen always tended to spill over into Europe). It would fail if the dollar started to fall again because the mark would then bounce as high as the dollar falls low, while the weaker currencies in EMS would stay down with the dollar. The $500 billion loose in the Eurocurrency markets was, and is – to recall a graphic simile once used about monetary disorders by President Hoover – like an iron cannon that breaks its chains on the firing deck of a man-o'-war. It does not take a very heavy swell in the markets to send it crashing through any barriers set up by central banks.

And just to emphasize the point made by M. van Ypersele about exchange rates shifting in excess of what would be allowed (i.e., explained) by differential rates of inflation, it is worth noting some calculations made by the London Business School in 1979. These suggested that for Community currencies to stay in line with each other, it was probably necessary for Germany to have a rate of inflation 2 percent above the rest – such was then the market's bullish assessment of prospects for the mark. But if they could help it, this was a price the Germans did not want to pay. A monthly report made by the Bundesbank on the prospects for EMS in March 1979 categorically rejected, yet again, the notion that Germany would permit domestic inflation in order to help the Deutschmark's harmonization with the other European currencies. In the event, however, Germany was forced into accepting increased inflation not by her EC partners but by the inexorable need to respond to pressures originating in the United States and communicated through international markets. The reality of this dependence was in fact demonstrated by the experience of the winter of 1978/9. From November through to February, the dollar stayed remarkably stable. And although the EMS was not formallly inaugurated until March 1979 because of a French gambit on agricultural MCA's (i.e., compensatory payment to farmers), it did in fact function from early January on without great strain. According to the Bundesbank report just quoted, the indicators required market intervention only once in this initial period and then on behalf of a minor currency, the Danish Krone.

In retrospect, credit for this easy birth must go in large measure to the package of measures announced by President Carter on All Saints' Day, 1978 – November 1st. Recall that these included an impressive $30 billion reserve for the New York Federal Reserve Bank to draw on, the deliberate use of higher interest rates to stiffen the resolve of central banks to keep reserves in dollar assets and – perhaps biggest departure of all – a decision to issue U.S. government bonds denominated in Deutschmarks and Swiss francs. (This last measure recalls the dollar gurantees which the Bank of England finally had to offer official holders of sterling reserves in the Basle Agreement of 1968.)

According to the Federal Reserve Bank's Monthly Bulletin, these measures followed a four-month period in which $33 billion had been spent by the U.S. and other central banks in a vain attempt to prevent a decline in the dollar's exchange rate. The Bundesbank contributed $8.4 billion in DM to this effort contributing as the Monthly Bulletin admitted 'to a strong expansion in German monetary aggregates.' The need for the Bundesbank and for the Bank of Japan to come promptly to the aid of the dollar as a matter of their own self-interest did not end with the Carter measures and the arrest of the dollar's precipitate fall in the foreign exchange markets. But as the dollar subsequently strengthened, it has in fact been less marked.

Instead, the United States under the intelligent leadership of Mr. Paul Volcker, first at the Federal Reserve Bank in New York and later as chairman of the Federal Reserve Board in Washington, resorted increasingly to interest rates acting on the money markets to maintain the value of the dollar. Of course, this was not the only factor to which markets have reacted in 1980 and 1981: Afghanistan, the slowing of U.S. oil imports and the election of a hawkish, 'sound money' President have played a very large part. But if the EMS has had a relatively easy ride, domestic monetary management in Germany has not. It is no coincidence that volatility in U.S. interest rates from 11 percent up to 20 percent and back down to around 13 percent within a twelve month period has coincided with accelerated inflation in Germany, the emergence of a massive current deficit, and the decline of the DM to the bottom end of the EMS grid. In short, the susceptibility of Germany and of the rest of the European Community including Britain to arbitrary and often unexpected changes in American monetary nostrums and policy measures remains undiminished, despite the EMS. It becomes not more but less easy to devise means of reducing the vulnerability of European (and Japanese, OPEC, and LDC) economies to choices made in Washington. We must continually remind people, I believe, of the fundamental indicators of American monetary dominance – indicators which do not change much with the yo-yo ups and downs of exchange rates, interest rates, or overall balance of payments positions. They are (1) that the proportion of world reserves held in dollars remains around 76 or 77 percent; (2) that the percentage of Eurocurrency bank liabilities denominated in dollars is still around 80 percent; (3) that the proportion of U.S. government debt held by foreigners remains around one-sixth; (4) the value of dollar denominated bonds is still twice that of D-mark bonds and accounts for nearly 60 percent of the total international bond market; (5) that foreign direct and portfolio investment in the United States has risen higher and faster in the 1970's than in any other national economy; (6) that probably something around 75 percent of international trade transactions are invoiced and calculated in dollars, and that private buyers and sellers, therefore, respond most promptly to decisions made in Washington rather than anywhere else; (7) that U.S. corporations still dominate international business, accounting for 46 percent of total sales of all major transnational corporations and their share of all foreign direct investment is still over 45 percent compared with under 7 percent each for Germany and Japan.

What, the question inevitably follows, can the Europeans do about it? They cannot, it is clear, create their 'zone of monetary stability' unaided by the coincidence (when it happens) of U.S. interest. But they can perhaps use persuasion peppered with a touch of coercion. There are more and more voices in the United States today than there were in 1971 or 1975 calling for a return to monetary rectitude and responsibility. America's enlightened long term interest lies in presiding over a world market economy that offers reasonable prospects of justice, stability, and wealth to all those, great and small, rich and poor, who contribute to its daily miracles of production and exchange. The weapons of monetary power which the United States wields, can be used to exploit the system, shifting burden of risk and adjustment on the other shoulders. Or they can be used for the general welfare of the system in which American banks, insurance companies, and corporations now have an immense interest and commitment. The Europeans – and particularly those academics and others who are outside government – should not cease to join their voices to those from within the United States who perceive the short-run roses and raptures of monetary vice as being more ephemeral, and politically dangerous, than the sterner values of monetary virtue.

And it may be that persuasion would be more effective if it were reinforced with a touch of coercive competition. The introduction of a European reserve asset or parallel currency such as Roland Vaubel and others have imagined would offer a monetary asset representing not merely (like the SDR) the weighted value of the participating currencies but a stable value in terms of real goods and services. Of course, this would precipitate all the conflicts with the Americans that the Germans especially have been anxious to avoid for so many years of cold war and detente. Of course, the sacrifice of independent monetary options would be considerable. But the Europeans cannot continue to complain that through international inflation the Americans are subjecting them to 'taxation without representation' if they remain supine and passive and take no steps to help themselves – and incidentally, I believe, to help the long-term interests of the United States, even if few Americans as yet see it that way.

NOTE

(1) R. Triffin, "Gold and the Dollar Crisis: Yesterday and Tomorrow," <u>Foreign Affairs</u>, December 1978. Triffin footnotes this adding that the

combined surplusses of Japan, Switzerland, Germany, and Netherlands rose from $10 billion in 1972 and $8 billion in 1973, to $18 billion in 1977; and the combined current deficits of the US, UK, Canada, Italy, and France rose from $8 billion in 1972 and $6 billion in 1973 to nearly $25 billion in 1977.

REFERENCE

Ypersele, van M., Listener, October 5, 1979.

4 The IMF in Europe: Inflation Fighting in Britain, Italy and Portugal

Barbara Stallings

In the on-and-off battle against inflation in the postwar period, a major protagonist has been the International Monetary Fund (IMF). The IMF role has come about because inflation is one of the economic ills that the Fund tries to combat through its so-called stabilization agreements that are the sine qua non for governments seeking loans to tide them over balance of payments crises. Despite its prominence, however, the IMF's role has not been a very positive one. In fact, it is even possible to argue that IMF policies may lead to higher inflation rates.

There are many reasons for these negative findings. First, lowering inflation is only one of the multiple, and often contradictory, goals of IMF programs. Second, the IMF analysis and prescriptions are simplistic, if not actually wrong. Third, the political crises implicit in the programs lead governments to avoid implementing them fully and the Fund itself to acquiesce if the political crises are likely to produce a shift to the left. Fourth, the side effects of the programs – recession, regressive redistribution of income, and even political repression – are frequently seen as worse than inflation itself. Because of growing criticism, the IMF has been re-evaluating its approach over the past couple years. Larger amounts of money are being made available over longer periods of time. There are also some indications that inflation and balance of payments problems are coming to be seen as structural problems rather than purely ones of demand management as was previously the case. The effects of these changes, however, remain to be seen.

The strongest critics of the IMF are found in the third world. These critics argue, in increasingly strident terms, that the Fund misunderstands their problems and is an impediment rather than a help in development. The recent changes in Fund policies have not eliminated this criticism.(1) Because of these protests, most studies of the IMF center on its role in the third world. This chapter, by contrast, looks at the recent experience of the IMF in Europe. Thus, we are observing the Fund where its potential of having a positive contribution is greatest because the economies are stronger and political stability less delicate. Nevertheless, the same problems will be seen to exist in Europe as in Africa, Asia, and Latin America. This strengthens the impression that there are serious flaws in the approach itself.

The first two sections of this chapter will present some essential background information on the IMF analysis about the causes and remedies of inflation and on how inflation relates to other IMF concerns, especially balance of payments crises. Then we will turn to three recent Fund missions in Europe: Britain in 1976, Italy in 1977, and Portugal in 1978. Here we will look at the nature of the economic problems in each country, the political forces arrayed with and against the Fund, the Fund recommendations as contained in the Letters of Intent, and the effects of the stabilization programs. Finally, based on these three case studies, we will suggest some conclusions about the IMF approach to inflation.

THE IMF ANALYSIS OF INFLATION

In order to devise anti-inflation policies, there must be some notion about the causes of inflation. Trying to discover the IMF theory of inflation is complicated by two factors.(2) On the one hand, there is at least some disagreement on this matter among persons working for the Fund. On the other hand, the interest in theory, as well as the precision of views, is much stronger in the research department than in the area departments which actually prescribe policies. Nevertheless, a substantial degree of consensus seems to have emerged as a result of department views spreading through the rest of the organization.

This comes about in at least two ways. First are formal channels, e.g., the head of the research department is chief economic advisor to the managing director of the Fund who, in turn, supervises the teams that prescribe policies for governments. In addition, area department staff sometimes seek information on specific problems from the research department. Second and more important are informal channels. As one area department economist explained, "When you first come here, you quickly realize that everybody is talking with reference to a certain set of ideas. These ideas come from the writings of a few people like (J.J.) Polak (current head of the research department), (Robert) Mundell, and (Sidney) Alexander (former IMF economists). You have to become familiar with this body of literature or you simply can't communicate with your colleagues." Thus formal channels and informal indoctrination, together with the fact that economists who disagree with Fund analysis are unlikely to be hired, have resulted in a common position.

The position that prevails today can best be described as "eclectic monetarism." That is, although some economists in the research department are very strict monetarists, the area people continually repeat the phrase, "Yes, money is important. But it is not the only thing that is important." In the research department, it is possible to hear the standard monetarist line that if the money supply increases only with the increase in GNP, inflation is impossible. Wage increases cannot produce inflation unless they are "validated" by increases in the money supply. Outside shocks (even such strong ones as the 1973 oil price increases) are viewed in the same way. The mechanism presumed to be at work is that if the money supply does not rise sufficiently to validate wage increases, either profits must be cut to offset the rise in wages or many of the goods produced will not be sold for lack of effective demand, in which case unemployment will increase and wages will fall to their former level. The key assumption, of course, is constant velocity.

In the area departments, on the other hand, wage increases and international factors are assigned an independent role. Policy prescriptions are not limited to monetary targets, but usually focus on wages, budget deficits, credit policies, and exchange rates as well. In general, it is probably fair to say that the area department economists see their views as fairly eclectic (with some even verging toward Keynesianism) but saddled with a monetarist label for technical reasons. That is, the primary target which Fund economists monitor involves monetary aggregates, specifically Domestic Credit Expansion (increase in the money supply adjusted for surplus or deficit in the balance of payments), but they insist that this is for practical rather than theoretical reasons. Credit figures are available more quickly and are subject to less revision than other data. Other targets have been tried (e.g., budget deficits), but they are inaccurate in the short run, and months behind time, so that current monitoring is impossible.

INFLATION VIS-À-VIS OTHER IMF TARGETS

Concern with inflation was not one of the original aspects of the IMF mandate. The goals that were outlined in 1945 pledged the Fund to promote international monetary cooperation, expansion of trade, exchange stability, establishment of multilateral payments systems and the elimination of exchange restrictions, and smooth adjustment of balance of payments disequilibria (IMF, 1945; Horsefield, 1969). It was only a few years later that some economists realized that inflation could interfere with the achievement of the original goals. The 1948 Annual Report dealt specifically with this issue, and measures to control inflation began to be incorporated into the programs set out by the Fund (IMF, 1948). Several decades later, inflation is still considered an important evil in and of itself, and not just because of the side effects which it produces (e.g., uncertainty, redistribution, etc.). As one official explained, "I think it is accurate to say that the Fund has not adopted the view that indexation can obviate the need for combatting inflation."(3)

On the other hand, inflation cannot be said to be the Fund's top priority, nor do governments go to the IMF because they have problems with inflation.(4) They go because they have balance of payments crises, so it is crucial to understand how inflation is seen to relate to the balance of payments and other parts of the economy. As can be seen from the goals listed above, the IMF's main role is to open up the world for the free movement of goods and capital or, conversely, to prevent the imposition of restrictions. Exchange stability was seen as part of this process. One of the major reasons why countries impose restrictions is because they have foreign exchange crises or would have them if controls were eliminated. Thus, in practice, the Fund's main activity is working out ways to resolve balance of payments difficulties, including the provision of short-term loans, so that restrictions will not be needed. Such programs are known as stabilization programs.

What is a stabilization program, and how does inflation fit in? The IMF tends to see the relationship between inflation and balance of payments crises in terms of the so-called "monetary approach to the balance of payments" which Fund economists were influential in developing (IMF, 1977). Again, however, it is necessary to think of the Fund adopting a more flexible or eclectic version of the theory (Blackwell, 1978). According to the monetary approach, a balance of payments crisis is chiefly caused by excess credit expansion which will then leak out into imports. This same phenomenon, of course, is thought to contribute to (or cause) inflation. In addition – and here the IMF eclectic outlook reappears – there are some direct linkages between inflation and exchange crises. The most important is probably lack of competitiveness in countries which have high inflation rates relative to their trading partners so that their exports become more expensive and imports cheaper in relative terms. Devaluation should be able to overcome this handicap, but that infringes on the exchange stability which the Fund tries to promote, and it also further fuels inflation.

The elements of a stabilization program generally include devaluation, cuts in the budget deficit (usually by cutting spending but sometimes by raising taxes), cuts in credit expansion and higher interest rates, elimination or lowering of price controls, and sometimes the imposition of wage ceilings. These elements are incorporated into a "Letter of Intent," addressed to the IMF managing directors and signed by the country's finance minister. The goals mentioned, however, are not all of equal importance. Some represent the country's own intentions over the period (e.g., target rates for inflation and wage increases). Others are official "performance criteria," meaning that if they are not met, the loan which accompanies the stabilization program will be cut off (Stallings, 1981).

Stabilization programs vary in severity, depending in part on how large a loan the country is requesting in relation to its drawing rights in the Fund. (Other reasons will be discussed below.) That is, each country has a quota representing the amount it has paid in and therefore can borrow. The first 25 percent – the so-called gold tranche – can be drawn at will. The second 25 percent – the first credit tranche –

can only be drawn after a Fund mission has examined a country's economy and approved the general policy lines being followed. Further drawings carry much stricter requirements, including precise performance criteria to be met, usually focusing on credit expansion, budget deficits, and the balance of payments.

Four types of effects typically result from a stabilization program. First is a recession, as demand falls because of lower wages, lower government spending, and lower credit availability. Second is a shift in income from wage earners toward capital because of wage ceilings and the lifting of price controls.(5) Third is a temporary easing of the balance of payments crisis, because of a drop in imports, due to recessionary conditions and, possibly, any increase in exports. The fourth effect, and the one which is most directly relevant for this chapter, is that inflation often increases in spite of the avowed intention to slow it down.

Increased inflation comes about through higher import costs after devaluation, higher interest rates, and higher domestic prices as price controls and subsidies are eliminated. Fund economists deny that these changes will bring about an inflationary spiral, however; rather they say a one-time rise and readjustment of relative prices will occur. This is true under one crucial condition which reveals the inherent bias of Fund programs. There will be no inflationary spiral, if and only if, wage increases are not allowed to keep up with the jump in prices.(6) Thus workers must accept a substantial cut in their purchasing power; otherwise the effect of the stabilization policies will accelerate inflation.

This is not to say that some capitalists – mainly small ones – will not be hurt through falling demand, higher interest rates, and limits on credit. The chief beneficiaries tend to be foreign firms operating within the country as restrictions on their activities are lowered, and some of their competition is driven out of business. Because of the international scale of their operations, they can get credit in other markets and sell elsewhere until better times return to the country. Domestic firms do not have this alternative, at least in the short run, since breaking into the international export market is a very difficult feat.

It would be a mistake, however, to see this process as one where the IMF is simply trying to help the rich and hurt the poor. In fact, the Fund is an organization that believes the capitalist system offers the greatest advantages for all. The aim is, therefore, to make the economy "healthy" again so that private capitalists will invest. The only way to do this is to insure that high profits will be earned, and thus it is workers who must be squeezed in order to eliminate exchange crises and inflation.

It would also be a mistake to see the IMF as unilaterally imposing stabilization programs on governments that are totally opposed to such policies. Fund officials realize that a program imposed from the outside is extremely difficult to enforce and is not likely to succeed. Rather what happens is usually a coalition between the IMF team and certain factions of the government and business groups of the country concerned. Under such circumstances, the IMF plays several roles. It can bolster the forces of domestic groups desiring stabilization-type policies. It can also be used as a type of "scapegoat" for the negative effects such policies will produce. Finally, it can provide access for money to partially offset these negative effects in the short run; that is, they can be spread over a longer period of time. This third role is more important than it might appear at first. IMF loans per se are relatively small, but some bilateral as well as other multilateral money has traditionally been made contingent on the IMF "seal of approval" as evidenced by the acceptance of a stabilization program. Recently, many of the private banks have also begun to tie their loans in the same way.(7)

Europe, the IMF, and Inflation

In the 1950s and 1960s, stabilization programs were mainly directed at Latin American governments which continually got into exchange crises through what the IMF considered faulty economic management, that being especially large increases in the money supply. Some European countries had occasionally gone to the Fund for "stand-by" arrangements (permission to draw money any time within a year if problems arose) (Gold, 1970; IMF Annual Report, 1970-80). Recently, however, the number of European stand-bys has increased significantly. Here we will be looking at the most important agreements over the last several years – Britain (1976), Italy (1977), and Portugal (1978).(8)

Nature of economic problems

From a superficial point of view, the economic problems of the three countries appeared quite similar. All had high inflation rates, large budget deficits, and large deficits in the current account of the balance of payments. All had suffered serious drains on reserves as well. In spite of these surface similarities, however, there were both quantitative and qualitative differences among the three.

In quantitative terms, Britain's problems were less serious on almost every count than those of Italy or Portugal. This can be seen in table 4.1 which shows figures for the four quarters preceding the respective IMF agreements. The British inflation rate was "only" 15 percent, while that of Italy was 19 percent and Portugal 29 percent. The budget deficit in the UK represented five and a half percent of the GNP,(9) while Portugal's deficit was eight percent and Italy's over eleven percent. Balance of payments figures showed Britain with a current account deficit of 0.7 percent of GNP, while Italy has 0.5 percent, and Portugal a whopping nine percent. In relative terms, then, it is possible to identify Italy's most obvious problem as the budget deficit and Portugal's as the balance of payments and inflation. The British situation was a more balanced one, though the Fund was mainly concerned with the budget deficit.

Table 4.1. Economic Conditions in 4-Quarter Periods Preceding IMF Agreements.

	Britain[a]	Italy[b]	Portugal[c]
Inflation[d]	16	19	29
Budget deficit[e] GDP	5.6	11.3	8.0
Budget deficit[e]/expenditures	14.2	36.3	25.1
Balance of payments deficit[f]/GDP	0.7	0.5	8.9
Growth in GDP	3.0	5.0	5.4
Unemployment	5.3	5.3	9.5

[a]1st quarter 1976-4th quarter 1976

[b]3rd quarter 1976-2nd quarter 1977

[c]1977 (no data available by quarters)

[d]consumer prices

[e]Public sector "net lending" (Britain) "enlarged" public sector (Italy), public sector (Portugal)

[f]current account

Sources: IMF, International Financial Statistics; OECD, Main Economic Indicators and Economic Surveys (Britain, Italy, and Portugal), various issues.

Qualitatively speaking, there were also major differences. Britain was the classical example of a stagnant economy. Alternating Labor and Conservative governments presided over a public sector that continually grew in size (in the 1970s, it accounted for over half the GDP) and power (regulator capacity, plus ownership of a large number of key industries) but never assumed the dominant role in directing the accumulation process (Shonfield, 1965). The large size but ambivalent nature of the government produced a stalemate with private capital so that neither the public sector nor the private sector was willing to invest. For example, during the 1950-73 period, Britain's rate of growth of capital stock was only 3.7 percent, while its major competitors' was 8.2 percent. At the same time, the labor unions increased their power aand militancy so that wage hikes led to a profits squeeze. The before-tax profit rate dropped from 14.2 percent in 1960 to 8.7 percent in 1970 to 3.5 percent in 1975 (Glyn, forthcoming).

The result of these and other factors was a slow-growing economy in general, but much more importantly an economy suffering from what has been called the process of "deindustrialization." Referring to the decline of the industrial sector, deindustrialization can be measured by trends in output, employment, and competition. By all of these measures, Britain's industrial sector has been ailing in the last 20 years, both in comparison with its own past performance, and with the performance of other major industrial countries. In terms of manufacturing output, Britain's average annual growth rate between the early 1960s and 1973 was 3.0 percent compared to 6.6 percent for other major industrial countries; for growth rates of employment in manufacturing, the comparable figures were -0.9 percent and 1.1 percent (Singh, 1977). Since 1973, Britain's industrial performance has declined even faster. For the same period, the British share of exports to industrial countries fell by almost one-third; all others' increased except the United States whose share fell by about one-sixth. Even more damaging were trends for import penetration. The share of the domestic market supplied by imported manufactured goods increased by almost two-thirds between 1969 and 1974 (Moore and Rhodes, 1976).

De-industrialization is an example of Myrdal's cumulative causation process. It is a vicious spiral whereby low investment leads to a lack of competitiveness. This in turn leads to a lack of demand which leads to higher unit costs. This results in lower profits which lead to lower investment rates. It has had a particularly devastating effect on the economy for at least two reasons. First, the poor performance of the manufacturing sector has had serious repercussions for the trade balance, both through exports and imports. When this factor is combined with the fact that the British balance of payments is especially vulnerable in any case because of that remnant of empire, the "sterling balances," the context is set for the stop-go economic cycles that have characterized post-war economic policy in Britain. The stop-go cycles, in turn, fed back into the problem of stagnation because they produced a slow-growing domestic market and because it was investment that tended to be cut back in a "stop" period, while consumption was stimulated in a "go" period (Caves 1968; Cairncross, 1971). A second reason for being concerned about the deindustrialization process is that the industrial sector has traditionally been the main source of technological progress, economies of scale, productivity, and economic growth (Kaldor, 1966). Thus, a decline in industry has important ramifications in other sectors as well.

By the mid-1970s, these structural trends, exacerbated by conjunctural factors such as the oil crisis, put the British economy in a state of crisis. The 1975 figures showed inflation at 22 percent, a growth rate of 1.9 percent for the previous decade and -1.9 percent for the year, over one million persons unemployed (about four percent of the labor force), and a balance of payments deficit of almost $2 billion (OECD, 1979). The only bright spot was North Sea oil, which was due to begin production for export in the late 1970s, but the oil reserves were small and already heavily mortgaged. The important question was whether they would be used to improve British industry, and thus its long-run competitive position, or whether there would be a brief period of consumption-led growth, followed by a return to stagnation.

If Britain represented an overripe economy, Italy and Portugal had gotten into trouble by trying to catch up too quickly. Italy had finished World War II as a semi-industrialized country, with low per capita income, low productivity, and high rates of protection. All of this changed, however, with the installation of a Christian Democratic government in 1948 and the political-economic line it followed. In political terms, the left was excluded from political participation and the unions from a role in industrial relations. In economic terms, the economy was opened up, and a long boom period of export-led growth enabled Italy to reach living standards approaching those of other European countries. That growth was achieved at the expense of cheap labor, made possible by the Christian Democratic political stance, on the one hand, and a large supply of surplus labor, on the other hand. The state also contributed by investing heavily in energy, roads, and basic metals (Salvati, forthcoming; Proctor, 1976).

Although average per capita income rose rapidly, such figures hid two kinds of economic divisions, in addition to that between labor and capital. The first concerned the division between the fast-growing industrial North and the relatively stagnant agricultural South. The second division lay within the industrial sector itself, between the modern high-productivity sectors such as chemicals, automobiles, and steel compared to textiles and food which were more traditional, low-productivity sectors (Lutz, 1962).

By the 1960s, the political-economic context had begun to change significantly. The tightening up of the labor market provided the objective conditions necessary for growing union strength, and this was matched by greater organizing. Furthermore, the erosion of the Christian Democratic electoral power forced the party to make an alliance with the Socialists which, in turn, brought about a less coercive political environment (Proctor, 1976). The result was rising wages, plus other labor demands with respect to employment guarantees and social services. At the same time, however, the Christian Democrats managed to protect their position through greater use of patronage, both through the social services system and the growing state enterprise system. The latter had been inherited from the fascist regime, but was enlarged in the post-war period both by taking over bankrupt companies and by investing in new industries. The government is now estimated to account for 55 percent of industrial production, but – as in the British case – this potential power to direct the economy has not been used in practice (Posner and Woolf, 1967; Shonfield, 1965). The use of the state sector in support of a single political party in Italy, however, never had a counterpart in Britain.

By the 1970s, the last traces of the "Italian miracle" had disappeared. The economy was coming to be dominated by the stop-go policies begun in the 1960s to dampen the wage boom, and trend growth had slowed as well. For instance, GDP growth rates from 1950 to 1969 averaged 5.7 percent, while between 1970 and 1976 the average was only 2.6 percent (Posner and Woolf 1967; Basevi, 1977). Unemployment again became a serious problem, especially for young people who represented almost 50 percent of total unemployment. Real wages nevertheless continued to rise, mainly because of the *scala mobile*, an escalator clause which partially protected labor from inflation. In 1975, this clause was strengthened and workers today are able to recover about 90 percent of purchasing power lost through inflation (Bank of Italy, 1975). In 1973, oil price increases drove the balance of payments into deficit for the first time in decades. The deficit continued until 1977, exacerbated by runs on the lira in 1974 and 1976, and caused the government to seek emergency loans from the IMF, the EEC, and various individual governments and private banks. High inflation rates and a huge budget deficit rounded out a dismal economic picture (OECD, 1977 and 1979; Vivo and Pivetti, 1980).

The 1970s problems were also heavily involved with politics. The Christian Democratic-Socialist coalition fell apart in 1975. In the general elections the following year, the Communist Party gained 34.4 percent of the vote compared to the Christian Democrats' 38.7 percent. Since the Socialists refused to participate in a government that did not include the Communists, the stage was set for a series of inconclusive arrangements and political crises. The Communists supported the Christian Democrats for a period, without actually forming part of the government, and the resulting uncertainty exacerbated domestic and international economic problems alike.(10)

The Portuguese situation was a more dramatic one, resulting from revolutionary, rather than evolutionary, change. After nearly 50 years of right-wing dictatorship, the Armed Forces Movement (MFA) led a revolution in April 1974. The MFA was primarily interested in ending the dictatorship, moving toward democracy, and – above all – ending the colonial war in Africa. They also had vague economic goals of greater development and equality, but no exact strategy was spelled out. In fact, a precise strategy would have been difficult to work out because of the disparate elements making up the MFA, ranging from committed socialists to equally committed capitalists. The situation was made somewhat clearer after the Communist Party began to take a more active role in the process in September 1974. It was then that the so-called "flower revolution" became firmly linked with the goal of establishing socialism in Portugal (Maxwell, 1976; Bruneau, 1981).

The new revolutionary government faced serious economic problems from the beginning. On the one hand, it had to deal with the most backward economy in Europe. Almost one-third of the work force was still in agriculture; per capita income in the last year of the dictatorship was $1,350, compared to $4,500 for the OECD as a whole (OECD, 1977). National income was also distributed in a highly uneven manner in geographical, sectoral, and class terms. Although most agricultural land in the north was held in fairly small units, the south was characterized by very large estates and landless workers. Productivity and income also varied across sectors, with agriculture far behind industry and even services (Vasconcelos and Garrido, 1977(1)). Most conspicuous was the domination of the entire economy by a small number of conglomerates, which had been very closely associated with the state, thus enjoying protection and privileges of various kinds (Santos, 1977; Martins, 1975).

Another aspect of inequality concerned unemployment. On the surface, Portugal had no unemployment problem, but in reality the country was unable to provide work for its own people. There were 700,000 emigrant workers out of a labor force of three million; this did not include the tens of thousands who were fighting the colonial wars in Africa (OECD, 1977). Emigrants were also important for the balance of payments since their remittances had been a key factor in maintaining a positive balance on the current account in spite of chronic deficits on the trade balance. The colonies were also important, providing captive markets and cheap raw materials, thus supporting the balance of payments and enabling the inefficient industrial sector to survive and prosper (Marques, 1978).

On the other hand, the revolution took place just as the worldwide economic problems made their way to Portugal. Oil price rises were a serious jolt to the country, which imported most of its oil. Food imports were also beginning to become significant, as a legacy of the neglect of agriculture over the years. Inflation began to rise during the 1970s and especially in 1973 and the first quarter of 1974 (Vasconcelos and Garrido, 1977 (2)).

One of the first moves of the new government was to end the colonial empire which meant that the soldiers came home, together with an estimated 400,000 Portuguese citizens who had been living in Africa. At the same time, recession hit Europe, thus forcing emigrants to return home. The government also made significant changes in domestic economic policy, raising real wages and increasing public spending. Real wages increased by about nine percent during 1974-75 (Banco de Portugal, 1973-77; Kurgmand and Macedo, 1981), due to high nominal increases, price controls, a pegged exchange rate, and subsidies. There were also attempts to increase the equality of the wage structure. Public expenditures over the same period increased by 31 percent in real terms which created a large deficit in the public sector budget (IMF, 1979). Likewise, there was a large balance of payments deficit, brought about partly by running the economy at a higher growth rate than other countries, but oil price increases, the end of the empire, a slowdown in tourism and emigrant receipts, and capital flight also contributed as well. The other aspect of economic policy was structural changes as part of the projected move toward socialism. The most important changes were a large-scale agrarian reform and nationalization of the banking sector and certain industries. As would be expected, the combination of structural change, expansionary policies, and external forces created major disequilibria in the economy which were exacerbated by political polarization.

When elections were held in April 1976, the moderate Socialist Party won a plurality victory and formed a minority government. Although not completely repudiating their predecessors, the Socialists put great emphasis on restoring equilibrium in the economy and order in general; socialism was shelved in the process. They quickly announced a set of austerity measures and were rewarded by aid from the U.S. government, the EEC, and the IMF. The programs were only partially implemented, however, and failed to eliminate the high inflation rate and the huge balance of payments deficit (Stallings, 1981).

Political struggles over stabilization

These economic problems, in both their structural and current aspects, provided the background for the political struggles which erupted around the stabilization programs in the three countries. The political struggles varied, however, since there were different interpretations of the economic problems by different political groups, different weights were put on the various problems, and different remedies were recommended. In each case, the IMF allied itself with the most conservative faction.

In Britain, the main battle took place among factions of the Cabinet in alliance with certain members of the Civil Service.(11) The process began with the falling pound during the first half of 1976. Caused by a combination of bad performance by the British economy, jitters on the part of holders of the sterling balances, and the strategy of the British Treasury, the situation reached crisis stage by mid-year. The government negotiated a $5.3 billion stand-by loan from European and American central banks and the Bank for International Settlement, believing that this would permit them to stabilize the pound and continue with the mild austerity program begun the previous year. This view, however, did not take the U.S. Treasury and the Federal Reserve into account. Top Treasury and Fed officials, who regarded the British government as "profligate," took this opportunity to force it to go to the IMF and thus cut spending drastically. This was done by putting an unusual six-month time limit on the stand-by and insisting that the British go to the IMF if they could not repay (Fay and Young, 1978). The IMF entry was guranteed when the pound plumetted again, and the Bank of England had to spend huge sums trying to stop the fall.

True to U.S. expectations, the IMF team which arrived in London in November demanded large cuts in the budget deficit and a brake on the money supply. These demands immediately triggered divisions in the Cabinet over the proper response. In the beginning, only Denis Healey, Chancellor of the Exchequer, supported the IMF position. A middle group, led by Foreign Secretary Anthony Crosland, opposed any but the most minor spending cuts; this group thought that policy should continue along current lines, possibly using import deposits if the balance of payments situation became critical. Finally there was the left-wing faction which not only opposed spending cuts but – what the IMF would not tolerate – supported the use of import controls to resolve Britain's economic problems (Fay and Young, 1978).

Prime Minister James Callaghan did not take an open position in the initial stages, but tried to mount an international campaign, aimed at Washington and Bonn, around the idea that the IMF conditions could undermine democracy in Britain and thus destabilize the entire West. That campaign failed, thanks in large part to the vociferous opposition of the U.S. Treasury, and Callaghan then turned to support the Healey-IMF line. The Fund helped somewhat by compromising on the amount of spending cuts it required. Once Callaghan announced his position, the battle was over. Those who opposed him had to go along or resign; the latter course would split the party and precipitate an election which Labor could not win. The only question then became how to divide up the spending cuts (Fay and Young, 1978).

The nature of the struggles over IMF policy in Italy was quite different from that in Britain (Payer, 1978). No important intra-government divisions occurred in Italy; rather on some key issues, it was the government and the IMF on the same side opposing the unions. The government did oppose the Fund, however, over budget cuts. Only the immediate reason for negotiating with the IMF was the same in the two countries: a run on the currency.

Italy had had trouble with the lira for several years beginning in 1974. That crisis had been stemmed by loans from the IMF, the EEC and the Bundesbank. In early 1976, however, the problem returned in force, fueled partly by fears about the upcoming election. There were also economic reasons – a heavy foreign debt and low reserve level – but a key factor again seems to have been the United States. This time the U.S. agency was the Comptroller of the Currency which announced a new policy on private bank loans to Italy. The Comptroller decided that some banks had exceeded the legal limit on loans to one borrower (the problem was the still-current one of whether loans to separate government agencies should be considered loans to a single borrower). The impression given was that Italy was considered to be a poor risk, and the run on the lira speeded up.(12) The EEC stepped in with a $1 billion loan, and Italy began negotiating with the IMF. The negotiations reached no conclusion, however, because the Fund was apparently unconvinced that the government would really limit spending.

The Italian answer was to impose a temporary system of import deposits which the IMF and the EEC reluctantly approved. Although the back of the crisis was broken, negotiations with the IMF continued. The Fund aimed its guns at two targets in Italy: the budget deficit and the _scala mobile_. These were thought to be the main factors responsible for Italy's inflation and balance of payments problems. The political lineup on the two issues was quite different.

As explained previously, the _scala mobile_ is an escalator clause designed to guarantee that wages more or less keep up with inflation. The government (and business as well) was very happy with the IMF attacks on the _scala mobile_ and saw them as the only way to undermine the unions. Guido Carli, former president of the Bank of Italy and now head of Confindustria (the industrialists' organization), made the point very clearly: "The function of the IMF loan is really to focus attention on what has to be done. What is being talked about, and openly now, is the restricting of income in real terms, and that is always a politically difficult matter" (International Herald Tribune, 1977). Here was a clear example of the use of the IMF as scapegoat; eliminating the _scala mobile_ could be portrayed as a necessity imposed from outside. The fact that Italy persisted in its negotiations with the Fund, when the loan involved was relatively small and the need was not apparent, prompted the conclusion that help in eliminating the _scala mobile_ was the main reason.

On the other hand, the IMF was also interested in lowering the budget deficit, and here it ran straight into government opposition for, as was pointed out earlier, the budget was a major tool in maintaining the Christian Democrats in power. Prime Minister Andreotti opposed the IMF on this point in much the same way that Britain's Callaghan had done; he mounted an international political campaign, again primarily aimed at Washington and Bonn, around the theme that if the IMF conditions were too stringent, democracy could be threatened in Italy. Andreotti was more successful than Callaghan because the Italian Communist Party was seen as a much more serious threat than the left wing of the British Labor Party. In the end, the IMF loan was given, in spite of the fact that the scala mobile remained intact and there was little hope that the Christian Democrats would live up to their budget promises (Payer, 1978).

Despite a balance of payments surplus, the Italian government returned to negotiate a $1 billion jumbo credit from the Fund in mid-1978, in hopes of getting outside support for its three-year economic plan that included an incomes policy, credit controls, and higher taxes. Political crisis, including the fall of the Andreotti government, inconclusive general elections, and caretaker governments resulted in the temporary shelving of the plan in 1979, but officials indicated continuing interest in negotiating a new standby (Financial Times, 1978 and 1979).

Portugal presented yet another type of political line-up around the IMF negotiations (Stallings, 1981). There the main divisions were neither intragovernment nor government-union but inter-party. Such a situation was perhaps inevitable since Socialist leader Mario Soares insisted on establishing a minority one-party government. After obtaining a first-tranche IMF loan in early 1977, the government ended up in a foreign exchange crisis in mid-June. The IMF was invited back partly because of this reason and partly due to U.S. Treasury manipulations once again.

In this instance, Undersecretary for Monetary Affairs Ed Yeo (one of the main people behind the move to force Britain to the IMF) had undertaken to obtain a large loan for Portugal from the major Western governments. This was very important since Portugal was in critical balance of payments trouble. Yeo's plan was for the money to be managed by the IMF (Financial Times, 1976), but the Fund refused because of a principle of not administering other people's money. The final arrangement, however, tied release of the $750 million to Portugal's signing a second-tranche stand-by agreement, thereby giving the IMF the right to prescribe austerity measures and to monitor the economy.

Like the British and Italian Prime Ministers, Soares also tried to obtain concessions on the terms of the IMF agreement by using leftist scare tactics. He even took his campaign directly to IMF headquarters, where he told Managing Director Johanes Witteveen that "the Communists will be in the Azores" if the conditions were too stringent. He did indeed get some concessions, principally on the amount of the balance of payments deficit which was raised from $800 million to $1 billion. At home, the Soares government played a different game, vociferously denouncing the IMF in press statements, but taking a much more compromising line in the negotiations themselves.(13)

When Soares presented the austerity measures to Parliament in December, however, the IMF scapegoat was not sufficient to carry the day. The program was defeated on a vote of confidence with all three other major parties (the Center Democrats, the Social Democrats, and the Communists) voting against the Socialist proposals. The government was brought down as a result, and the measures were only approved when Soares finally formed a coalition government with the right-wing Center Democrats.

In early 1979, the IMF returned to renew the agreement. Domestic political problems exacerbated economic differences between the Fund and the government, as one prime minister succeeded another. Portugal wanted more lenient targets than in the previous year since the balance of payments had improved well beyond the agreement projections. The IMF, however, insisted on continued austerity because of the still-large budget deficit and the high inflation rate.(14) No agreement proved possible under the circumstances; nevertheless the private banks stepped in to provide a $300 million loan on the basis of the strong balance of payments position. As a top Central Bank official said, "An agreement with the IMF isn't as important as it was a year ago" (Wall Street Journal, 1979; Financial Times, 1979).

The Letters of Intent

Although the IMF claims that the conditions it prescribes are determined by purely economic conditions, an examination of the performance criteria of the three Letters of Intent indicates otherwise.

Table 4.2 shows the three sets of economic targets in terms of comparisons with the previous twelve-month period. Thus it is possible to judge the relative stringency of the targets by seeing how much deflation they required. These figures can then be compared with those in Table 4.2 which showed the extent of the economic problems found in each country. If economic factors were the only criteria influencing the design of the stabilization programs, presumably those countries with the most severe problems would have the most deflationary targets.

As might be expected, this was not the case. In fact, close to the opposite was true. Britain, whose economic disequilibria were generally less severe than those of the other two countries, had had the most deflationary program. This was especially true in terms of the budget deficit, where the government pledged itself to cut the deficit by 22 percent in the first year <u>before</u> taking inflation into account. Credit was to be cut by 14 ½ percent, while the current account deficit was to be halved (Financial Times, 1976).

Italy, on the other hand, the country which had by far the most serious problem with its budget deficit, was only asked to cut the deficit by 12 percent. Furthermore, credit was allowed to increase by 10 percent.

Again these figures are before inflation. The balance of payments was supposed to make a huge leap into surplus. Because of the issue of the scala mobile, described in the previous section, Italy also had a special condition written into the Letter of Intent. For the first time, an inflation target was made a performance criterion. Generally this is not done because it is thought that the government does not have sufficient control over the inflation rate. In the Italian case, however, the IMF was so worried about the effects of the scala mobile that the government was ordered to make sure that the particular inflation index that triggers the escalator clause did not rise above 13 percent (Mondo Economics, 1977).

Portugal also had a relatively lenient program (although Fund officials described it as "average" or even "tight"). The budget was to remain constant in nominal terms, while domestic credit expansion was to be cut by 15 percent. The latter target was especially tight because Fund officials believed that the previous year's stabilization program in Portugal had been ruined because of a high rate of credit expansion. The balance of payments deficit was to be cut from $1.5 billion to $1 billion (Diario de Noticias, 1978).

Of course there is no proof that Italy and Portugal got off easily in comparison to Britain because the political threat in the former two countries was more credible than in Britain. IMF officials deny the charge. On the one hand, they say "We are not yet in the business of keeping the Communists out of the Azores." On the other hand, they offer the opinion that the Communist Party is one of the most responsible forces in Italy. (The difference between the Italian and Portuguese parties might not produce the same evaluation for the latter.) Nevertheless, it seems hard not to come to the conclusion that the threat of being seen as responsible for major gains by either the Italian or the Portuguese Communists, or for further radicalizing already highly polarized societies, did not have a significant effect on the type of stabilization programs which were negotiated. The possibility of U.S. pressure being brought to bear on Fund negotiators cannot be ruled out either. (The admitted U.S. interference in the British case will be remembered.) The U.S. antipathy for Communist Party members in European cabinets is well known. The U.S. government definitely is in the business of keeping the Communists out of the Azores and out of key positions in Rome.

Such a respected source as the London Economist argues along similar lines: "The IMF is letting Italy off more lightly than it let off Britain. The simple reason is that sick Italy is much frailer and there is a lingering suspicion that strong medicine could do more harm than good. Armoured vehicles quelling last week's student riots in Bologna were an ugly reminder of the dangers. Workers, fed for years on hopes now impossible to fulfill, are dangerously sullen."(15)

Effects of the stabilization programs

In evaluating the three programs, in line with the focus of the chapter, we will concentrate mainly on trends in inflation. Table 4.3 shows inflation figures by quarter for the period since 1976. As can be seen, price rises fell off significanly in both Britain and Italy, following the signing of the stabilization agreements. In Britain, low rates persisted for six quarters, beginning the first quarter of 1978, while Italy saw marked improvement in price rises during the year 1978. In the case of Portugal, no significant change can be observed. The question then becomes: what was the role of the stabilization programs in lowering the rates of inflation? Such a question is always difficult to answer because of other factors present, but some very rough answers can be suggested. In all cases, though for different reasons, it would seem that the IMF programs can claim little credit.

Table 4.2. Conditions on the IMF Loans to Britain, Italy, and Portugal.

Country	Prev. 12 Months	Target	% Change[a]
Britain			
Budget deficit[b]	£-11.2 bil.	£-8.7 bil.	-22.3
Credit expansion	9.0 bil.	7.7 bil.	-14.5
Balance of payment deficit	-2.0 bil.	-1.0 bil.	-50.0
Italy			
Budget deficit	-Lit 18,700 bil.	-Lit 16,450 bil.	-12.0
Credit expansion	27,218 bil.	30,000 bil.	+10.2
Balance of payment deficit	-2,380 bil.	500 bil.	
Inflation[c]	22%	13%	
Portugal			
Budget deficit	-E°43 bil.	-E°45 bil.	+ 0.2
Credit expansion	167 bil.	142 bil.	-15.0
Balance of payments	-$1.5 bil.	-$ 1.0 bil.	-33.3

[a]Nominal changes [b]PSBR [c]Inflation index for *scala mobile*

Sources: Letters of Intent (Britain, *Financial Times*, December 16, 1976; Italy, *Mondo Economico*, April 23, 1977; Portugal, *Diario de Noticias*, May 19, 1978); IMF, *International Financial Statistics*, August 1978).

In the British case, the rate of inflation had been falling fairly steadily ever since its peak in 1975. The main reasons would seem to be the incomes policy which the Labor government had negotiated with the Trades Union Council (TUC) and the appreciation in the exchange rate for sterling. The incomes policy was a voluntary one which began in 1975, was renewed in 1976, and partially renewed in 1977. It provided for a halving of the growth rate of average earnings from 28 to 14 percent in Phase I and a further decline to eight percent during Phase II. This meant that real earnings fell by about seven percent (OECD, 1978). At the time that Phase III was to be negotiated in the summer of 1977, the TUC voted to return to collective bargaining, but agreed to go along with the "12-month interval rule" between pay increases after Phase II settlements.

Table 4.3. Inflation Rates[a] in Britain, Italy, and Portugal, 1976-80.

Quarter and Year	Britain	Italy	Portugal
I 1976	21.3%	12.1%	18.4%
II 1976	15.1	16.1	14.9
III 1976	13.4	16.7	18.0
IV 1976	14.0[b]	21.0	25.8
I 1977	16.0	22.5	23.8
II 1977	17.2	19.8[b]	36.1
III 1977	16.7	19.8	31.1
IV 1977	14.2	15.7	24.0
I 1978	10.9	13.3	22.8
II 1978	8.7	12.4	19.7[b]
III 1978	8.3	12.1	22.6
IV 1978	8.3	12.0	25.5
I 1979	9.3	13.4	24.7
II 1979	10.3	14.5	23.3
III 1979	16.0	15.7	23.9
IV 1979	17.2	18.9	22.9
I 1980	19.5	21.4	27.5
II 1980	22.3	20.9	--

[a]Consumer Price Index, percentage change on previous annual period

[b]Quarter when IMF agreement signed

Source: Calculated form OECD, Main Economic Indicators, various numbers.

Since there is strong evidence in Britain that industrial prices are set on a cost-plus basis (Nordhaus and Godley, 1972), and that wages are the major aspect of costs, it seems clear that the fall in real earnings would have led to a decline in the inflation rate. Further, the important rise in the value of sterling vis-à-vis the dollar and some other currencies – amounting to 18 percent between the second quarter of 1977 and the last quarter of 1978 – is a significant element in a country where imports are equal to 30 percent of GDP (IMF, 1979). These two factors, then, would seem to be the major ones in the drop in inflation rather than the budget and credit limitation – which, incidentally, were overachieved. Fund officials deny this proposition and point to their contribution as having convinced the Labor government that government spending should increase no faster than the GDP. This, they say, was the crucial decision.

In the Italian case, the reasons for the fall in inflation are less clear, but it would seem strange to attribute it to a program which was not carried out. The Italian stabilization program was in trouble from the beginning. It had to be re-negotiated even before it was signed because the government had agreed to certain conditions without consulting with the unions. In addition, the quantitive targets were overshot so far that, in spite of the limit on the budget deficit being raised, drawings on the loan were cut off before the end of 1977. The 1977 annual deficit was Lit 20,500 billion, compared with the originally agreed on Lit 16,450 billion. Domestic credit expansion totalled Lit 35,000 billion as opposed to the Lit 30,000 billion target. Deviations for 1978 were much larger (Financial Times, 1978). The IMF's own analysis, shared by other international observers such as the OECD, placed major emphasis for the temporary drop in inflation rates on improvements in Italy's terms of trade. This turnabout had both direct – slowing the rise in import prices – and indirect effects – strengthening of the lira due to the resulting surplus in the balance of payments (OECD, 1979).

Portugal, unlike Britain and Italy, did not even obtain temporary respite from inflationary pressures so the Fund can obviously claim no credit in this case. Economic improvement was limited to the balance of payments where the target was more than met. Estimates for the 1978 budget deficit, however, were for E°84 billion or almost twice the E°54 billion target. In fact, at 10.7 percent of GDP, the 1978 budget deficit was worse than 1977 (8.0 percent). The credit expansion target was formally met but only by using a loophole, and inflation was higher than planned.(16) Both Fund and OECD economists refer to current Portuguese inflation as profits-led since wage increases have been well below the inflation rate and below government targets as well. Another key factor in the 1978 inflation rates was the government decision to let controlled prices rise; this is important because almost half of consumer expenditure is subject to price controls. Price rises are not only keeping up with the current increase in costs, but also catching up for the entire period since 1974 (OECD, 1979).

Whatever can be said about the short-term effects of the three stabilization programs on price rises, by 1979-80 inflation had once again become a serious problem in all three countries. In fact, the 1979-80 figures for Britain and Italy were as bad or worse than the pre-stabilization periods: 19 percent for Britain (compared to 16 percent in the four quarters before the December 1976 IMF agreement), 19 percent for Italy (compared to 19 percent), and 23 percent for Portugal (compared to 29 percent)(OECD, various issues). Even more perverse from the point of view of IMF analysis, however, these high inflation rates were accompanied by strong and/or improving positions on the balance of payments, thus contradicting the monetary theory of the balance of payments. Italy had huge current account surpluses of $2.5 billion in 1977, $6.4 billion in 1978, and $5.9 billion in 1979, while Portugal managed to lower its deficit from $1.5 billion in 1977 to $776 million in 1978, and a surplus of $150 million for 1979 (IMF, 1977-79; Bank of Portugal, 1977; Financial Times, 1979). Only Britain conformed to the expected pattern as the 1978 current account surplus faded into deficit in 1979. International observers, such as the OECD, attribute the decline to fall in competitiveness, however, not the IMF-predicted mechanism. In a more expected vein, the stabilization efforts led to low growth rates and worsening wage and/or employment positions for the working class. The exception to the latter is Italy where workers are protected by the scala mobile.

This analysis has a natural ending point in 1979 since all three countries had general elections leading to shifts to the right and administrations that are much more forcefully committed to IMF-type economic policies. The Thatcher government in Britain and the Sa Carneiro government in Portugal are clear-cut cases. The situation in Italy is somewhat murkier since the elections were inconclusive. Nevertheless the lower Communist share of the vote, together with the withdrawal of the Party's support for the government, marked a turn toward more reliance on the private sector and a more hostile policy vis-à-vis labor.

CONCLUSIONS

On the basis of the recent British, Italian, and Portuguese stabilization programs, what can we say about the role of the IMF in combatting inflation?

Four points can be made:

First, it seems clear that the nature (both quantitative and qualitative) of stabilization programs is not determined by inflation rates. In the examples used in this chapter, the country with the lowest inflation rate in the 12 months preceding the IMF agreement (Britain) was saddled with the most deflationary program. The nation with the highest inflation rate (Portugal) had the most lenient stabilization targets, while Italy was in an intermediate position in both respects.(17)

Rather than inflation rates, the first factor of importance is the balance of payments. That is, the amount of money which a government wants to borrow (together with its previous borrowing) will determine the tranche into which it falls and therefore an initial estimate of the nature of the program. In addition, however, the evidence presented in this chapter indicates that political factors also play an important role in determining just how deflationary a program can be imposed in a given country. If an immediate and credible threat to the political system exists, this may mean that a government will be allowed space for a positive growth rate to avoid increasing political conflict.

Second, in an ironic twist, stabilization programs may actually increase inflation rather than decrease it. This comes about through policies introduced to readjust relative prices which are thought to be out of line; since it is very difficult to lower prices, the readjustment comes through price increases. The prices that are likely to be increased are the exchange rate, the interest rate, indirect taxes, and consumer prices in general as subsidies are lowered or eliminated and price controls are lifted. The inflation resulting from such changes is termed "corrective inflation" by IMF officials and is said to be a one-time phenomenon. As was pointed out earlier, however, this is true only if wage increases are held below the other increases; otherwise a wage-price spiral is likely to result. In theory, wages could be increased to keep up with rising costs, but profits would have to be cut to compensate. Such a move would run counter to the Fund's reliance on private enterprise. That is, higher profits are a necessary prerequisite for stimulating recalcitrant private investors.

Third, and on the other hand, the IMF can be useful in combatting inflation. The resources that the Fund itself controls, and much more importantly the resources which are tied to its "seal of approval," can enable a country with a high inflation rate to slow it down gradually rather than through a "shock treatment." A higher growth rate can be maintained through the use of outside resources, and subsidies can be provided to individuals and sectors which are hit hard in the process of restructuring the economy which is usually the only long-term remedy for inflationary pressures.

The IMF itself has been moving in a useful direction in the last couple of years, both through increasing the amount of money it can offer to governments in trouble and through increasing the time span over which stabilization is expected to take place. Many programs are now routinely negotiated for two years rather than one, with even longer periods available through the new Extended Fund Program and the Witteveen Facility. In a more controversial vein, there seems to be a move toward softening the Fund's conditionality requirements. In March 1979, the IMF Executive Board adopted a new set of guidelines that could legitimate a more lenient approach. The key points were: (a) contractual language should be avoided in Letters of Intent; (b) performance criteria will be limited to those necessary to evaluate implementation of the program; and (c) "the Fund will pay due regard to the domestic social and political objectives, the economic priorities, and the circumstances of members, including the causes of their balance of payments problems" (IMF, 1979). More recently, the managing director, Jacques de Larosiere, has reportedly been trying to overcome member governments' hesitation to submit themselves to IMF requirements by "advertising a softening-up of conditionality" (especially de-emphasis of devaluation) and advocating the use of loopholes to give jumbo loans (The Economist, 1979).

Fourth, given this potential, the question about the possibility of realizing it remains. This takes us back to two of the points raised at the beginning of the essay: the adequacy of IMF analysis and thus prescriptions and the side effects. The Fund's own evaluation of its success rate is quite pessimistic. In the most recent internal evaluation, which covers the period 1973-75, the conclusion is that

> . . .less than one third of the programs included in this survey can be deemed as having been successful, in the sense that policies were broadly implemented, the balance of payments and the general economic situation at the end of the program period was better than at the beginning, and that this improvement was sustainable with a continuation or some adaptation in policies (IMF, 1978).

The cases analyzed in this chapter cast further doubt in at least two directions. On the one hand, the simultaneous existence of high inflation rates and strong balance of payments performance found in Italy and Portugal is clearly contrary to Fund analysis (similar to the problems stagflation posed for Keynesian economics a decade earlier). On the other hand, the recurrence of high inflation rates points to a much more serious problem. This cannot be dealt with in any detail here, but must be explored further in another context. The Fund's habit, deriving from its mandate, of concentrating exclusively on the short run places it in a very weak position. Inflation, like any other economic disequilibrium, may have short-term policy causes, but it may also derive from structural problems. By ignoring the latter, the IMF tends, at best, to cure symptoms while paving the way for the same problems to return later, perhaps in exagerated form. A more integrated analysis, that combines both long and short-term problems and remedies, is the only way that a more "permanent" resolution can be found.(18)

In terms of side effects – especially unemployment and regressive redistribution of income – more difficulties arise. The type of stabilization programs designed by the IMF have an inherent bias such that the working class (and especially the weakest among the workers) must pay the vast majority of the costs of stabilization. The reason for this fact is clear: the IMF is a key link in the capitalist system and, by definition, must support that system. This means that it must look for ways to support private accumulation, and private accumulation in turn requires high profit rates. It is, therefore, hard to imagine stabilization being achieved at the cost of profitcutting in the context of an IMF program. It is also difficult to imagine stabilization at the cost of tax cuts since this would require even larger expenditure cuts (given that governments who go to the IMF always have budget deficits). Cutting state expenditure in modern capitalist society would imply cutting many of the services that capital has come to rely on as part of the stimulus to investment. The main factor remaining then is wages.

The assault on the scala mobile in Italy is a prime example of the philosophy behind IMF programs. Although even the Bank of Italy admits that the scala mobile only enables workers to defend themselves – it does not itself go beyond to start an inflationary spiral – nevertheless it is a hindrance to private accumulation and must be eliminated. Although lobbying is going on in the U.S. Congress to link U.S. approval of stabilization programs to consideration of "basic human needs," the requirement of capitalism are against such a scheme.

NOTES

(1) Two basic fora for third world criticism are the Committee of 24 (that represents third world interests within the IMF framework) and UNCTAD. Committee of 24 statements can be found in the biweekly IMF Survey while the most extensive UNCTAD critique is The Balance of Payments Adjustment Process in Developing Countries (UNDP/UNCTAD Project INT/75/015), Jan. 1979. A recent volume of case studies, in addition to those contained in the UNCTAD study, is R. Thorp and L. Whitehead, eds., Inflation and Stabilization in Latin America, Macmillan, 1979. An older study, which is the take-off point of many of the more recent critiques, is C. Payer, The Debt Trap, Penguin, Middlesex, 1974.

(2) This analysis of the IMF theory of inflation was based on interviews with IMF officials and various printed materials. The most important of these are the Staff Papers and the IMF Survey. See also the article by former Managing Director Johanes Witteveen, "Inflation and the International Monetary Situation," Papers and Proceedings of the American Economics Association, May 1975.

(3) Interviews with IMF officials.

(4) One prominent former IMF official has, in fact, criticized the Fund for not paying enough attention to inflation. See Fred Hirsch's statement: "Too weak to impose price stability on national economies, international organizations have in effect served the second-best objective of the liberal community, of maintaining an open international economy at whatever inflation rate has to be accepted to attain this. This ordering of priorities is openly visible in the lending policies of the International Monetary Fund, which by giving primacy to liberalization of trade and payments, typically require large devaluations and consequential domestic price rises" (F. Hirsch, "The Ideological Underlay of Inflation," in F. Hirsch and J. Goldthorpe, eds., The Political Economy of Inflation, Martin Robertson, London, 1978, pp. 278-9).

(5) Another mechanism is via devaluation (See Stallings, 1981).

(6) In theory, profits could be cut rather than wages, but this contradicts IMF views on the necessity for private investment. See discussion below.

(7) See B. Stallings, "Peru and the U.S. Banks: The Privatization of Financial Relations," in R. Fagen, ed., Capitalism and the State in U.S. Latin American Relations, Stanford University Press, Stanford, 1979, pp. 217-53.

(8) Other recent European programs include Spain, which is not included because the government was only applying for a first credit tranche loan, and Turkey, where negotiations were still under way when this paper was written. An agreement was finally approved in June 1980. On Turkey, see A. Oncu, "The Recent Turkish Encounter with IMF: Notes on the Political Limits of Dependent Economic Development," in N. Smelser et. al., eds., Social and Political Challenges to the New International Economic Order, Sage Publications, forthcoming.

(9) The definition of the British budget deficit used in Table 4.1 is public sector "net lending." This is the figure which is comparable to the public sector deficit in other OECD countries (see OECD, Economic Surveys: United Kingdom, March 1977, p. 19). The Letter of Intent was framed in terms of the so-called Public Sector Borrowing Requirement (PSBR), the more commonly used deficit figure in Britain itself, and so it appears in Table 4.2. The difference between net lending and PSBR is that the latter includes government financial transactions.

(10) For example, the U.S., France, Germany, and Britain are reported to have agreed to withhold economic aid to Italy if the Communist Party was permitted to join the government. See C. Payer, "The Italian Crisis," mimeo, 1978.

(11) Highly detailed information, based on interviews with leading participants, is found in S. Fay and H. Young, "The Day the Pound Nearly Died," Sunday Times (London), May 14, May 21, and May 28, 1978. IMF officials confirm the accuracy of these articles though saying that they "overstress the American role a bit."

(12) The director-general of the Bank of Italy attacked the Comptroller's position, saying that it had "objectively created an atmosphere of uncertainty about the international financial credibility of our country." See The Times (London), January 23, 1976.

(13) See press statements in Expresso, Tempo, and O Jornal in the March-May 1978 period. Informtion on behavior in negotiations comes from interviews with IMF officials and Portuguese negotiators.

(14) Interviews with Portuguese economic officials.

(15) The Economist (London), April 2, 1977. An argument might be made that it is instability, rather than leftism, that the IMF is concerned about. In the three European cases, however, as well as the third world, the threat has definitely come from labor and the left. This is logical since it is the workers who bear the main brunt of stabilization.

(16) Interviews with Portuguese economic officials.

(17) The Spanish case reinforces this conclusion. Spain had an inflation rate of 24.5 percent in the four quarters preceding the IMF program signed in early 1978. Nevertheless, its targets included a 32 percent increase in state expenditure, a 17 percent rise in credit, together with a fall of 30 percent in the balance of payments deficit. The reason, of course, was that Spain was only applying for a first credit tranche loan.

(18) These comments, of course, leave open the question of the kind of long-run planning and structural changes that are needed. Whether they can be achieved under a capitalist economic system is a discussion that must be carried on elsewhere.

REFERENCES

Banco de Portugal, Indicadores Económicos, 1973-77.
______, Annual Report, 1977.
Bank of Italy, Abridged Version of the Report for the Year 1975.
Basevi, et al., "Italian Stabilization Policies under Social Constraints and International Shocks, 1972-76," paper presented at the Conference on National Stabilization Policies in Industrial Countries, 1972-76, Brookings Institution, Rome, May 30-June 3, 1977.
Blackwell, D., "Monetary Approach to the Balance of Payments Needs Blending with Other Lines of Analysis," IMF Survey, February 20, 1978 and March 6, 1978.
Bruneau, "The Pattern of Politics in Portugal Since the April Revolution," in J. de Macedo and S. Serfaty, eds., Portugal Since the Revolution, Westview Press, 1981.
Caincross, A., ed., Britain's Economic Prospects Reconsidered, George Allen and Unwin London, 1971 (especailly chapters by Matthews and Worswick).
Caves, R. et al., Britain's Economic Prospects, Brookings Institution, Washington, D.C., 1968 (especially chapter by R. and P. Musgrave).
Diario de Noticias, May, 19, 1978.
The Economist, December 15, 1979.
Fay, S. and Young, H., "The Day the Pound Nearly Died," Sunday Times (London), May 14, May 21, and May 28, 1978.
The Financial Times, November 25, 1976.
______, December 16, 1976.
______, July 7, 1978.
______, July 19, 1978.

______, April 28, 1979.
______, October 11, 1979.
______, October, 1979
Glyn, A., The Internatinal Economic Crisis, forthcoming.
Gold, J., Stand-By Agreements, (IMF, Washington, D.C., 1970).
Horsefield, Keith J., ed., The International Monetary Fund, 1945-65, IMF, Washington, D.C., 1969, Chapter 2.
International Herald Tribune, May 17, 1977.
International Monetary Fund, Articles of Agreement of the International Monetary Fund, (IMF, Washington, D.C., 1945).
______, Annual Report for 1948, (IMF, Washington, D.C., 1948).
______, The Monetary Approach to the Balance of Payments, (IMF, Washington, D.C., 1977).
International Monetary Fund, International Financial Statistics for Britain, and International Financial Statistics for Italy, (IMF, Washington, D.C., 1977-79).
______, "Experience with Stabilization Programs Supported by Stand-By Agreements in the Upper Credit Tranches, 1973-75," February 28, 1978, mimeo.
______, International Monetary Fund Survey, (IMF, Washington, D.C., March 19, 1979).
______, International Financial Statistics, (IMF, Washington, D.C., 1979).
Kaldor, N., Causes of the Slow Rate of Economic Growth of the United Kingdom, (Cambridge University Press, Cambridge, 1966).
Krugman, P., and J. Macedo, "The Economic Consequences of the April 25th Revolution," in J. Macedo and S. Serfaty, eds., Portugal in the 1970s: Political and Economic Perspectives, Westview Press, 1981.
Lutz, V., Italy: A Study in Economic Development, London, 1962.
Marques, Walter, "Interview with Walter Marques," Euromoney, March 1978, pp. 22-3.
Martins, B., Sociedades y grupos em Portugal, Lisbon, 1975.
Maxwell, K., "The Thorns of the Portuguese Revolution," Foreign Affairs, 54, 2 (Jan. 1976), pp. 250-70.
Mondo Economico, April 23, 1977.
Moore, B. and Rhodes, J., "The Relative Decline of the UK Manufacturing Sector," in Economic Policy Review, Vol. 2, (March, 1976), pp. 36-7.
Nordhaus, W. and W. Godley, "Pricing in the Trade Cycle," Economic Journal, 1972.
Organization for Econmic Cooperation and Development (OECD), OECD Economic Survey: Italy, March 1977.
______, OECD Economic Survey: Portugal, December 1977.
______, OECD Economic Survey: United Kingdom, March 1978.
______, OECD Economic Survey: Italy, January 1979.
______, OECD Economic Survey: Portugal, July 1979.
______, OECD Economic Survey: United Kingdom, March 1979.
______, OECD Main Economic Indicators, 1980.
Payer, "The Italian Crisis," Mimeo, 1978.

Posner, M. and S. Woolf, Italian Public Enterprise, Harvard University Press (Cambridge, Mass., 1967).

Proctor, J. and R. Proctor, "Capitalist Development, Class Struggle, and Crisis in Italy, 1945-75," Monthly Review, January 1976, pp. 21-36.

Salvati, M., "The Italian Inflation: 1968-1976," in L. Lindberg, ed., Global Inflation and Recession, Brookings Institution, forthcoming.

Santos, A.R., "Desenvolvimento monopolista em Portugal, 1968-73," Analisis Social, Volume 49 (1977).

Shonfield, A., Modern Capitalism, Oxford University Press, London, 1965, Chapter 6.

Singh, A., "UK Industry and the World Economy: A Case of Deindustrialization?" Cambridge Journal of Economics, II, 1. (June 1977).

Stallings, B., "Portugal and the IMF: The Political Economy of Stabilization," in J. Macedo and S. Serfaty, eds., Portugal in the 1970s: Political and Economic Perspectives, (Westview Press, 1981).

Vasconcelos, L., and C. Garrido, "Structural Changes and Development Trends in Portugal since 1974," September 1977, mimeo.

______, "Survey on Portugal," The Economist, May 28, 1977.

Vivo, G. de and M. Pivetti, "International Integration and the Balance of Payments Constraint: The Case of Italy," Cambridge Journal of Economics, Vol. IV, No. 1 (March 1980), pp. 1-22.

Wall Street Journal, May 29, 1979.

5 The Bucks Stop Here: The Politics of Inflation in the United States

Michael J. Mumper
Eric M. Uslaner

The first law of democratic politics is: To protect your political position, protect the economy. It was recognized as early as 1905 by the eminent statesman and ward boss, George Washington Plunkitt of Tammany Hall (New York): "The district leader promises and that makes a solemn contract. . . .But if he only looks after his own interests or shows no talent for scenting out jobs or ain't got the nerve to demand and get his share of the good things that are goin', his followers may be absolved from their allegiance and they may up and swat him without bein' put down as political ingrates" (Riordan, 1963, p. 36). One needs only think of other great upheavals in American politics to recognize the potential impact of the economic issue. Most recently Ronald Reagan defeated Jimmy Carter for the presidency in 1980 by asking inflation-torn voters, "Are you better off today than you were four years ago?"

The great political transformations of our time are all associated with economic issues, ranging from the fiscal foundations of the Civil War (which also marked the birth of a new political party, the Republicans, and the death of an old one, the Whigs), the "Cross of Gold" speech of William Jennings Bryan at the Democratic National Convention of 1896, and the severe depression of the 1930's which ushered the Democrats into power and kept them there – at least in the Congress – for almost half a century. One of the few interruptions occurred in 1946, also a time of high inflation, when "(e)xasperated with government controls and the shortage of meat, the voters marched to the polls that November to answer the question we Republicans had been asking them all fall, 'Had enough?" (Martin, 1960, p. 179). At least that was the interpretation of the new Speaker of the House Joseph Martin (R., Mass.).

*The support of the General Research Board, University of Maryland – College Park, is gratefully acknowledged.

Yet there remains debate as to whether economics and politics are so intricately intertwined. It is almost a commonplace in American politics to acknowledge that the Democrats are considered the party of "war," the Republicans the party of inflation. And, according to Plunkitt's logic, even international conflicts should not be sufficient to cause voters to depart the party of stronger economic performance and this strong concern for the economic interests of supporting coalitions has, according to some authors (Mayhew, 1966, pp. 146-160; Fiorina, 1978b), kept the party dominant electorally even in the face of other issues. However, this view of the electorate is not universally accepted. First, the unsophisticated electorate does not pay much attention to issues; the most powerful determinant of the vote for president or Congress is party identification, and this is more of a rational response to electoral choices than is perusal of economic stands. George Stigler (1973, p. 166) argued an economist's point of view: "There is no difference between the Republicans and Democrats with respect to the ardent pursuit of high levels of employment and high and steady rates of growth of real income. . . .Prosperity is even more uncontroversial than motherhood. . . .Nor do the parties differ in their intellectual or political resources to deal with macroeconomic policy."

Second, voters' responses to economic conditions may not be particularly sophisticated, but the impact on elections may be quite pronounced anyhow. And the reactions are not necessarily symmetrical with the economic trends. This argument has two components. One maintains that voters reward strong economic performance. An early statement of this thesis (Kent, 1928, pp. 110-111) is: ". . .in a period of prosperity, with plenty of work for everybody willing to work and good wages, the party in power, if normally the majority party, is absolutely invincible. Save through some extraordinary piece of luck or stupidity, it cannot be beaten." This perspective may not imply that people vote <u>for</u> the party which maintains prosperity; instead, they may become less concerned with economic issues and just vote the party.

In this case the second thesis becomes relevant to account for economic voting, as again Frank Kent (1928, p. 192) noted: "It is when the value of their holdings go down, the dividends are dropped or decreased, that these millions of small stock and bond holders with whom the country is now cluttered get politically restive, become receptive to new ideas, ready for progressive (and, now conservative!) proposals." This is not straightforward economic voting on the issues, such as asking yurself: "Will I be better off four years from now under Reagan than under Carter?" It is but a simpler form of reaction which requires no comparison among alternative candidates and platforms. The question posed is of the sort Republicans asked in 1946 and 1980: Are things good or bad <u>now</u>, particularly compared to a few years ago? If the latter, throw the rascals out! This is "negative voting" (Kernell, 1977) or "retrospective voting" (Fiorina, 1978a) compared to "future-oriented" balloting.

These perspectives envision American national elections as referenda on the performance of the government on the economy. The economic issue, because it is fundamental to achieving the "good life," is preeminent and voters are not posited as being so concerned with social issues (from race relations to abortion) or international politics to let such factors actually determine their voting behavior. The preeminence of economic issues in electoral cycles is traceable to the lack of any deep-seeded interest in other questions on the part of most voters. Further evidence in support of this thesis is that the major upheavals in the American party system have been occasioned by similar problems in the economy; the major realignments of partisan support for the parties among the electorate occurred in 1860, 1896, and 1932. The first realignment was, of course, marked by the Civil War – but even in this case, the slavery issue was at least as much of an economic one as a racial conflict between the North and the South (there was little love for blacks even among many abolitionists); the contests of 1896 and 1932 were more clear-cut examples of new cleavages emerging on the basis of economic issues. The view of elections from the perspective of retrospective voting is one based upon evaluations of the in-party's performance, generally on economic issues, in periods of calm and of profound crises when faith in traditional party ties no longer coincides with long-term economic expectations. The voter is not necessarily a rational calculator measuring distances between his or her own ideal preferences across a wide range of issues and then determining where each of the parties stands on those issues. The task is much more straightforward and, as we shall see, there are substantial data which support the thesis of retrospective voting.

But even this more restricted view of the interaction of politics and economics has its critics. Stigler (1973, pp. 164-165) argues that many outside events determine the state of the economy at any particular time and that the policymaker's knowledge about what to do about inflation or unemployment is imperfect: thus it is "foolish" to vote retrospectively in anticipation of happier days being here again once the dolts are thrown out of office. Similarly, V.O. Key, Jr. (1942, p. 628) states: "If the party control of the national Government (sic) had little or nothing to do with (the economic condititions of the country). . .(t)o throw the 'ins' out probably had about the same effect on economic conditions as evangelical castigation of Satan has on the moral situation." Yet there is considerable evidence that farmers, whose income probably fluctuates more than most others, quite regularly "punish" the in-party for weakness in the agricultural markets, even when the bad times may be caused more by the weather than by the deeds of politicians (Key, 1942, pp. 624ff.).

The debate as to whether there is a "political business cycle" – a correspondence between economic conditions in the nation and election results – should not concentrate on whether such a cycle is a reasoned response to the state of the economy. As Fiorina (1978a, p. 429) responded to Stigler: "Is retrospective voting silly? Perhaps, but so what?" It is of little comfort to the politician who is tossed out of office during periods of economic hardship that his or her policies were misperceived by an unthoughtful electorate or would only have worked given more time. Instead the debate should focus upon, as most of it has; 1) the conditions under which the electorate will rise up in wrath and vote retrospectively; and 2) what the politicians do to try to manipulate first the economy and then the voters in anticipation of such reactions.

There is no single "political business cycle" because the issues involved are quite complex. First, we need to consider the impact of economic conditions upon the evaluations of the president and his political party as reflected in public opinion surveys. Second, there is the question of how these evaluations translate into votes for president and the Congress. Normally, the party of the president loses seats in the Congress in off-year elections. To what extent are such elections referenda on the economic performance of the administration? How do we handle complicating factors such as international crises and domestic scandals? Our task is not made any easier when we recognize that in two Congressional elections within recent history in which dramatic gains were made by the party out of power in the White House, some degree of scandal was intermixed with economic and international problems. In 1952, the GOP charge of "Communism, Corea (sic), and Corruption" helped to unseat the Democratic majority in Congress as well as to install a new Republican chief executive; in 1974, inflation and unemployment only added to the problems that Republicans faced in the wake of Watergate and President Gerald R. Ford's pardon of former President Richard M. Nixon. Third, recent trends show inflation to be more important as a factor in the political business cycle than unemployment. Why is this the case and what implications does it have for future political trends? Fourth, does it really make much difference which party runs the economy? Is Stigler right when he claims that both parties have similar commitments to economic prosperity and that neither knows how to achieve it? Does this mean that George Wallace was correct in 1968 when he charged that "there's not a dime's worth of difference between the parties"? If so, has the situation become worse in the interim? Or, stated somewhat differently, how much is George Wallace's dime worth in the inflated political currency of 1982 real dollars? We shall examine each of theses questions in turn, but first we shall consider the ways in which politicians react to economic conditions, what Tufte (1978) has called the attempt to assert "political control of the economy."

POLITICS AND INFLATION

Economists have traditionally viewed politics as constituting "a messy interference with rationality, a combination of misplaced and doomed good intentions, wooly mindedness and downright corruption" (Crouch, 1978, p. 217). Political factors are surely a bad guide to macroeconomic policy and it is fortunate indeed that the overall economy is not easily subject to manipulation by political decisions. Politicians also generally foreswear their fealty to promoting the common weal regardless of the electoral consequences of what may be unpopular decisions on macroeconomic performance. It is hardly surprising to find the most vehement denials of the existence of a political business cycle among these factors.

However, both perspectives are overly simplistic. Few other people than those directly associated with political leaders would maintain that such high-minded philosophical principles always guide macroeconomic policy formation. Certainly members of the opposition party, or candidates within the incumbent's own party who might attempt a primary challenge, are often very able to perceive a political dimension to economic policy formation. On the other hand, many economists have either subsumed the effects of politics under the rubric of an "invisible hand" or even gone so far as to maintain that the course of the economy is largely independent of the decisions made by a few highly-placed politicians (including the president). We do not want to argue this point here, but we are concerned with, first, how political leaders do attempt to manipulate macroeconomic policy to increase their own popularity and reelection prospects and how the citizenry responds to such leadership actions. Many economists now do recognize that politics and macroeconomic outputs are intertwined (see, inter alia, Hoadley, 1980; Hirsh and Goldthorpe, 1978). Before examining the actions taken by specific administrations to control the economy, we first put the overall political economy picture in perspective by considering the social pressures toward such attempts at manipulation and the literature examining how politicians react.

The withering away of the old economic and social consensus seems the most obvious of the political causes of inflation. Indeed, the cleavages among and between contending groups have grown progressively deeper and the schism in social values ever wider. This myriad of rival interests now seems more concerned with securing an ample slice of the economic pie than expanding it size. On the one hand this social disintegration may reflect what Jimmy Carter called a moral "malaise" or a "crisis of confidence." On the other, it may reflect what others see simply as widespread confusion and disagreement about the proper direction of American society. In any case, this lack of political consensus in the electorate has resulted in a Congress which is unwilling to depart from its own narrowly defined interests. Similarly, labor, the media, and the general public increasingly refuse to cooperate with policies they question and whose efficiency they doubt (Yankelovich, 1980, p. 28).

Additionally, political barriers to optimal macroeconomic policy result from a structural weakness in the American political system. Decisions seemingly irreconcilable with sound monetary and fiscal policy often result from the inability of political leaders to achieve a working economic compromise. The political system accelerates inflation partly as a consequence of the inability of public officials to reconcile their differences and arrive at an agreed upon strategy for economic management. The pursuit of high priority national objectives is made impossible by increased sectional conflicts of interests which cannot be peacefully resolved except by tolerating inflation. In this context, Lawrence Whitehead (1979) sees the stimuli to inflation administered from the U.S. presidency in 1965-67 and again in 1972 as not deliberately expansionary policy by the imperial presidency, but as an attempt to escape the onslaught of constitutional paralysis.

The desire of public officials to maximize votes as an election approaches, is perhaps the most rigorously examined of the political causes of suboptimal macroeconomic policy. Nordhaus (1975) argues that voters make myopic judgements about the performance of elected officials. Because this model sees voting as retrospective, politicians are encouraged to discount the future costs of macroeconomic policy which maximize short-term benefits. The result is expansionary policies which reduce unemployment immediately but increase inflation in the future. Following the election there is a severe, induced, recession with the object of getting the increase in inflation over as quickly as possible. This sets the stage for another stimulus administered just as the next election approaches. The electoral benefit is compounded by the decaying memory of the voters. This minimizes the negative effects of recession at the next election. If this scenario is correct, politicians act strategically by pursuing pre-election policies which are expansionary and employment oriented. Tufte (1978) claims that Western democracies often pursue "covert economic policies with concealed priorities."

The manipulation of macroeconomic policy to maximize votes is possible because of the existence of lags in the mechanism of inflation. If monetary expansion led to an immediate levying of the full inflation "tax," it would be no more attractive than a straightforward tax of similar magnitude. These lags also provide an element of uncertainty about the reasons for post-election inflation and make causal relationships difficult to establish.

This crucial inflationary time lag occurs because monetary expansion can give output and employment a short run boost of the Keynesian type. If there were no such lag, there would be an immediate cost to all governmental spending, whether financed by taxes, borrowing from the public, or monetary expansion, and in the latter case the inflationary tax would accept its payment immediately.

Thus, the literature regarding the political business cycle requires three fundamental assumptions. First, it is possible to boost output and employment by a monetary or fiscal stimulus. But this can only be done at the cost of an eventual higher rate of inflation. Second, there is a lag between the effects of a monetary or fiscal expansion on real activity and its inflationary consequences. Finally, the electorate's memory is subject to fairly rapid decay so that the loss rate from poor economic performance early in a term of office is substantially less than the gain from better economic performance just prior to the election (Brittan, 1978, p. 168). Further, because of retrospective voting or imperfect foresight, voters do not give full weight to post-election consequences of current economic policy.

While pre-election manipulation of macroeconomic policy may contribute to the current economic spiral, it is certainly nothing new. Adlai

Stevenson referred to this phenomenon as the "liberal hour" when all but the sternest believers in fiscal restraint embrace, for a moment, the need to spend more on things they believe the voters want (Wilson, 1980, p. 468). Compounding these political causes of inflation is a political process which operates over a much shorter time horizon (two or four years) than that necessary to address most serious economic problems. Understandably, political decision makers tend to resist policy alternatives whose benefits are long term but whose costs must be paid at the next election. No less of a tactician than Henry Kissinger (1978) realized that:

> . . .as the pressures of their electoral process have increased, governments have become more and more tactically oriented. The more tactically oriented they are, the more short-term their policies. The more short-term their policies, the less successful they are. So we have the paradox that governments following public opinion polls begin to look more and more incompetent.

This is not only a powerful statement about the concerns which motivate political decisions, but it is also an indication of the kinds of incentives which drive individual leaders to choose the policies they do. We turn now to an examination of how several recent American Presidents have attempted to control the political business cycle.

PRESIDENTS AND ECONOMIC CYCLES

Richard Nixon was especially aware of the links between macro-economic activity and electoral behavior. He recalled in his Six Crises that as vice president he had watched the Republican Party suffer sizable congressional losses in the mid-term elections of 1954 and 1958. He attributed these losses to sagging economic performance. He woefully recounts:

> The power of the pocket-book issue was shown more clearly perhaps in 1958 than in any off-year election in history. On the international front, the administration had had one of its best years. . . Yet, the economic dip in October was obviously uppermost in people's minds when they went to the polls (Nixon, 1962, p. 309).

Then, as a presidential candidate in 1960, Nixon is again reminded that, as John Kenneth Galbraith (1977, p. 70) writes: "In recent elections, economists have far outpaced even the generals and cold warriors as the architects of domestic political disasters." So when Arthur Burns warned him in 1960 of an upcoming slump in economic activity, the vice president was quite receptive to the message. But such politically sensitive economic advice was ignored by the policymakers in the Eisenhower administration. Nixon (1962, pp. 310-311) recalled:

> Unfortunately, Arthur Burns turned out to be a good prophet. The bottom of the dip came in October and the economy started to move up in November after it was too late to affect the election returns. . . .All the speeches, television broadcasts and precinct work in the world could not counteract that one hard fact.

When Richard Nixon did finally assume the office of the presidency, eight years later, he would not forget the political realities of macroeconomic policy.

The initial impetus for the current round of inflation is usually traced to the Johnson administration's attempt to obscure the cost of the Vietnam War by hidden deficit finance. Thus, 1968, the incoming Nixon administration faced accelerating inflation and very tight labor markets. Predictably, the Republican president pursued a contractionary macroeconomic game plan in an effort to control inflation. Arthur Burns, now Chairman of the Federal Reserve Board, compounded the impact of the contraction by simultaneously decreasing the real money supply. This in turn produced the 1970-71 recession which lowered the reat rate of inflation more than two percent.

But by the spring of 1971, Americans were losing patience with the Nixon administration's economic policies. The recession had driven unemployment to more than six percent and the president was running substantially behind Senator Edmund Muskie in many polls. President Nixon needed a policy to increase output and employment while maintaining relative price stability. The politically optimal solution was to stimulate the economy while simultaneously putting the lid on inflation through mandatory income policies. So as Douglas Hibbs (1978, p. 3) observes, "The policy of restraint was jettisoned in a successful attempt to stimulate an election year boom." This stimulation, coupled with the dramatic leaps in food and oil prices, produced an unprecedented double digit inflation in less than two years after instituting wage and price controls.

The newly installed administration of Gerald Ford responded to the economic crisis by launching the "Whip Inflation Now" media campaign and, more tangibly, by cutting back the rate of growth in government expenditures. Burns again accommodated the administration's policy of restraint by cutting the money supply at "a crushing rate" (Hibbs, 1978, p. 4). This combination yielded the most severe contraction in postwar U.S. history, unemployment shot up to 9 percent and consumer price increases declined by half the rate of the previous year. While the reasons for the slowing of inflation are far from clear, the economic forecasts encouraged the Ford administration.

Consequently, just prior to the 1976 election, President Ford and his conservative economic team elected to pursue moderately expansionary policies. But this was to be only a short-term deviation in an overall strategy which recognized, as Ford said, that "After all, unemployment affects only 8 percent of the people while inflation affects 100 percent" (Hibbs, 1978, p. 5).

By the time Jimmy Carter took office, the economy was heating up from the pre-election fiscal stimulation of the Ford administration. Still the domestic economy was operating well below its full employment potential. It was this problem of underutilized resources and reserve capacity that the new president was to address first. In January of 1977, the Carter administration proposed a fiscal stimulus package which included a rebate of personal income taxes quite similar to the Ford tax plan of 1975. Although the proposal was later withdrawn, owing to a slight economic recovery and a hostile Congress, it reveals the sharp distinction in economic policy orientation between the new administration and its predecessors.

The level of resource utilization increased substantially in 1977. But the Carter economic team still confronted the task of stimulating aggregate demand sufficiently to ensure the reemployment of reserve capacity. The administration hoped to bring about that continued growth without the return of inflationary wage and price increases. In this regard 1978 "was a critical year in the management of the economy" (Weatherford, 1980, p. 1). It was not until then that the economy had fully recovered from the massive recession of four years before. Until the economy had achieved the levels of resource employment that prevailed prior to 1975, the transition Carter hoped to make from straightforward economic stimulation to the more complex balance of fiscal and monetary policy required for equilibrium growth was impossible.

By the end of the year the economic indicators yielded a mixed set of results. Economic growth slowed and the increase in per capita income was down nearly a full point from the previous years of economic recovery. However, the most disturbing aspect of the 1978 economy was the dramatic rise in the Consumer Price Index from 6.8 percent in 1977 to 9.0 percent. Moreover, unlike the previous inflationary surges of the 1970s, this one could not be attributed to increased levels of government spending or to some external economic shock. The food and energy components of the C.P.I., in fact, remained constant. Closely following this unexpected shift in both the quantity and source of inflation came an economic anxiety that would grow into what Sidney Weintraub (1980) called the "Hoover Syndrome."

By late 1978, the public had begun to perceive the administration as one committed to retrenchment rather than economic growth (Weatherford, 1980, p.8). Also the image of economic drift was beginning to take shape around Carter administration policy. Continuing to shift the policy focus from unemployment to inflation, the president proposed a new voluntary incomes policy along with a program of wage-price "insurance." The plan was greeted with skepticism by business, labor, the media, and the public. As the mid-term election approached, congressional leaders were less than enthusiastic about the administration's economic leadership.

The economic slowdown persisted through 1979. This recession was further aggravated by Paul Volker and the Federal Reserve Board who continued their predecessors' contractionary monetary policy. Double-digit inflation, record interest rates, and a virtual collapse of the housing and auto industry, combined to shake public confidence in the administration's economic policy as the nation moved into a presidential election year. In early 1980, Jimmy Carter finally seemed to discover that political considerations make anti-inflationary macroeconomic policy extremely hazardous. Shortly before the election, he firmly announced that "this is not time for an economic stimulus program" but embarked on a "long term economic renewal" which nevertheless looked conspicuously like economic stimulus (Stanfield, 1980, p. 1468).

In September, the economy began to make a modest recovery. With the administration now running counter to the Federal Reserve Board's contractionary policies, unemployment declined from an annual rate of 18 percent in March to 7 percent. Even more significant, the Consumer Confidence Index of the Conference Board rose 34 points between May and September. This seems to confirm the hypothesis that as people become more optimistic about their personal futures they become less critical of the incumbent. The modest economic recovery, however, was not enough to salvage the White House for Jimmy Carter, thus giving Ronald Reagan the opportunity to command an economy with both increasing inflation resulting from the preelection spurt and unemployment still well over 7 percent.

The new administration committed itself to an economic policy of governmental austerity and fiscal constraint. The primary economic enemy was inflation. In this respect, Reagan is supported by a Federal Reserve Board still committed to tight monetary policy. However, tight money, governmental retrenchment and the persistence of near double-digit inflation, could result in two or more years of no economic growth. During that same time, unemployment could rise to over 9 percent and stay there. The Reagan plan to avoid this gloomy scenario calls for a series of dramatic steps, beginning with deep cuts in the federal budget and strong declarations of the administration's determination to stop inflation. If the expectations of inflation are lowered, interest rates may follow. If investors are persuaded that inflation is slowing, presumably they would be willing to accept lower rates.

Changing public expectations offers the key to the Reagan economic policy. Director of the Office of Management and Budget, David Stockman, describes the first 24 months as an "economic Dunkirk." If the new administration cannot quickly lower inflationary expectations and spur economic expansion, Stockman warns, it "will be thrown on the defensive" and face a "plethora of Capitol Hill initiatives to 'fix-up' the housing, auto and steel sectors, hype up exports, subsidize capital formations, provide municipal relief, etc." (Samuelson, 1980b, p. 2108).

Disagreements, he said, would "quickly destroy the present G.O.P. consensus on economic policy, pitting the tax cutters against the budget cutters and capital formation boosters against Kemp-Roth supporters" (Samuelson, 1980b, p. 2108). Thus, the administration faces a political as well as an economic battle to control inflation. In order to have a chance to work, the administration must convince the public that the policies will work. But if it fails, the slow effects of inflation, coupled with rising unemployment could create political pressures to modify administration policies, making it impossible for them to work.

PARTIES, PERCEPTIONS AND ECONOMIC POLICY

Models of the political business cycle are founded on a conventional view of democracy involving competition between two or more political parties that advocate and implement the interests of their clientele. But do American political parties differ substantially in either their goals or methods of macroeconomic policy? And equally important, does the mass public perceive the parties as different? Clearly, only if the impression of interparty competition exists can political control of the economy translate into increased support for incumbent politicians.

Compelling accounts of the differences in macroeconomic policy objectives are developed independently by Hibbs (1977) and Tufte(1978). Based primarily on the familiar Phillips Curve, party competition is said to result from different notions of the optimal point on the curve for policymakers to strive. The Phillips Curve presents elected officials with a dilemma – a trade-off between unemployment and inflation. If full employment is the prime policy objective, then the social cost of obtaining that objective is a rise in price levels and vice versa. Certainly, the two parties do not slavishly pursue identical macroeconomic policies. Yet, both Hibbs (1978) and Tufte (1978) find that the two parties differ in their weighting of the relative desirability of unemployment and inflation. Not surprisingly, these differences seem to correspond quite well to the objective interests and subjective preferences of their traditional support groups. Specifically, Tufte finds that as measured by platforms, by statements of Presidents, and by preference of party rank and file, Republican party ideology places a higher priority on low inflation while Democratic ideology favors low unemployment.

Hibbs indicates that public attitudes regarding the relative seriousness of inflation and unemployment are largely class based. Preferred economic outcomes are thus related to occupation, social class, and income of the citizens in ways that correspond to the differences in clienteles of the two parties. Lower income and status groups are more concerned about unemployment while higher income and status groups are more concerned about inflation.

While objective measures are important in determining party difference, unless citizens perceive a difference in the parties' economic goals, or the efficiency with which they pursue their goals, real economic conditions are irrelevant to electoral choice. In this context, the public's image of the two major parties confirms the common impression that Americans distinguish between the parties in terms of their economic class constituencies. Republicans are the party of business and Democrats are the party of the working man. Further, voter differentiation is made in terms of their economic management. The Republicans are the party of economic retrenchment and relative price stability, while the Democrats are the party of growth and the party of inflation. However, the recent "stagflation" which combines conditions of low growth and persistent inflation poses a dilemma to which traditional party responses seem inadequate. If the public perceives that no one quite knows how to improve economic conditions, then this dimension of party choice becomes irrelevant.

To complete the picture, Hibbs finds the actual macroeconomic policies of parties in office corresponds to both their ideological preference and the interest of their traditional support groups. A complex analysis of American unemployment data from 1947 to 1978 shows that even with a control for wartime, partisanship of administration is correlated with the national unemployment rate, Republican administrations producing more unemployment while Democrats seem to produce less.

A different relationship between party and economic policy has been put forth in another series of studies. These findings imply that party differences are simple, straightforward, and short term. What matters to citizens is whether conditions are good or improving now, rather than which party might best serve some long-term interest. Voters are thus myopic satisfiers who view elections as a referendum on their short term economic condition.

Both of these approaches to the relationship between economic policy and political behavior strengthen the notion that meaningful party differences exist in terms of policy outcome. However, it must be added that these distinctions revolve mainly around a short term decision to throw out one or another set of rascals.

INFLATION AND PRESIDENTIAL POPULARITY

The previous discussion of the effects of politics on economic policy at the macro-level implies a corresponding link between economic performance and political behavior at the micro-level. Political control of the economy is useless to a president if it has no impact on the level of his support. For this relationship to exist, of course, it is not necessary to suppose that citizens follow the cyclical movements of fiscal and monetary policy closely. It need only be that the general trends of the economy play a role in determining levels of presidential support. A brief look at recent economic and political trends seems to bear this out.

During the preceding decade, the fluctuations in sentiment as to which of the two parties could best preserve prosperity corresponded closely to changes in the inflation rate. This is clearly shown in figure 5.1. In 1972, when the C.P.I. increased only 3.3 percent, the Republicans were thought to be the "party best for prosperity." But as the inflation rate soared to 11 percent in 1974, public opinion shifted and the Democrats came to be considered a party for prosperity by an overwhelming 47 to 17 percent. With the inflation rate taking another dramatic jump in 1980, the tables turned again. In a poll taken shortly before the election the GOP received their best economic rating in 8 years, only slightly behind the Democrats as the "party best for prosperity."

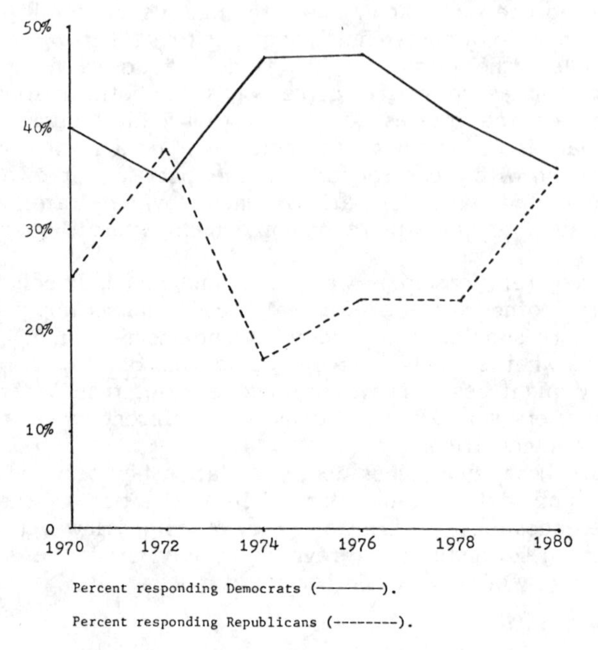

Fig. 5.1. Party best for prosperity, 1970-1980.

Similarly, presidential approval appears to follow changes in the rate of inflation. Again, during the years with the largest consumer price increases, presidential support was low. In 1974, President Nixon's approval level never rose above 28 percent. This was down 40 percentage points from the previous year's high. Much of this dissatisfaction, of course, resulted from the president's involvement in the Watergate scandal. But that same year, the combination of the enormous economic shock resulting from the dramatic increases in OPEC oil prices, and the lifting of the wage and price controls, produced unprecedented double-digit inflation. A Gallup poll taken just before Nixon's resignation found that the president's handling of the economy was rated no higher than his performance in the Watergate affair – despite the fact that a majority still approved of his foreign policy. In 1979, President Carter's approval hovered around 30 percent for the six months prior to the seizure of the American Embassy in Tehran. This was down 25 percentage points from 1977 when the inflation rate was less than 7 percent. By contrast, when inflation was relatively low in 1971 and 1972 presidential approval seldom dipped below 50 percent. The correlation between the percent change in the Consumer Price Index and the annual high in the Gallup Index of Presidential Approval was .62.

More sophisticated study of the relationship between economic conditions and presidential support, however, has yielded a mixed set of results. In attempting to establish the determinants of executive popularity Thomas Cronin (1980, p. 327) observes:

> No matter what Presidents do, their popularity declines. It hardly seems to matter what they attempt or even who is President. When news is good, a President's popularity goes down; when news is terrible, it merely goes down further and faster.

Evidence to support this pattern is produced by James Stimson (1976) who constructs a model of the factors determining presidential support. Looking at the data from 1945 to 1972, Stimson uncovers a recurrent cycle which operates independently of all factors but time. The cycle begins with the publc's expectations about the possibilities of presidential performance. As a president's term progresses, regardless of his performance, unfulfilled hopes inevitably turn into disillusionment. This slump ends only as the executive struggles to rebuild his supporting coalition and produces a late presidential rally. The performance of the economy is found not to have a dramatic impact on levels of presidential support.

But aside from a few such finishes to the contrary, the bulk of study confirms the common sense notion that a healthy economy usually means a healthy president at the polls. Kristen Monroe (1975) employs a distributed lag regression model to assess both the immediate and cumulative effects of a variety of economic factors on presidential support. Neither unemployment nor real personal income are found to have a significant effect on presidential support between 1952 and 1974. However, a significant negative relationship between inflation and support was discovered. The political impact of inflation is found to be quite powerful, but this effect does not appear to be fully felt until a year or more after it has occurred.

In a series of more complex analyses, Monroe (1977) and others (Kenski, 1977; Frey and Schneider, 1977; Kernell, 1978) experiment with a great variety of statistical models. But most of them conclude that high inflation carries a significant political impact.

Schneider (1977) disaggregates presidential support data, 1967-1975, according to social class. He retests the hypothesis of the previous studies and finds that lower and middle class citizens adjust their support for the president on the basis of changes in unemployment levels. Support among upper class respondents, however, is more closely related to changes in inflation rates. More importantly, Schneider finds that a rise in unemployment has a stronger negative impact on support among lower and middle classes. This finding is reversed for inflation rates. Thus, while economic factors strongly influence support trends, that impact appears to vary considerably across different classes.

This presentation should make several things clear. First, serious disagreement exists about the effect of economic factors on presidential popularity. Even among those studies which show a significant relationship between economic policy and political support, the nature of that relationship is disputed. Still, successful presidential politics seems to imply successful macroeconomic performance. It remains to be seen, however, if these factors influencing presidential support levels translate into votes at election time.

INFLATION AND THE ELECTORATE

While we have seen that the level of inflation and perceptions of which party can better handle economic problems affect presidential popularity, we must consider the question of whether these macroeconomic conditions also affect voting decisions. From our data presented in figure 5.2, we can see that inflation rates do correspond to the three landslide elections in the past decade: 1972, 1974, and 1980. In the latter two contests, the party out of power in the White House swept to electoral victories in November as inflation soared above 11 percent. On the other hand, in 1972 Nixon founded Eisenhower's prediction and not only won reelection, but did so by a huge margin. For 1972, inflation was the lowest (3.3 percent) in the entire decade.

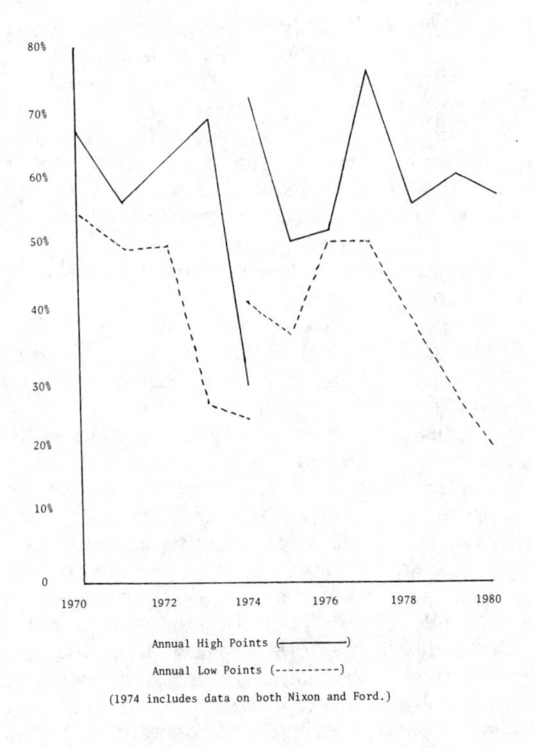

Fig. 5.2. Annual high and low points in presidential approval 1970-1980.

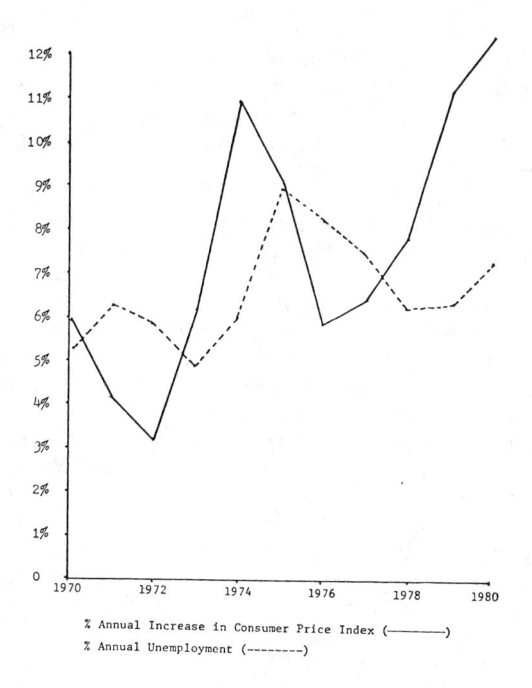

Fig. 5.3. Unemployment and consumer prices 1970-1980.

These impressionistic findings are confirmed by aggregate time-series analyses conducted by Kramer (1971) and Tufte (1978, ch. 5). The latter study indicates that economic conditons, specifically the yearly change in real disposable per capita income, affect both presidential and congressional races significantly. Specifically, a one percent improvement in real disposable income per captia benefits the incumbent Presidential candidate (in races from 1948 to 1976) by 1.3 percent of the national vote (Tufte, 1978, p. 121). An impact of 0.6 percent is found for the same economic conditions for off-year congressional elections from 1946 to 1974 and 1.1 percent for on-year elections for the House. To be sure, presidential popularity, as measured in Gallup polls has a much greater effect upon aggregate vote shares received by the party currently occupying the White House and this in turn may explain why there is a greater impact for economic conditions in on-years than in midterm contests. But our analysis, together with those of others (see Monroe, 1979 for a summary of the literature), suggests that economic performance affects the vote both directly and indirectly. The indirect impact is, of course, based upon the impact that economic conditions have upon presidential popularity, which in turn affects aggregate seat losses for the House of Representatives. While the overall shift in vote percentages for the two major parties may be greater for on-year contests, Tufte recognizes that the party controlling the White House normally loses congressional seats in off-years and estimates that a year of prosperous growth (a 3.0 percent increase in real disposable income) compared to a mild recession (a decline of one percent) would translate into an extra 20-30 seats in the House (1978, p. 112), while a similar scenario for on-year contests would mark a shift of 25-45 House seats (p. 119). Thus, Tufte (1978, p. 115) concludes that "(t)he vote cast in midterm congressional elections. . .is a referendum on the performance of the president and his administration's management of the economy" and furthermore that the in-party benefits from prosperity as well as losing ground during hard times (p. 126). Kramer's longer time series (1896 to 1964) confirms these findings.

There is a huge literature on the question of the impact of economic conditions on congressional voting, and there is agreement that economic performance affects presidential contests. The debates on Congressional contests focus upon whether unemployment and inflation do indeed have symmetric impacts upon the elections, whether the impacts occur through changes in partisan attitudes or by changes in the rates of participation by various groups within the population, and over issues of data and method (cf. Monroe, 1979). We shall not summarize the debates here, in part because there are not clear-cut battle lines which lead to sharpening of the issues involved and also because many of the questions raised are methodological and outside the scope of this essay.

The debates on congressional elections have been more focused as the success rate of House members seeking reelection has dramatically increased while that of Senators has declined. Members of the House have been enormously successful – at a rate of over 90 percent and often much higher – in retaining their seats and the margins for House members, at least prior to 1980, were increasing at an even more rapid pace (cf. Light, 1979). Senators, on the other hand, are becoming much more vulnerable; in 1978 and 1980, over 40 percent of incumbents seeking reelection were defeated. It thus becomes critical to try to figure out what differentiates these elections, since both cannot be responding to the same national economic factors. To be sure, there are other confounding events which make analysis at the aggregate level difficult: Did Nixon win by such a huge margin in 1972 because of low inflation or because his Democratic opponent, George McGovern, conducted such a weak campaign (one in which he had to ask his vice-presidential nominee to withdraw from the ticket)? Did the Democrats sweep the Congress and state and local offices in 1974 because of the high rate of inflation or because of Watergate and Ford's pardon of Nixon? Did the Republicans score heavily in House contests and win control of the Senate in 1980 because of the state of the economy or because of the Iranian hostage situation? At the aggregate level, it is virtually impossible to disentangle these factors, so many observers have looked at survey data.

Fiorina (1978a) found a significant role for economic factors, particularly inflation, upon individual decisions in presidential voting, but little evidence of retrospective voting in House contests. Kuklinski and West (1981) confirmed Fiorina's results for the House, but found evidence of future-oriented economic voting in the 1978 Senate contests: Senate voters cast ballots not on the basis of past performance, as a referendum on the president's performance, but upon their expectations for the future. These analyses suggest that House races are largely local contests, no longer influenced by national economic conditions (if they ever were in the past two decades). Members benefit most in their reelection bids by personal contacts with voters and constituency service, thus making them largely immune from the normal ebbs and flows of the economy. Senators and their opponents are better known than House members and particularly House challengers, so voters do have an idea of where they stand on the issues. Thus, elections to the upper house probably do constitute a referendum on the state of the economy, broadly defined.

To be sure, House incumbents are never completely safe (cf. Uslaner, 1981): When voters do have issue concerns, they tend overwhelmingly to choose economic matters. Under "normal" circumstances, lower house members may be able to deflect the impact of national economic conditions; in virtually all situations, the personal economic status of voters does not affect voting for the House. But when inflation becomes particularly high – or, conversely, when times are very good economically – the impact of economic conditions may indeed be felt. The 1974 and 1980 elections were marked by above-normal losses in the House for the party controlling the White House and many stories from the districts revolve around the effects of economic conditions. One cannot disaggregate the impacts of other events (Watergate, Iran) from those of the economy, but it is more than likely that such factors interact with each other to produce electoral landslides rather than serving as independent determinants of the vote.

A distressing problem in research on the political-business cycle has been the failure to disentangel the effects of inflation and unemployment. The evidence from aggregate studies is inconclusive, probably because of the strong negative correlation between the two variables. Prior to 1978, the Center for Political Studies did not ask separate questions in their surveys so that individual level analyses could only focus upon the voter's overall satisfaction with his or her own economic situation or the state of the national economy. Kuklinski and West (1981) believe that the latter variable should be more important: "No economic condition is more debilitating – physically and psychologically – than the lack of gainful employment. . . .The obvious expectation is that the unemployed will be more disenchanted with the current state of political affairs than the employed, and thus be more likely to focus their wrath on the imcumbent party." They further argue that unemployment is a more likely target of issue voting than inflation because the two parties have more clearly defined differences on the former policy than upon the latter. Yet, there is no impact for unemployment on voting for the House and the effect in Senate contests is in the wrong direction!

Two explanations for this anomalous finding may be offered. First, unemployed voters are more likely to believe that the Democratic party is better able to handle the unemployment problem and also that people who are unemployed are more likely to comprise that strata of the electorate who identify with the Democratic party (Kuklinski and West, 1981). Second, inflation may be a more salient problem for most voters than unemployment. As noted above, Ford maintained that unemployment affects a relatively small proportion of the citizenry compared to inflation; furthermore, the unemployed are less likely to vote than are those who hold jobs, and for many unemployment is only temporary. The unemployment figure at any given time reflects people who may be between jobs; indeed, most of the hard core unemployed do not show up in such statistics since they are not actively looking for work. These factors are put into perspective by the observation of Hibbs (1980, p. 11): ". . .unemployment no longer poses an economic disaster for many of those affected directly. In the 1930s the unemployed often went hungry. Today public transfers to the unemployed provide a significant cushion against the economic pain and most suffer temporary reductions in income. . .the private costs of unemployment are much lower now than in the past." While Hibbs also found that real changes in income do not justify the large jump in public concern about inflation as opposed to unemployment in recent years, the pervasiveness of inflation of such commodities as food and petroleum probably accounts for the level of concern of the public on inflation (1981, pp. 8-9).

The increase in public concern for inflation will probably continue throughout the foreseeable future. Even if the politicians and economic planners do succeed in reducing the rate of inflation, the prospects for prices for petroleum and food point to continuing increases over the long term. To be sure, should a decline in the rate of inflation be accompanied by an increase in the rate in unemployment, the relative standings of the economic issues may change again. But the prospect is for continued inflation and there should be little doubt that public concern for inflation will decline over the immediate future. The question thus becomes: To what extent can politicians effect changes in the economy? Or, more appropriately, the question might be to what extent do voters believe that politicians can do so and how do politicians respond to such beliefs?

DOES IT MAKE A DIFFERENCE?

Tufte maintains that politicians can make a difference in the economy, at least marginally, and in a way that many voters will recognize (1978, p. 57):

> The real income cycle is especially the product of election-year increases in transfer payments, administrative messing around with the timing of beneficiary payments, and decreases or postponements of taxes. Thus election-year enhancement of real disposable income is significantly a political and a bureaucratic problem: legislation must be passed, room for discretionary

> spending found, and agency administrators energized. The successful maintenance of the two-year real income cycle does not require, nor does it demonstrate, any great skill at macro-economic planning, management, or theory.

But Tufte does not disagree with Stigler about the overall impact of politicians on the larger questions of macroeconomic policy. Changes in economic situations brought about by politicians are generally marginal on this view, particularly with respect to unemployment cycles.

On the other hand, Pomper and Lederman (1980) and Hibbs (1977) have argued that there are significant differences between the parties in terms of economic platforms and performance. Specifically, they argue that the Democrats, when in power, pursue economic policies designed to reduce unemployment rates whereas the Republicans have acted more to control inflation even at the expense of higher unemployment. Thus, these authors conclude that there are indeed noticeable policy differences between the parties in the government. Furthermore, surveys have demonstrated repeatedly over the past three decades that voters _do_ perceive differences in orientations towards macroeconomic policies for the parties (cf. Monroe, 1979, pp. 159-161). What we do not understand very well – and what should be the focus of intensive analysis – is the extent to which party control of the economy affects not only unemployment and inflation but also the underlying factors in the economic infrastructure. We simply do not know whether this is the case. The politicians wish us to believe that they can when times are good – or, as in Reagan's campaign in 1980, when times are bad and the candidate is running against an incumbent. For the incumbent when times are bad, there is a tendency, hardly unique to Carter (although he did appear to raise it to an art form), to maintain that the economy is beyond the control of mere politicians. Yet all politicians, regardless of their beliefs about the impact that the policies they favor will resolve economic problems, recognize that they will be held responsible for whatever actions they take. Sir Ivan Gilmore, Lord Privy Seal in Great Britain, stated the dilemma very well with respect to Prime Minister Margaret Thatcher's supply-side economics approach to resolving Britain's rampaging inflation and unemployment in 1979 (Apple, 1979, p. A2): "While I agree that we are embarked on a program that could take two parliaments to carry through, I also note that between the first Parliament and the second one the electorate will have its chance of a say."

REFERENCES

Apple, R.W. Jr. "No Honeymoon for Mrs. Thatcher, Just Political Setbacks," _New York Times_ (March 19), p. A2, 1979.

Blinder, Alan. _Economic Policy and the Great Stagflation_, New York: Academic Press, 1979.

Brittan, Samuel. "Inflation and Democracy" in _The Political Economy of Inflation_ edited by Fred Hirsch and John Goldthorpe, Cambridge, Mass: Harvard University press, 1978.

Cronin, Thomas E. The State of the Presidency, Second Ed. Boston: Little, Brown & Co., 1980.

Crouch, Colin. "Inflation and the Political Organization of Economic Interests" in The Political Economy of Inflation edited by Fred Hirsch and John Goldthorpe, Cambridge, Mass: Harvard University Press, 1978.

Fiorina, Morris P. "Economic Retrospective Voting in American National Elections: A Micro-Analysis," American Journal of Political Science, 22 (May), pp. 426-443, 1978a.

______. "Legislative Facilitation of Government Growth: Universalism and Reciprocity Practices in Majority Rule Institutions." Paper presented at the Conference on the Causes and Consequences of Public Sector Growth, November, Dorado Beach, Puerto Rico, 1978b.

Frey, Bruno and Frederich Schneider. "Economic and Personality Determinants of Presidential Popularity." Unpublished manuscript, Universities of Zurich and Basel, 1977.

Galbraith, John K. "Let Us Now Praise (Faintly) Famous Economists." Esquire 87 (May) p. 70, 1977.

______. "Political Parties and Macroeconomic Policy," American Political Science Review, 71 (December), pp. 1467-1487, 1977.

Hibbs, Douglas A. Jr. "Public Concern About Inflation and Unemployment in the United States: Trends, Correlates and Political Implications." Paper prepared for the National Bureau of Economic Research Projeact on Inflation, Cambridge, Mass., 1980.

______. "The Mass Public and Macroeconomic Policy: The Dynamics of Public Opinion Towards Unemployment and Inflation." Paper presented at the 1978 Meeting of the American Political Science Association, New York, New York, 1978.

Hirsch, Fred and John Goldthorpe. The Political Economy of Inflation, Cambridge, Mass: Harvard University Press, 1978.

Hoadley, Walter. The Economy and the President. Englewood Cliffs, N.J.: Prentice Hall, 1978.

Keech, William. "Elections and Macroeconomic Policy Optimization," American Journal of Political Science 24, (May) pp. 345-367, 1980.

Kenski, Henry. "Inflation and Presidential Popularity," Public Opinion Quarterly 41 (Spring), pp. 86-91, 1977.

Kent, Frank. Political Behavior, New York: William Morrow and Company, 1928.

Kernell, Samuel. "Politics and Economic Performance in Modern Industrial Democracies." Paper presented at the 1978 Annual Meeting of the American Political Science Association, New York, New York, 1978.

Kernell, Samuel. "Presidential Popularity and Negative Voting: An Alternative Explanation of the Mid-Term Electoral Decline of the President's Party," American Political Science Review, 71 (March), pp. 44-66, 1977.

Key, V.O. Jr. Politics, Parties and Pressure Groups, first ed. New York: Thomas Y. Crowell, 1942.

Kissinger, Henry. "Is There a Crisis of Spirit in the West?" Public Opinion 1 (May/June) pp. 3-9, 1978.

Kramer, Gerald H. "Short-Term Fluctuations in U.S. Voting Behavior, 1896-1964," American Political Science Review, 65 (March), pp. 131-143, 1971.

Kuklinski, James H. and Darrell M. West. "Prospective Economic Voting in House and Senate Elections," American Political Science Review, 75, forthcoming, 1981.

Light, Larry. "For Many Incumbents, Running for Reelection Is Now a Full-Time Job," Congressional Quarterly Weekly Report, 37 (July 7), pp. 1350-1357, 1980.

Martin, Joe. My First Fifty Years in Politics (as told to Robert Donovan), New York: McGraw-Hill, 1960.

Mayhew, David R. Party Loyalty Among Congressmen, Cambridge: Harvard University Press, 1966.

Monroe, Kristen R. "Econometric Analyses of Electoral Behavior: A Critical Review," Political Behavior, 1 (Summer), pp. 137-173, 1979.

______. "God of Vengence and of Reward?" Paper presented at the annual meeting of the Public Choice Society, 1977.

______"The Economic Influence on Support for the President." Unpublished manuscript. State University of New York at Stony Brook, 1975.

Nixon Richard M. Six Crises, Garden City, N.Y. Doubleday, 1962.

Nordhaus, William. "The Political Business Cycle," Review of Economic Studies XLII (April), pp. 169-191, 1975.

Presser, Stanley and Jean Converse. "On Stimson's Interpretation of Declines in Presidential Popularity," Public Opinion Quarterly, 40 (Winter) pp. 538-541, 1976-1977.

Pomper, Gerald M. with Susan Lederman. Elections in America. Second ed. New York: Longmans, 1980.

Riordan, William L., comp. Plunkitt of Tammany Hall, New York: E.P. Dutton, 1963.

Samuelson, Robert J. "Carter Rides the Economic Waves," National Journal (October 11), p. 1707, 1980a.

______. "Will Reagan of the Federal Reserve be Calling the Economic Signals?" National Journal, (December, 13), pp. 2108-2112, 1980b.

Schneider, Frederich. "Presidential Popularity Functions of Different Classes." Paper presented at the Annual meeting of the Public Choice Society, 1977.

Sigelman, Lee. "The Dynamics of Presidential Support: An Overview of Research Findings," Presidential Studies Quarterly (Spring), pp. 206-217, 1979.

Stanfield, Rochelle L. "Don't Call it Economic Stimulus, Call it Long-Term Economic Renewal," National Journal (September, 6) pp. 1468-1472, 1981.

Stigler, George. "General Economic Conditions and National Elections," American Economic Review Papers and Proceedings (May), pp. 160-167, 1973.

Stimson, James. "Public Support for American Presidents," Public Opinion Quarterly, 40 (Spring), pp. 1-22, 1976.

Tufte, Edward R. Political Control of the Economy, Princeton: Princeton University Press, 1978.

Uslaner, Eric M. "Ain't Misbehavin': The Logic of Defensive Issue Voting Strategies in Congressional Elections," American Politics Quarterly, 9 (January) pp. 3-22, 1981.

Weatherford, M. Stephen. "Alternative Sources of Politico-Economic Demands: Carter Policies and the 1978 Congressional Elections." Paper presented at the Annual meeting of the American Political Science Association, August, Washington, D.C., 1980.

Weintraub, Sidney. "Carters Hoover Syndrome." New Leader, 63 (May 24), pp. 7-8, 1980.

Wilson, James Q. American Government, Lexington, Mass: D.C. Heath & Co., 1980.

Yankelovich, Daniel. "Economic Policy and the Question of Political Will," in the Economy and the President, edited by Walter Hoadley. Englewood Cliffs, N.J.: Prentice Hall, 1978.

6 Inflation Policy in Germany: The Institutional and Political Determinants

Richard Medley

The West German concern with inflation forms the central nerve of most discussions regarding the country's post-war economic recovery. The point which is often missed is that inflation-avoidance is a part of West Germany's larger policy of avoiding any significant amount of economic destabilization. The overriding concern of most economic actors, both public and private, has been the same: economic stability.

Economic stability does not mean simply low inflation rates, although they are an important element of any stabilization program. The range of concerns that run through economic planning are set forth in the 1967 Act to Promote Economic Stability and Growth, they are: stable prices, appropriate growth, high employment, and balanced trade. There is general agreement that all of the policies are important, and that the successful implementation of any one of them requires stability in the other areas.

This consensus, which relies upon all economic sectors, from the private bankers to the trade unions, is reinforced by the formal and informal arrangements that characterize the German system. At the center of this system stands the Deutsche Bundesbank. Since its creation in 1957, the Bank has carved out a reputation for intelligent planning and forceful implementation that keeps all other sectors of the economy reacting to its moves. That is exactly the way the Bundesbank wishes it to be.

The Central Bank's policy decisions are taken with respect to the overall economic conditions of the country, and not to suit the needs or desires of any particular sub-group of the economy, or to please any particular acedemic sect. Furthermore, the Bank is aware that its success depends upon the cooperation and understanding of all sectors of the economy. For these reasons, the Bank is in constant touch with all major interests in the country including both private and public sector representatives.

This chapter will examine the formal and informal mechanisms by which monetary and inflation policies are arrived at in Germany. The chapter's structure will parallel the economy in concentrating on the five pressure points that make nearly all important economic decisions in the Federal Republic. These five pressure points are the government, the Bundesbank, the banking sector, the company sector, and the unions. Many of the formal organizations within West Germany display a curious blend of concentration and federalism, as high-ranking bodies from banking, business, and labor meet with officials of the government and the Bundesbank to explain and negotiate for policies that their members consider important. Such discussions, which often lead to widely-accepted decisions, are crucial to the overall stability of the economy.

The first section will give a brief historical setting to the essay which is important to any understanding of current inflation policy in the Federal Republic. Two cataclysms stand out: hyper-inflation of the 20s and late 40s and, the vast destruction of life and property that Germany experienced in the Second World War. They have produced the wide-shared need for security which gives Germany the consensus that forms its economic foundation. While this essay will focus on German economic institutions, it must not be forgotton that the political, psychological, and historical aspects of Germany's national life are crucial to the success of its economy. Many decisions taken by the Bundesbank and the federal officials are made with these factors in mind, and any recounting that ignores them in favor of strictly formal institutional presentations will not give an accurate representation of the economy.

Immediately following the historical overview will be institutional analyses of the major economic actors in Germany. Because so much has been made out of the monetary control procedures of the Federal Republic, a thorough-going discussion of the Bundesbank will occupy the largest part of this section. Finally, we will look at Germany's reactions to the two oil shocks during the 1970s to have a glimpse at this stability-oriented machinery in action.

HISTORICAL OVERVIEW

An understanding of the economic and political life of modern Germany requires familiarity with the last century of this troubled country's history. Not only its vaunted fear of inflation, but many of its institutional arrangements arise from the ashes of previous errors.

The over-arching concern with stability and security has been forged by two hyper-inflations, as well as the personal and social losses from wars, political turmoil, and the destruction of industrial capacity by relentless Allied bombing and conquest during the Second World War. The best estimates are that 15 percent of the country's population was killed during the war, and many more people were permanently crippled. On top of this was the blow to German transportation facilities as all bridges spanning the Rhine, Wesel, and Main rivers were destroyed, and the railroad system obliterated. When the war ended the German economy faced total collapse.

From 1945-48, unemployment continued to grow, while production and housing remained at minimal levels. The people, many of whom had been wiped out by social and economic chaos twice in their lives, came to value security above all else. The consensus that grew out of this shared deprivation has continued to dominate Germany to this day.

The first postwar leaders, Adenauer in politics and Erhard in economics, knew very well that security was uppermost in citizens' minds, and that any form of government or economic arrangement which failed to provide such security would not survive. For our purposes it is Erhard's accomplishments that matter most.

The first order of business was to recontruct the country's steadily deteriorating production and supply capabilities. By early 1948, Lucky Strikes had replaced the disgraced Reichsmark as Germany's accepted currency. With the previous excessive inflation of 1922-3 burning in their minds, officials recognized that a stable and hard currency was necessary for further progress. With this in mind, on June 20, 1948, the American Government unleashed Operation Bird Dog. The plan was to replace untold billions of the worthless Reichsmarks with 10 billion newly minted Deutschmarks.

It was announced that each German citizen could exchange 400 Reischsmarks for 40 Deutschmarks. Two months later citizens were allowed to exchange 200 more Reichsmarks for 20 more Deutschmarks. That was it. The government estimates that 93 percent of all paper wealth was wiped out by this conversion.

Its effect was immediate, astonishing, and positive. As Henry Wallich has noted:

> It transformed the German scene from one day to the next. On June 21, 1948, goods reappeared in the stores, money resumed its normal functions, the black and gray markets reverted to a minor role (Hartrich, 1980).

But the longer-term performance was even more impressive than the immediate impact. In the 22 months after introduction of the Deutschmark, industrial production rose by 83 percent.

The overwhelming importance attributed to maintaining the strength of this currency can be seen in the government's fierce determination to keep the Mark stable, and prices down. The pride with which Germans view the Deutschmark is illustrated by the festivities held in 1968 to commemorate the currency's 20th anniversary. The other side of this pride, however, is the dark fears of losing the security this currency brings to their lives. These fears are reflected in Heinrich Bölls words:

> The ownership of land, of real estate . . . has remained the sole stable factor; and a currency, a mark that has already reached

> 28 years (after two other marks had melted away within 25 years), has likewise become a stable factor, and anyone interfering with either of these factors has little chance of obtaining votes (Böll, 1976:19).

The obsession with security that dominates economics discussion is evident in the campaigns between the conservative Christian Democrats and the more progressive Social Democrats. While there are a few major economic issues separating the two parties that dominate the political landscape, they are minor compared to the divisions among parties in other Western European countries. The Christian Democrats speak resoundingly about stopping socialism, and the Social Democrats speak about the dangers of war and labor strife under Christian Democrat rule, but when the talk turns to details of economic programs for the country, the differences begin to melt away. The two parties often find themselves in the position of a Christian Democratic gubernatorial candidate who had to admit that he "didn't know what his party would do differently for the economy if it were elected."

In this, like in most areas of German economic life, it was the Christian Democrat economics wizard, Ludwig Erhard who set the pace, by combining a free market orientation with social welfare concerns, to arrive at what he termed Soziale Market wirtschaft or the social market economy. As the first, and dominant, voice in post-war economic planning, Erhard implemented this hybrid approach which seeks to assure that all sectors of the economy benefit from any general economic improvements. This led to an extensive social welfare system, strict labor laws, a form of industrial democracy, and three decades of relative labor-management peace.

The compromises since 1945 have not been made solely by the Christian Democrats. After the Social Democrats lost the first decade of elections to their Conservative counterparts, it was clear their Marxist tenets did not appeal to most citizens. Therefore, in an historic conference at Bad Godesburg in 1959, the Social Democrats renounced Marxism and accepted a much more conservative stance. It was only then that the Social Democrat's electoral share began climbing until 1969 when they achieved a parliamentary majority in coalition with the Free Democrats.

Even though the Social Democrats had moderated a great deal by the time of their victory, fears of destabilization and socialist-led wave of expropriation caused some businessmen to hustle suitcases full of Marks into Switzerland shortly after the election. The decade of leadership under Willy Brandt and Helmut Schmidt has erased any lingering fears about the dangers of their rule, and a 1980 Christian Democratic national campaign based on stopping the socialist threat from the Social Democrats fizzled and expired well before election day.

The country's stability consensus is important not only for politicians but also for central bankers, as it helps set the conditions under which the Bundesbank wields the considerable power that it does over the country's economic course. The Bundesbank is perceived as an able and determined guardian of monetary stability, and its power has only been increased by the few clashes with the Government in its 23-year history. Its goals have not changed, and its policies are directed singlemindedly at stabilization of the Deutschmark, as long as that goal does not threaten severe destabilization of other economic concerns such as employment and trade balances. Although other sectors have had disagreements with the Bank on specific issues, there is widespread agreement with its goals, and admiration for its skill.

Crucial to economic recovery was the system of German banking which had developed during the century before the war, and which the Allied forces did their best to destroy after the war. The Occupation forces broke the big three banks into thirty successor banks, with each of the three having one new bank created in every state (Land) of Germany, and in Berlin. The demands of history and reconstruction were too much, however, and these banks slowly recombined into the original Big Three so they could afford the massive loans necessary to finance postwar recovery. The existence of very large banks, with the attendant capital facilities and investment expertise are a part of German history, and could not be successfully purged by foreign intervention. The banks and businesses have traditionally worked hand in hand in ways that violate most received ideas about sound banking in Anglo-Saxon countries.

All sectors of the economy had learned hard lessons about the great intrinsic value of stability, in the first half of the twentieth century, but laborers paid the highest tuition. It was largely the laboring class which fought the war, and the same class that was left without any real estate or capital goods after the conversion from the Reichsmark to the Deutschmark. While there has been some redistribution of the wealth remaining after the war, and subsequent currency change, laborers suffered demonstratively more than capitalists as a class. To help protect itself against renewed destruction, labor has forged a record of cooperation with capital that is the envy of most Western European nations.

The dual lesson labor seems to have taken up is a fear of destabilization, and an appreciation for the rewards of the social market economy which has developed in the last thirty-five years.

While there are reasons to wonder about the medium-term future of the German economy, there is no denying the overwhelming successes of the postwar period, and most particularly of the 70s, when most other industrialized nations were suffering prolonged doldrums. The past is part of the explanation for the country's success, but institutional arrangements within the public and private sectors are also important to the economic "miracle" of modern Germany.

THE PUBLIC SECTOR

The federal, state, and local governments in West Germany are involved in many aspects of the economy, as are all West European governments.

Their concerns range from labor and social security to housing and agricultural support. For our purposes, however, only two areas are important: money-related policies and industrial policies. Not including the powers of the Bundesbank, the various levels of government exercise influence over monetary developments through tax and exchange-rate policies.

In addition to the government's standard taxation on income, sales, and gasoline, the federal government has a series of short-term counter-cyclical tax instruments at its disposal that were given to it in the 1967 Act to Promote Economic Stabilization and Growth. This act grew out of the 1965-1966 recession when it became clear that monetary policy, as practiced by the Bundesbank would be insufficient to keep the economy on an even keel through all conditions. The powers granted to the government represent the high point of fine-tuning hubris, and were greeted by then chief of the Economics Ministry policy division, Dr. Otto Schlect with the words:

> The ad hoc economy, the economy of the light hand is dead . . . we have a new economic system now . . . a tailored economy.

The oil shock and subsequent events have knocked much of the wind out of the fine-tuners' sails, but the powers remain on the books. Their greatest period of use was in the early 70s, with 1973-4 being the last major wielding of these instruments.

Under the 1967 Act, the government – at the behest of the Economics Minister, and subject to the endorsement of parliament within six weeks – may take a range of measures to affect the liquidity and investment prospects in the economy. It may raise of lower income taxes by up to 10 percent, for up to one year. The receipts from this excise tax are placed in a blocked account with the Bundesbank and returned at the end of the embargo, usually as part of a secondary counter-cyclical policy. One use of this policy in 1973 caused a minor stir when the Social Democrats invoked the tax rise only for higher income Germans, which stimulated renewed fears of vast expropriations of wealth. The concern was ill-founded and floundered quickly.

A second set of policy tools allows the government to accelerate, slow down, or even suspend tax depreciations for industrial capital investments. Such changes would almost certainly affect investment decisions, especially as the one-year time limit is known in advance and businessmen would seek to take advantage of the breaks or avoid the penalties, as the case may be.

Another group of weapons center on the budgets of federal, state and local governments. On the federal level, the Finance Minister can be empowered by the cabinet to order partial freezes in spending by all units. The government cannot specify which programs are to be cut, such decisions being left to the departments. The money from such freezes is placed in a blocked account as well, and becomes known as an "eventual budget," which will be released in future counter-cyclical moves. Additionally, the Ministry may order accelerated repayment of government loans to the Bundesbank.

These programs offer strong medicine for an economy, but the dangers of application to situations where there is not an underlying robustness is great enough to warrant extreme caution in their use. As mentioned, these instruments have largely gone out of favor with government officials.

The other major instrument of monetary control at the disposal of the federal government is exchange-rate policy. In setting such policy, the government naturally works closely with the Bundesbank, but it is not obliged to follow the Bank's directives. Before the large revaluation of the Mark in 1969, the Central Bank had been publicly pressuring the government to take some action in this direction for some time. The government remained convinced that strongly worded intentions against revalution would be enough to cure the speculative capital inflow caused by the Bank's obligation to support the parity arrangements of the old Bretton-Woods agreement. Only after the national election of that year was the Mark revalued (by 9.3 percent against the dollar). It should not be thought that the government does not take the Bank's opinion seriously, but the Bank is officially charged with maintaining monetary stability, while the government must worry about all aspects of the economy. Furthermore, all sides agree that while revaluation does not occur whenever the Bundesbank wishes, the government would never revalue against the preference of the Bank.

A major factor in promoting the stable postwar economy has been the strong direction given the overall monetary policy of the Federal Republic by its central bank, the Deutsche Bundesbank (DBB). Its impact comes through its dedication to steadying the currency and through its competence at this task.

THE CENTRAL BANK

The German Central Bank (Deutsche Bundesbank) was created in 1957 by merging the state (Länder) banks and the Bank Deutsche Länder. Its primary goal is to assure the continued high perfomance of the Deutschmark. It is secondarily charged with assisting the federal government's economic policy, but in the case of conflict between the two goals, it must choose to assure the Mark's stability. This ordering of goals is evident in the DBB reply to questions from the U.K. House of Commons Treasury and Civil Service Committee in June 1980:

> The accepted interpretation of the relevant sections of the Bundesbank Act, which has never been disputed by the Government, is that in the event of a conflict with the objectives of the Government's general economic policy the Bundesbank has to give priority to its primary task, namely safeguarding monetary stability.

The few outbreaks of conflict between the Central Bank and the federal authorities illustrate that this is the true state of affairs and not merely public relations.

One of the most interesting tests of DBB autonomy came in March 1970. At this time, the stability of the Mark was threatened from many sides. First, there were foreign exchange pressures. The Mark had been upvalued by over nine percent only six months before, in the wake of its emergence as the second major reserve currency in the world, after the dollar. Because of the small German economy, in relation to that of the United States (roughly one-eighth the size), the reserve currency status left the DBB faced with profound difficulties in its attempts to control the domestic money supply. Compounding this was the Bundesbank's pledge to support the dollar, if not within the old Bretton-Woods parity range, then at least within moderate parameters. Finally, the DBB had to note a surging inflation rate that officials believed was in danger of destabilizing the entire economy. The coincidence of all these circumstances was thought sufficient to spawn the widespread inflationary psychology the Bank was determined to avoid.

Following the Federal Government's failure to invoke the strong inflationary program proposed by then-Economics Minister Schiller, the DBB raised the rates at which it loans to banks to their highest level since World War II. It took this action against the advice of labor, management, banks, and the government itself. Coupled with this was a 30 percent increase in the reserves which banks had to hold on deposit with the Bundesbank against non-resident liabilities. This double-barreled action was intended both to slow credit expansion and to decrease the huge foreign capital inflow resulting from speculation about new upvaluations of the Mark.

This did not end the DBB action to slow the economy. It continued to pressure the Federal government for strong fiscal measures to dampen inflationary pressures in the economy. Political pressure from business and labor to avoid such "restraining policies" caused the newly-elected SPD coalition to reject the Bank's pressure. Finally, after four months of behind-the-scenes lobbying with no results, the Bundesbank took a step it had never taken. It announced considerations about raising the Banks' reserve requirements by 10-20 percent. While the effects of such a squeeze would be severe, the DBB chose this announcement of intent as the most dramatic signal it could give of its seriousness to follow whatever course necessary to smother the rising inflation rate.

The cabinet met shortly after this announcement to reconsider anti-inflationary measures it had shelved in March, but no action was taken. After seeing that no governmental action was forthcoming, on July 1, the Bundesbank raised the reserve requirements by 15 percent hitting the middle of its threatened range. It believed no more increases in its lending rate were possible, since higher rates would attract more speculative capital from abroad compounding the liquidity glut. The continued pressure of the Bank and its clear determination to blunt the economic upsurge finally outweighed private sector pressures, and the parliament ratified a government plan to increase personal and corporate taxes and suspend certain capital depreciation provisions. On the same day that this measure passed the Upper House of Parliament the DBB reduced the rate at which it lent to banks to guard against more speculative capital inflows.

It is exactly the DBB's willingness to press its case against strong political opinion, along with the undeniable intelligence it has brought to its goal of monetary stability, that makes the Bank a major force in determining the course of the German economy. The Bank is fully aware that public perception of its determination, and a thorough understanding of its instruments and goals are crucial to its task. It does not operate in a vacuum guided only by neo-Keynesian or monetarist theory, but recognizes the importance of presentation, persistence, and consensus for the success of its policies.

The Organization and Instruments of the Bundesbank

The first thing to note about the Bundesbank's power is the number of institutions covered by its regulatory powers. Any institution that performs banking functions in Germany is considered to be a bank. This covers more ground than might be suspected at first, since the definition of banking functions is broader in Germany than in the United States. Under the Federal Republic's rules, any credit institution that deals with deposits, loans, security transactions or the safekeeping of securities for others is a bank, for regulatory purposes.

A few credit facilities, such as insurance companies, escape control by the DBB, but they play almost no role in the creation of short-term capital, so their exclusion has no significant impact on money creation.

Tools of the Bundesbank

The control of money and credit by the Bundesbank is centered on interest rate and reserve requirements manipulation. Open Market Operations, while used more frequently in the last few years, play a limited role in policy control due both to the relatively small size of these markets, and to the small number of institutions who participate in bond purchases and sales. Still, such operations are used to give signals and to mop up small amounts of excess liquidity.

Although the Bundesbank argues that it follows neither an interest rate nor a liquidity management policy, *per se*, its instruments may be divided between the two for analysis. It should be clear that the Bank does not, in fact, seem to pursue one or another of these policies single-mindedly, but tries to mix and match with overall stability as its goal.

Longer Run Rates Policy

Interest rates

The Bundesbank has three interest rates it can wield within its policy arsenal. The discount and Lombard rates are the charges for which the DDB will advance money to banks. Of late, the higher Lombard rate has set the open money market rates within fairly narrow limits. The third rate is that at which the Bank offers government and Treasury paper on the open market. Used in concert with the discount quotas and other liquidity measures, the Bank has maintained impressive control over the monetary system during the past decade.

Discount rate

The Discount Rate is the basic rate at which the Bundesbank will rediscount commercial bills of exchange and checks. This facility is available only to credit institutions, and maturities never exceed three months.

Lombard rate

The Lombard Rate is the rate at which the Bundesbank will loan to banks who have reached the limit of their rediscount quotas. Such a rate is made necessary by the strict adherence of the DBB to its rediscount quotas. Although well-developed overnight money markets now help to perform some of the tasks of the Lombard Rate it maintains its significance as a leader of interest rates in this market.

Longer-Run Liquidity Management

Rediscount quotas and Lombard ceilings

The quotas and ceilings are effective and frequently used medium-term instruments of the Bundesbank. Their existence is made necessary by the seriousness with which the Bank takes its role as lender of the last resort. It will not refuse money to a bank, as long as the bank has not exhausted its available quotas and ceilings. Since the DBB does not play a discretionary lending role, it must establish limits to its facilities at the outset.

Although the Bank is, in principle, able to set individual quotas and ceilings for credit institutions it rarely does so. Quotas are normally established on the basis of coefficients that vary by size and type of institution. Although the exact details of these quotas are not published, there is a general formula for discount quotas.

Reserve requirements

Reserve requirements are a finely honed set of selective policy instruments at the Bundesbank's disposal. Through them, the DBB can reach down to influence small sections of the banking system. Used together with the rediscount quotas and Lombard ceilings, they form an effective liquidity control mechanism.

Fine tuning

As many commentators on the DBB have remarked, including the Bank's own officials, Open Market Operations are best viewed simply as adjuncts to Bank policy which is mainly directed by use of the rate and liquidity management techniques discussed above. Since the scope of open market operations is limited – though expanding – in Germany, the Bundesbank can use a change in rates on its short-term paper or other government bills to display a concern for the movement of capital markets without greatly changing the liquidity of the system.

Such a demonstration occured in October 1980, when the Bank wanted to demonstrate its awareness of an extreme liquidity crunch it would have liked to ease, but could not. The DBB was faced with large capital outflows to the U.S and U.K. because of high interest rates in these countries, and with a quickly-developing recession within Germany. The Bank ideally would have lowered interest rates, signalling an easier money policy. It felt unable to risk the lower rates in this case for fear that they would increase the capital outflow, and add to the country's unusual, and disturbing current account deficit. For this reason, the Bank maintained its high interest rates, while dribbling liquidity into the market as a show of concern.

The exchange outflow and current account deficit of the Federal Republic is the converse of the problems it faced throughout the early 70s, when massive capital inflows and bulging trade surpluses made Germany the target of speculators and the object of anger for many of its OECD and EEC partners. At one point in 1968, this anger boiled over to cause Britain's Prime Minister Wilson to remark that if the Germans failed to upvalue the Deutschmark, he qustioned the future security of West Berlin. It was a remark that could not have been more pointed at a natinal obsession.

Both the problems of the early 70s and those of the current time are a result of Germany's fervid avoidance of exchange controls. Not only do such controls strike at the heart of the country's free market ideology, but they are tainted through use by Hitler's economics adviser Hjalmar Schacht.

One of the most ferocious political battles about economic issues in the last decade centered on a requirement that West German corporations keep 50 percent of any overseas loan they acquired in non-interest bearing accounts with the Bundesbank. By going abroad for loans, corporations were virtually nullifying the effect of DBB tight money policies. The fight led to the resignation of Finance and Economics Minister Schiller. This resignation was shocking for its suddenness and bitterness, as well as for its timing 3 months before a national election. But its occurrence is an indication of the strong emotions that direct controls of any sort evoke from German politicians.

The Bundesbank has established a series of indirect mechanisms designed to give them some control over the flow of capital across the country's borders. Beside the reserve requirements detailed above, the Bank has an active swap policy, offering to buy back foreign currency at especially favorable rates in the forward currency markets. In addition, the government can choose to support DBB attempts to clamp down on foreign capital inflow by prohibiting interest payments on non-resident deposits. When it chooses to do this, it must also control the purchase of fixed interest securities by foreigners, or money simply moves to those facilities.

The restraint of Federal Repubic politicians in not imposing elaborate direct exchange control measures is an important indication of the depth of their commitment to free market incentives rather than command economy directives. Capital flow problems have been almost overwhelming at times for this country, but to date the authorities have preferred the less effective incentive measures, to the direct control measures other countries have employed.

CENTRAL BANK MONEY STOCK

The intermediate target at which all these policy instruments are formally aimed is the growth rate of Central Bank Money Stock. The Bundesbank's transition to published monetary targeting, which was greeted with as much misunderstanding as ballyhoo, resulted from the coincidence of a waxing economic theory and a waning supply of alternative monetary control instruments. One point must be made at the outset. The Bundesbank has not become soley concerned with the growth of central bank money, since the inception of published targets.

The Central Bank views the control of monetary growth as part of the complex of tools it can use to influence the planning environment for all other serctors of the economy. A stable growth in money supply affords great advantage to individuals making investment or wage decisions. Stability is the raison d'être of monetary targeting, and not a theoretic conviction that by controlling the money supply per se major problems in the German economy can be solved. The Bank, in answer to the House of Commons, wrote:

> The paramount importance accorded to the Central Bank money stock as a monetary indicator is based not on any specific analytical tenet but rather – in addition to economic factors – on political and psychological considerations.

TRANSITION TO MONETARY TARGETING

The Federal Republic was the first major OECD country to begin publication of monetary aggregate targets. This, together with its success in controlling inflation, has made it a frequently referred to case of successful monetarist policy. On the evidence, however, monetarist theorists would be wise to think twice before using Germany as an example of their theory being successfully implemented. In order to frame the discussion of the move to monetary targeting, Table 6.1 will indicate other major OECD transitions to targeting, as well as the relative successes which have been achieved.

Table 6.1. OECD Transitions to Targeting.

Country	Aggregate	Projection Period	Target (In Percent)	Outcome (In Percent)
Germany	Central Bank Money Stock	End 74-End 75	8	10.0
		Average 75-76	8	9.2
		Average 76-77	8	9.0
		Average 77-78	8	11.5
		1978 Q.4-1979 Q.4	6-9	6.3
		1979 Q.4-1980 Q.4	5-8	4.8 (est.)
		1980 Q.4-1981 Q.4	4-1	
United States	M1/M2	March 75-March 76	5-7½	5.0
			8½-10½	9.6
		75 Q.2-76 Q.2	5-7½	5.2
			8½-10½	9.5
		. . . .		
		1978 Q.1-1979 Q.1	4-6½	4.8
			6½-9	7.1
United Kingdom	Sterling M3	Fiscal year ending April 1977	9-13	7.8
		Fiscal year ending April 1978	9-13	14.9
		Fiscal year ending April 1979	8-12	11.4
		Fiscal year ending April 1980	7-11	11
		April 80-Sep. 80	7-11	31
Japan	M2	77 Q.3-78 Q.3	11-12	12.0
		77 Q.4-78 Q.4	12	12.6
		78 Q.1-79 Q.1	12	12.2
France	M2	Dec. 76-Dec. 77	12.5	13.9
		Dec. 77-Dec. 78	12	12.3
		Dec. 78-Dec. 79	11	

WHY PUBLISH MONEY STOCK TARGETS?

The framework for publication of a monetary aggregate was established seven years before the program began, when then-Economics Minister Schiller began to keep all sectors of the German economy briefed on developing trends in, and government plans for, the economy. Schiller and other ministers published aggregate targets for such things as unemployment and inflation, as required by the 1967 Law to Promote Stability. With the law came an activist government role in the economy. While this did not mean the beginning of a command economy, it did mean that the government would publish its targets and projection in yearly reports, as well as promote meetings of business, labor, bank, and government officials to help provide a consensus on actions needed to keep the economy strong. This was the founding of a policy which Schiller dubbed "concerted action" and which was to help lead Germany through the first oil shock in relatively fine style.

While aggregate publications of the federal government provided the background, developments in the economy during 1974 furthered the transition to monetary targeting. The first and most pressing problem was the general uncertainty created by the 1973 oil shock. Coupled with that were two years of wage negotiations in which settlements set post-war records. A wage-price spiral seemed to be in the offing, and strong action was necessary to halt inflationary expectations before they set in. Nothing would be better suited to moderate the atmosphere for wage and investment decisions than a stark announcement of limits the Bundesbank planned for economic growth in the coming year. Since it was a new instrument it could not be discredited by the economic performance of 1973 and 1974, and a dramatic new policy would attract attention throughout the country.

Reinforcing the psychological value of money stock targets was the virtual disappearance of "free liquid reserves" held by banks. The DBB defines free liquid reserves as "excess reserve balances, open market paper which the Bundesbank has promised to purchase and unused rediscount quotas." Because of the extremely tight liquidity situation the Bank had imposed as it tried to prevent the cost of energy and wages from being passed through into price increases, banks had reduced these liquid reserves by well over half from 1972 to 1973. The problem was that free liquid reserves had been the aggregate employed by the Bundesbank as an intermediate target. Their disappearance created problems for the credibility of this policy.

The other major external factor affecting the timing of this transition was that the DBB had just been released from its requirement to maintain the then-surging Deutschmark within the rough limits of the 1971 Smithsonian agreements. Once floating was allowed, the Bundesbank felt more confident of controlling the money supply without the destabilizing effects of having to purchase and sell large amounts of foreign currencies.

While the above-mentioned economic and political factors were vital to this transition, it cannot be maintained that monetarist ideology had no part in the decision to move to money stock targets. Bundesbank officials say that the monetarist theory held powerful sway in the early 70s within the bank. Following the guidelines, a decision was made to use a version of the monetarist's "high-powered money" for their published monetary aggreagate.

These same officials, however, caution against an overemphasis on the ideological content of their target, noting that the Central Bank money definition was – and is – viewed as an experiment, and that controlling the money growth rate is not the sole concern of the Bank. The experimental nature of this construct can be seen with a look back at Table 4.2. Here it is obvious that both the projection periods, and the nature of the targets have changed considerably since their introduction 6 years ago.

EVOLUTION OF THE TARGET

The overriding goal in setting the CBM targets, from the Bundesbank's perspective, is to provide a relatively smooth pattern of growth for the economy. Both the continuity of measurement provided by constant reserve ratios, and the gradual alterations of targeting emphasize this goal.

When the DBB decided to publish targets it set one-year intervals for its projection. There was pressure both for shorter and longer term pronouncements, but neither direction was deemed sufficiently useful for Bundesbank goals. It was feared that short run targets could require massive DBB intervention, to hit the goals on a regular basis. The other option – to allow its targets to be missed consistently - would undermine CBM credibility and destroy its stabilization possibilities.

At the other end of the spectrum, the Bank does not feel that any institution is capable of predicting the economy's movements, domestic and foreign, for periods longer than one year, if that. During the late 60s the Federal Government, under Minister Schiller, posted five year plans for aggregate economic variables, only to be forced into adjusting those plans each year. The effect was yearly targets, with the lessened credibility that comes from having to recant on predictions.

In fact, the Bank has discovered that even one year targets are too long to be accurately set, and has moved to a two-tiered announcement procedure that incorporates the stable decision making environment of one-year targets, with the accuracy that comes from shorter term projections. As a result, the Bank announces a range within which it will allow CBM to grow during the coming year, and mid-way through the year, refines that prediction by announcing which end of the range it will aim at.

The point in each year at which measurement of money stock growth is taken is as much a result of successive experimentation as is the length for which targets are predicted. When the targets were first published, in December 1974 (for End 74 – End 75) DBB shot at a specific growth rate (8 percent). As it was, they overshot that goal by 2 percent. The Bank concluded that December was a bad month on which to base its growth statistics since currency in circulation figures for that month are unrepresentative of the other eleven months.

December figures were used only for the first year of targeting, after which the Bank concentrated on entire year averages for CBM growth during the following three years. The Bank was eventually convinced that averages for the entire year were too cumbersome, and failed to reflect the corrective actions taken by the Bundesbank. A few months of high money growth during the early part of a year could result in overshooting of the monetary targets for the year, even if the Bank brought growth rates under control in the final months. Again, the Bank was faced with the prospect of overshooting its targets consistently, or of taking actions to hit the targets and, in the process, severely distorting interest rates or general liquidity.

The system in effect at the time of this writing targets the growth of CBM from the fourth quarter of one year to the fourth quarter of the next year. This, Bank officials believe, avoids both the errors of the two previous measurement periods.

The other major change in calculation moved the target from a single point (usually 8 percent) to a range (6-9 percent in the first year of the new policy), with a mid-year refinement to indicate which part of the range the DBB will try to hit.

The situation precipitating this change is a perfect illustration of the pragmatism that has formed the Bank's policy decisions throughout its monetary experiment. In 1978, the Bank targeted a CBM growth rate of 8 percent for the year. At year's end, CBM had grown by 11.5 percent. Through it all, the DBB remained committed to stability in other areas of the economy, purposely sacrificing its chances of hitting the 8 percent target.

The growth occurred as the Bank tried to cope with a surge of speculative demand for the Deutschmark. If it did not adopt an easy money policy, the Bank knew that it would halt the strong investment recovery then underway. On the other hand, easy money policies would destroy any chance of hitting the 8 percent targt. The Bank decided to unleash the CBM for the year and concentrate on sustaining the economic recovery. In addition, it wanted to keep money market interest rates near the DBB's low bank lending rates of 3-4 percent, and to maintain adequate free liquid reserves in the banking system. In all these goals the DBB succeeded as well as can be expected.

The Bank sought to explain its 3.5 percent overshooting in every available public forum, and, to emphasize its concentration on the overall stability of monetary conditions, it announced the end of point targets with its 1979 CBM predictions. As the Bank explained to the House of Commons:

> In one extreme situation, in which exchange rate movements bearing no relation to the underlying economic situation threatened to endanger the ultimate objectives of monetary policy (i.e., growth and imployment) in 1978, the Bundesbank was

forced to temporarily disregard its annual monetary growth target. This is one of the reasons why the monetary growth target has been formulated in terms of a range since 1979. . .

The Bank authorities are now convinced that this change is the best of all possible worlds. They sought to combine a more realizable forecasting arrangement with strongly worded advice that the range would be the actual guidelines for CBM growth in the coming year. No overshooting would be allowed.

The loss of a single point of reference for monetary base growth was more than made up for by the Bank's success in hitting its refined mid-year targets during the first year of the new experiment, and barely undershooting it in 1980.

SETTING THE TARGET

The Bundesbank uses information from its econometric models, other government agencies, and direct or indirect contact with banks, business and labor in establishing its target ranges for the year. While the "concerted action" plan of formal meetings among these sectors has broken down, informal contact remains a strong part of the target-setting process for the DBB.

The formal econometric model used by the Bank employs four aggregate econometric indicators to establish the year's preliminary target ranges. They are:

- the expected rate of growth in productive potential in the year ahead;
- the predicted rise in capacity utilization;
- the unavoidable rise in the price level;
- any necessary adjustments due to the cyclical phase of the economy.

Once these predictions have been made, the Bank meets with representatives of the federal government, particularly from the Ministries of Economics and Finance, to compare projection results. Officials on both sides of these meetings maintain that there have been no great differences in their respective results since the process began in late 1974.

In December, based on aggregate predictions which emerge from these meetings, the CBM target is created, and published by the Bank. The government publishes its version of economic predictions in a state of the economy message during January.

These announcements are timed primarily to make their influence felt on the year's first round of wage negotiations. Two aspects of the labor situation make the timing crucial. First, German trade contracts run for one year, so the authorities must keep inflationary expectations down year by year, if a wage-price spiral is to be avoided. Second, there is a long-standing tradition that the first wage settlement of the year sets the pace for all remaining settlements. The importance of wage talks in DBB target announcements is emphasized in the Bank's statement to the House of Commons:

> Stabilization policy in Germany relies on the basic consensus between management and labor and on their sense of responsibility. To help entrepreneurs and trade unions to inform themselves about the non-inflationary behavior desired, the Federal Government and the Bundesbank announce objectives for the key economic variables as well as a monetary growth target.

A second, and clearly subsidiary, advantage of these announcements' timing is that they occur shortly before the annual EEC foreign ministers meetings in Brussels, and provide a pre-defined negotiating position for representatives of the Federal Republic.

With the target range set in December, the Bank refines it in mid-year, using all the information made available to it since December. Both years of this projection process have seen the refinements directed to the lower end of the target range.

In concluding the CBM discussion, it must be reemphasized that the Bank does not view CBM growth as an end in itself. The Bank is bound to consider its final goal of monetary stability above all else. In doing this, the Bundesbank is not unwilling to abandon particular monetary targets under the impress of ecnomic conditions. In doing so, however, it insists on explaining fully the reasons for its actions, and it feels that such explanations enhance rather than weaken its power. As the Bank wrote to the House of Commons:

> In the end. . .the decisive factor is the credibility of the arguments which a central bank uses when exploiting the flexibility inherent in its control of the money supply, regardless of whether it revises a target, announces a new position within the target range, or simply deliberately tolerates a failure to meet the target.

SUMMARY OF BUNDESBANK OPERATIONS

The Bundesbank is nearly unique in the world of western central banks in its appreciation of the social, psychological, and political forces that may support or erode its economic goals. It is also singularly capable of rallying those forces by trading on its well-deserved reputation for knowledgeable, well-thought-out plans which will be followed, unless the Bank itself decides to change. If there is a change, DBB officials are at pains to explain clearly, and at length, the reasons for the change. The final goal always remains the same: monetary stability couched within a framework of stability for all economic aggregates.

THE ROLE OF LABOR

The role cooperation of labor in Germany's industrial life is crucial part of its postwar success in stabilizing the nation's economy. The cooperation, and the social market principles that sustain it, have helped to place the German laborer among the most highly paid workers in the world. His per capita income surpasses that of an American laborer. In addition, the German worker has great security on and off the job, and social services consume 31.5 percent of total GNP. Over the last twelve years, there has never been so much as 5 percent of the workforce out of jobs at one time, and until the 1974 recession, vacancies generally were greater than the number of people looking for work. All of this was accomplished while real growth in wages and salaries increased by more than 50 percent in the last twelve years.

The role of labor in this development has largely been through its cooperation in restraining wage demands and strikes, as well as its ability to adapt to the increasingly technical training necessary to perform the highly skilled tasks on which German industry depends. A smaller, but growing, role has been played through the much-vaunted mechanism of "co-determination," whereby worker representatives sit on Supervisory Boards and Works Councils. Finally, the existence of a large "guest worker" population has provided a workforce for less-skilled, lower-paying jobs, and these workers have become a permanent part of the labor scene.

WAGES, STRIKES, AND JOB LOSSES

The smoothness of labor negotiations in Germany is well-documented, but cannot be overlooked in the effect this relative peace has on helping to control inflation. The cooperation has taken three main forms: moderation of wage demands; unwillingness to strike; and toleration of sectoral shifts in jobs. All of this has taken place with a workforce that counts only 30 percent of its number as union members. Without cooperation on all of these fronts, the German corporations, with their relatively thin margins of profits, would have had little choice but to pass on the increased wage costs, thus initiating the familiar wage-price spiral.

The willingness of labor to moderate wage demands has been pronounced enough to cause consternation in even conservative circles. In the late sixties, as Germany was recovering from the 1967 recession, the Economics Minister was forced to scold laborers because of their low wage demands. He alleged that they were not doing their part to pull Germany out of its slump. Furthermore, in only a few cases during the seventies did suggestions of the Bundesbank or federal government not succeed in moderating labor's wage demands.

The unwillingness of workers to strike is even more surprising than their wage demands. Germany has lost less time to work stoppages since World War II than any other industrialized, non-communist, country.

Strikes are rare enough that they are national news. One such strike in 1974 by the Public Employee's Workers, its first since the war, was sufficient to make Chancellor Brandt fold his opposition to double-digit wage settlements, offering the workers an 11 percent raise. This move set the pace for other settlements, which resulted in one of the two instances of high average wage increases during the 1970s.

The cooperation of labor with management is not based on worker delusion, or on weak leadership among the proletariat. German laborers have a high standard of material comfort, and are becoming a part of the decision making process that affects their lives through their work. In the first place, the worker has secure and well-paid working arrangements. This gives him a large measure of personal and social satisfaction as well as an investment in the stability and continued success of the German economy. In the second place, although it is not a panacea, co-determination has increased the worker's role in and understanding of, the needs of capital as well as those of labor.

The overwhelming emphasis on security and stability that marks the labor movement as well as all other sectors of the German economy may be understood as an outgrowth of German social history and perhaps also of the FRG's status as a frontline state in the Cold War. There is widespread acceptance of the thesis that only through low inflation and strong savings and investment can an economy remain strong. The results have been an inflation rate which peaked at 7 percent during 1973-74, and dropped to 2 and one-half percent in 1978, with a decade average around 5.8 percent per year, added to which is an average household savings rate of 13 percent of disposable income, compared to the 4 percent rate in the United States.

This concern has also led to the establishment of worker benefits which are among the world's best. In pay, security, fringe benefits, and safety the federal labor laws and the firm level labor contracts largely fulfill the "social market" principle of sharing the benefits from a successful economy between workers and owners, although not equally. In pay, the German worker ranks among the top of the industrialized world. He leads in per capita income. Real wages doubled during the 1970s, while productivity increased by 50 percent. The adjusted share of national income to wage and salary earners has remained nearly constant over those ten years, moving from 63 percent to 64 percent.

In fringe benefits he surges further ahead. The social security arrangements alone are enough to account for nearly a third of the GNP. They include complete health benefits, unemployment and disability benefits, strong pension benefits, and rent and child allowance for low wage earners. These are the government minima. Most labor contracts call for additional benefits that are negotiated by each plant's labor representatives.

For instance, job dismissals are not easy to accomplish. For all employees who have been working continuously six months or more, including foreign workers, the employer must prove that dismissal is brought about by:

> reasons which lie in the person or in the bahavior of that person or in the urgent interests of the business, which stand in the way of the worker continuing to be employed.

Furthermore, the employer must submit his proposed dismissal to the shop stewards, and either they, or the worker, can force the dismissal into labor courts for declaratory judgment. As long as the stewards join the worker's action, he may continue to work until a final judgment is rendered. The burden of proof on the employer is heavy in these cases and the length of adjudication in such cases makes the idea of dismissing a worker unattractive.

Factory closings have strict conditions attached to them. It should be mentioned that beside cash compensations and re-training for employees of closed plants, employers must notify the Federal authorities at least 30 days before the planned closing. Based on its finding, the government can delay or speed up the closings as it chooses.

From a primitive capitalist orientation this labor policy may seem suicidal in terms of productivity. The fact is that Germany has seen steadily increasing productivity throughout the 1970s. While U.S. productivity has inched forward at one percent or less in the last few years, German productivity increases have averaged 4-5 percent. One reason for this is the sense of involvement an employee has in his company when he is assured that employment will not be solely for the benefit of the employer. While this involvement is generated by a myriad of conditions, counted among the foremost determinants must be the knowledge that one's job is secure.

Such security and involvement seem to trigger a variety of positive responses that are reinforced by the formal and informal agendas for discussion of working conditions and future investments that come through the co-determination structure in German companies. Through such discussions, the workers are made aware of company plans before they are presented in the form of a pink slip, fait accompli. On the other hand, managers, faced with a decision about capital investments, are more likely to make them in consultation with labor if there is a reasonable assurance of cooperation in such procedures.

SUMMARY

The German worker has generally cooperated with the plans of capitalists throughout the country, and he has been greatly rewarded for his cooperation. The Federal Republic has been an island of relative stability during the last decade and has continued to increase its productivity, real wages, and leisure time. This required the actions of both private and public sectors to be moderate and ever-aware of the needs that other areas of the economy might be feeling. One of the truly remarkable results of this enterprise is that it did not spawn a centrally directed industrial policy, though there is a great deal of official direction coming from the Bundesbank. Still, it must be admitted that Germany has done as well as any industrial nation in living up to its purported belief in free markets.

To make this clearer, and to get a hint of possible problems in the 80s for the Federal Republic, this essay will conclude with a brief look at two periods in the last decade which are of special significance. The first, after the 1973 oil shock, shows a country springing back with amazing speed and actually increasing its trade surplus in the first year after the embargo. It will offer us a perfect chance to see the machine in full swing, as inflation, unemployment, and energy demands press on the economy, throughout which the authorities maintained their concentration of all sectors of the economy, not just on price stability. The second period will take us to the time of this writing as Germany attempts to swallow the second round of price hikes for oil. They have not been as successful in this recovery, and the question to keep in mind is whether the relatively firm commitment to nonintervention will succeed this time as it did in the mid-70s.

THE 1973 OIL SHOCK

While there is no good time for a 300 percent rise in oil prices, the final quarter of 1973 was a particularly bad time for such a rise in West Germany. The Federal Republic imports 96 percent of its oil, which accounts for more than 50 percent of total energy demand. The shock came as Federal authorities and Bundesbank officials were in the latter stages of policies designed to choke off an overheated economy, and bring some control to the massive capital inflows that plagued the country from 1968 through 1973. The government had revalued the Deutschmark upward by a trade-weighted average of 9.4 percent in the last year, while the Bundesbank continued to raise interest rates and reserve requirements.

By mid-73, the combined efforts of monetary and fiscal braking had managed to stagnate the domestic economy. Foreign demand for German products, however, continued unabated with the largest increase in trade surpluses of the postwar period being registered during the year. It was this surge of export demand that laid the groundwork for the Federal Republic's recovery after the shock.

By late December, the authorities were presented with a major dilemma. On the one hand, they were not sure that the inflationary pressure had been squeezed out of the economy. There were signs that wage-price spiral was still working through the system. Prices rose at an unacceptable rate in December, hitting the highest year-on-year inflation rate of the decade, at 8 percent. On top of this, wage negotiations had resulted in larger than expected average increase for the year of 11 percent.

On the other hand, they had to face the oil shock and its expected effect on export demand. Domestic demand had slumped sharply in response to the government's mid-year economic stabilization plan. Particularly hard hit were car sales which dropped 46 percent in

November. Unemployment, in November, was nearly double that of July, although only at 1.5 percent of the workforce, and short-time workers were up 600 percent over 1972.

This is a perfect test of the German commitment to price stability. If the authorities were predominantly committed to price stability, they could be expected to maintain restrictive policies, at the expense of further souring the country's economic bouyancy.

In the event, they followed a pincer strategy trying to knock the wind out of both the inflation and recession problems.

On the 19th of December, the federal government relaxed nearly all the fiscal measures it had put into effect during the February and May tightenings. Particularly important were reintroduction of depreciation tax credits, and the abolition of investment taxes. Meanwhile, the Bundesbank announced that it would continue to pursue its restrictive monetary policies in full force.

These actions provided incentives for the economy to begin a new cycle of growth, while trying to brake against renewed inflationary pressures. More importantly, they signalled investors and trade unions that the authorities would tolerate neither massive unemployment and large slumps in production, nor would they allow the full cost of energy and wage hikes to be passed through to price rises. Such signalling is a crucial element of government influence over economic decisions in the private sector. The need for massive direct controls is obviated to a large degree by the willingness of business and labor to follow the broad guidelines set in official policy. There is widespread respect for DBB and federal government decisions, coupled with the knowledge that such decisions are meant to stick.

The extent of manipulation authorities used to control the economy are indicated by a brief list of policy changes during 1973. There were nine budget freezings or releases, three bond floats, 14 tax changes, three discount rate raises, and six reserve borrowing authorization movements. Most of these changes were small, and most of them were coupled with announcements of the expiration dates. The size of, and rapidity with which, the private sector responded to government's mid-year stabilization programs, is exactly what authorities throughout Germany wish to have. The overarching desire is to send effective signals without unduly jarring the underlying fiscal and monetary structures. By staying away from large scale shifts, they allow themselves room to move away from previously announced policies should conditions shift. Furthermore, authorities shorten the lag times if their policies work through persuasion rather than waiting for monetary and fiscal changes to work their way through the markets. Finally, the cumulative effects of policy shifts, if small, are less drastic than would otherwise be the case.

The authorities were able to turn around in December on economic policies created less than six months before – without losing credibility. By leaving the Central Bank to guard monetary expansion, the federal government was able to smooth out the recessionary impacts of the 1973 oil shocks.

The effect of this dual-fronted policy was to create a shallow two-year trough with recovery picking up a great deal of steam in the first quarter of 1976. Only in 1975 was there negative growth in real GNP (-1.8 percent), and peak unemployment was 4.7 percent, with just over a million workers unemployed.

The Bundesbank was clear that the oil cost push would not be translated directly into prices, and that a profits squeeze would have to be tolerated by business. There was a short-lived attempt to moderate wage demands in 1974, but it failed and settlements averaged 13.7 percent. This made DBB's success at convincing business not to pass on the full amount of its increased costs the more remarkable. While the need to maintain market shares in a slumping world economy bears some responsibility for business's price moderation, Bundesbank pressure was still an important factor in the final analysis. As a result, 1974 was an extremely rough year for profits. In fact, while gross wage and salary income rose 10 percent for the year, profit and entreprenurial income rose only 1/10th of one percent. The increase in income to the two sectors from 72-75 looked like this:

Change in Percent Year-to-Year

	1972	1973	1974	1975
Gross Wage and Salary Income	9.9%	13.0%	10.0	4.1
Gross Property and Entreprenurial Income	7.6	7.5	0.1	5.4

Source: OECD

One startling result of this price restraint was that the Federal Republic's trade surplus spurted ahead to record levels in 1974, at a time when most other countries were moving toward large deficits.

The recovery from 1974 picked up steam in a way that displays the ability of various sectors to work together with some degree of trust. Largely because of the trust between labor and capital in Germany, government and business were able to present a convincing case to workers that the 13 percent wage increase in 1974 could not be repeated. Since neither the Central Bank, nor the world export market would allow businessmen to pass through increased labor costs, many medium-sized companies would have tottered toward bankruptcy if the 75 round of wage negotiations had not resulted in more moderate wage hikes. When the case was presented to labor, there was a significant drop in wage demands, as the 1975 round of bargaining ended in agreements that just about kept pace with the 7 percent inflation rate.

Labor's cooperation was not all due to high-minded public service. The facts of the economy convinced workers that the businesses were not hiding behind a facade of financial trouble. Firms could not afford to invest in capital if the 74 experience were repeated, and as they folded, jobs would be lost. Furthermore, in the crucial export markets producers had swallowed a 9 percent increase in the value of the Deutschmark over the 1972-3 rate. It was clear that they could not pass through much in the way of labor cost increases if their market share was to remain healthy. Finally the labor market itself was barely avoiding a collapse. While unemployment sat around 5 percent, short-time workers had jumped from an average of 44,000 during 1973 to 900,000 in February of 75. That is over a 2000 percent rise in two years. Unless wage demands were lowered, many companies would be forced to follow Volkswagen's example when it agreed to a 13 percent pay raise, and immediately put 33 percent of the workforce on short time.

While there were clearly self-interested motives for abstaining from large pay claims in 1975, the point is that this message could get through to workers in a believable way; unlike the experience in other Western European countries. If the businesses could be expected to absorb the first round of the cost-push in 1974, then labor must take responsibility in the second round for recovery to begin.

The result of cooperation and moderation on nearly all fronts by the various actors in Germany's economy was that after a mild two year slump, there was a rise in real GNP of 5.3 percent for 1976, and a rise in real fixed capital formation of 4.7 percent, after two years of decreases. The recession was moderate by most standards, and the recovery was complete, continuing to pick up steam through 1978 and 79.

The stability of Germany's economy during this turbulent period is the response for which its institutions and ideology are geared. The 1979-80 period has posed new challenges to this system which have not been so easily dealt with. It is to this we should now turn.

GERMANY IN THE EIGHTIES

The problems now faced by the Federal Republic are a mirror image of those it faced in the early 70s. After years of trying to fend off excessive capital inflows, trade balances and pressures to upvalue the Mark, authorities are now trying to keep money from leaving the country, and there is some talk of letting the Mark _fall_ in value. The primary weaknesses of the economy are (1) a recently developed current account deficit and; (2) a growing recession.

While the current account deficit did not begin to appear before the closing months of 1979, it has picked up considerable steam since that time and there is agreement that imbalance will remain through the first half of the decade. 1979 ended with Germany 4.9 billion Deutschmarks in the red, and according to the latest DBB preliminary findings the 1980 deficit will be 28.2 billion DM. There are at least six major causes for this downturn in foreign balances: (1) Giving in to ten years of OECD pressure, the West Germans agreed to try the vaunted "locomotive" theory in 1978 and to step up its growth rate – according to the optimistic outlook of OECD analysts, this move cost Bonn 9 billion DM toward its deficit in current accounts as German purchases of its neighbor's goods were stepped up; (2) the large price increases for oil combined with a deterioration in the trade balance between Germany and OPEC countries accounts for about 13 billion DM; (3) tourism by Germans, which accounted for an outflow of money equal to 2.4 percent of their GNP (about 33 billion DM), while they took in only an amount equal to eight-tenths of one percent of their GNP from foreign tourists, this differential is half as large as the total Federal Republic oil bill; (4) a drastic shift in direct investment by German companies in foreign countries with direct foreign investment rising by two-thirds since 1977, while foreign investment in Germany dropped to a low 2 billion DM; (5) a large capital outflow, due to the high interest rates in the United States and United Kingdom; (6) a large increase in the share of foreign-made consumer goods bought by Germans.

While the increase in consumer purchases of imported goods, and the compounding threats to traditional German export markets have been the responsibility of many countries from Korea to Rumania, it is Japan that occupies a prominent place in the concern of federal authorities. Attention was focused on the Japanese threat through shipbuilding, steel, photography, and other traditionally German enterprises, but it has hit especially hard with Japanese penetration into the domestic automobile sales market. During the late 1970s, the Japanese attempted to establish a sales network in Germany but were forced to retreat by consumer sales resistance. In 1980, the story was quite different as the Japanese zoomed from virtually no share in sales to command 10 percent of the domestic automobile sales.

The external market trends are compounded by domestic problems. In the first place, a recession is developing that is expected to send unemployment to 1 million by the middle of the winter. Although this is only 5 percent of the workforce, the one million level has served a symbolic role in measuring the success of economic policies. The Bundesbank, while it would like to back off of its historically high interest rates to help combat this recession, finds itself unable to do so, for fear that lower rates would simply compound the capitl outflow to the higher interest rates of the United States and Britain.

On the other hand, the federal authorities, who might be expected to take up the fight where the Bundesbank could not, a la 1973, find themselves unable to help recovery or further cushion the recession because of a mounting public sector deficit. The deficit became one of the few issues of any importance during the 1980 national elections. The overall government deficit, although limited by law, in the case of the federal government, to no more than the amount spent in investment programs, has been climbing for the last few years, reaching nearly 3.5 percent of GDP in 1980. Although this is down from its peak of 5.5 percent in 1975, the accumulated debt has reached a point where its interest nearly equals the total 1980 deficit.

German authorities point to three trends which lead them to a cautious optimism that the rocky weather will be smoothed considerably in the intermediate term. First, although more industrial jobs will be lost to foreign competition, the economy still has a great deal of room to move in expanding its service sector. It is the only one of the five largest industrialized economies with less than 50 percent of its workforce in services. Second, much of its current account deficit is due to oil import bills, and Germany is beginning to succeed in cutting back its energy consumption. While crude oil imports account for 16 percent of its total imports at present, consumption of crude oil has declined by 8 percent during the first half of 1980. Third, despite recent tensions in the management-labor sectors of the economy, productivity is still on the rise, and wage increases are still moderate. The average increases in the 1980 rounds were 6.7 percent, and no group deviated by more than one percent from that average.

Put together with continued emphasis on energy consumption reduction and production technique innovation, these positive signs are the beacons to which Germany looks for its future economic health.

REFERENCES

Boll, Heinrich, "The Specter That Still Haunts Germany, Inflation," The New York Times Magazine, May 2, 1976, p. 17.

Hartrich, Edward, The Fourth and Richest Reich, (McMillan, New York: 1980).

7 Reigning in the Surge: Inflation and Politics in the United Kingdom

Catherine B. Hill

INTRODUCTION

Under the leadership of Mrs. Thatcher the United Kingdom has embarked upon a macroeconomic policy giving 'overriding priority to reducing inflation and strengthening the supply side of the economy.' Short-run stabilization policies have been renounced in favor of creating conditions considered necessary for the sustainable growth of output and employment in the medium term. The central feature of the Government's economic program is its monetary policy, which is based on 'monetarist' doctrines and calls for a progressive deceleration in the growth rate of the money supply. Other Thatcher policies aim to improve the supply side of the economy, both by decreasing inflation and increasingly relying on the free functioning of the market economy.

The Government's monetary policy is motivated by the overriding priority given to inflation and by the belief that restraint of the growth rate of the money supply will necessarily lead to a decrease in inflation. The policy involves announcing to the private and public sectors and then consistently carrying out a monetary disinflation, regardless of the transitional consequences. The central component of this policy is a progressive deceleration over the medium term of the growth rate of the money supply. The Government believes that this policy can best be formulated in terms of targets for one of the monetary aggregates. For primarily institutional reasons, sterling M3, consisting of notes and coin in circulation plus all sterling bank deposits held by the private and public sectors, has been chosen as the appropriate aggregate to target. So as not to rely excessively on interest rates, the Government also announced its intention to decrease the Public Sector Borrowing Requirement (PSBR) as a percent of GDP over the medium term.

Thatcher's policies to improve the supply side of the economy generally involve attempts to decrease the interference of the government in the economy and to promote the free operation of markets.

Upon taking office, income taxes were reduced, with the stated purpose of restoring incentives to work. Mrs. Thatcher has declared that public expenditure as a percent of GDP should decline over the medium term. Public sector holdings in industry have been sold and financial assistance both to industry and regional development programs have been reduced. Foreign exchange controls have been lifted and quantitative credit controls have been removed. Finally, the government came to office intending to limit its intervention in the price and income determination process, stressing that the social partners in free collective bargaining, and not the government, would be responsible for excessive pay settlements. Attempts have also been made at limiting the power of the trade unions through trade union law reform.

After two years in office, the Government had not succeeded in carrying out the major elements of its economic program. In particular, both the growth rate of the money supply and the PSBR exceeded their targets. Sterling M3 grew at an annual rate of over 20 percent, compared to a target range for 190-81 of 7-11 percent. The PSBR in 1980-81 was approximately + 3 billion over the original projection of + 8.5 billion.

It has been suggested that the Government's lack of success in carrying out its economic policy program, and in particular in hitting their money supply and PSBR targets, has resulted from too many commitments entered into during the election of 1979. The Conservative Manifesto called for reducing the inflation rate, decreasing government spending and borrowing, cutting personal taxation, while increasing defense and 'law and order' expenditures. Initially, it was not clear whether the Government could successfully carry out all of its objectives simultaneously. After the unexpected oil price increase and the high public sector wage settlements, whatever possibility existed originally became more remote.

Others argue that the problem has not been one of incompatible policies, but of ineffective instruments. It is alleged that the instruments used by the Government to control the money stock are not sufficiently effective. In particular, it is argued that controlling the money supply by manipulating interest rates has been unsuccessful. Proposals to change to a system of monetary base control arise out of this line of argument. It is suggested that a switch from the current system of control, which relies on the relationship between interest rates and the demand for money, to monetary base control, which would rely on the more stable relationship between reserve assets and banks' liabilities, would increase the Government's control over the money supply in the short run and thereby contribute to more effective long-term control.

The above arguments center on whether there is not an alternative to the form of 'monetarism' adopted by Mrs. Thatcher. Other critics, more fundamentally, argue that there are alternatives to monetarism that would be more effective at attaining what should be the objectives of the Government, both in the short run and over the longer term.

Despite the Government's inability to implement its economic policy program, the Government's policies were contractionary and inflation has slowed. Both inflation and wage settlements at the end of 1980 were down from the previous year. The success in terms of inflation and private sector pay settlements was achieved at the expense of increased unemployment and lost output. Between January 1980 and January 1981, total unemployment (including school leavers) increased by just under 1 million to approximately 10 percent of the labor force. While real GDP declined by just over 3 percent in 1980. The Governments third budget of March 1981 reconfirmed its commitment to reducing inflation, regardless of the impact on employment and real growth of GDP. Because of this, nonmonetarists suggest that the Government's policies are not inherently different from policies adopted in the past and will only succeed in reducing inflation by restricting aggregate demand and increasing unemployment.

A wide spectrum of alternative strategies have been suggested by the non-monetarist critics of the Government's policies. At one extreme, it is argued that restrictive aggregate demand management is required, but that the mix of monetary policy and fiscal policy currently incorporated in the Government's policies is inappropriate. Toward correcting this, it is suggested that nominal GNP instead of sterling M3 should be used as a target. In addition, incomes policies are supported as a means of easing the real costs of transition to lower inflation. At the other extreme, reflation rather than deflation is proposed, on the grounds that deflation is both ineffective and inappropriate as a means of slowing inflation. Proposals favoring reflation are usually combined with an incomes policy and some form of industrial policy. Among reflationists, there exists a further dichotomy between those in favor of devaluation and those in favor of import controls.

HISTORICAL PERSPECTIVE

The Problems

Mrs. Thatcher's approach to the economy, which marks a major philosophical departure from that of previous governments, can only be understood in light of the problems of the U.K. economy has repeatedly suffered and the inability of previous governments to deal with these problems. Slow growth, low productivity, inflation, unemployment, and balance of payments crises have plagued Britain's economy on-and-off for over two decades. Successive governments have had little success with these problems in anything but the short run. Both Mrs. Thatcher's electoral victory and the policies she subsequently adopted can be explained partly by the inability of the previous governments to successfully manage the economy, and, in particular, to restrain inflation.

Turning to the longer-term problems, the United Kingdom's growth performance is generally considered to have been inadequate. Compared to most other developed countries, the growth rates of GDP and GDP per employee have been low in Britain. The average growth rate of GDP per annum for the United Kingdom was 2.6 percent between 1951 and 1969, compared to an average of 4.5 percent for West Germany, France, Sweden, and the U.S.A. More recently, the United Kingdom has continued to grow more slowly than these other developed countries. Between 1973 and 1978, the average annual growth rate of GDP in the United Kingdom was 1.1 percent compared to an average 2.2 percent for West Germany, France, the United States, and Sweden.

A low level and slow rate of growth of productivity have also been problems in Britain for over two decades. The growth rate of productivity in the United Kingdom averaged 2.6 percent on an annual basis between 1960 and 1970 and 1.8 percent between 1970 and 1977. The comparable rates for the European community countries were 4.4 percent for 1960 to 1970 and 3.3 percent for 1970 to 1977 (Dornbusch and Fischer, 1980, p. 49).

Shorter-term problems, which have both resulted from, and contributed to, the above problems, have included inflation, unemployment, and balance of payments crises. Up until 1967, the United Kingdom's inflation rate was low, averaging 3.0 percent between 1960 and 1967. This was in line with the rates experienced in other industrial countries. Between 1967 and 1971, the inflation rate increased rapidly in the United Kingdom, rising from 2.7 percent to 9.4 percent. After 1972, inflation accelerated more rapidly, attaining a high of 24.2 percent in 1975. The Labor Government succeeded in reducing inflation to 8.3 percent in 1978. It increased again in 1979 to 13.4 percent and reached 22 percent on a year-on-year basis in May 1980. Up until 1973, inflation in the United Kingdom was comparable to that experienced by other countries. Since 1974, however, prices have increased more rapidly in Britain than in the other major OECD countries.

Balance of payments problems have also troubled the United Kingdom since the 1960s. In the 1950s, the current account was generally in surplus. In the 1960s recurrent current account deficits, combined with a fixed exchange rate, led to capital account crises and "stop-and-go" aggregate demand management policies. Rapid growth leading to balance of payments deficits and speculation against sterling would be followed by restrictive aggregate demand policies and increasing unemployment. Finally, in 1967, sterling was devalued by approximately 14 percent. Following a 'J' curve effect, the current account moved into surplus in 1969 and stayed there until 1971. Between 1971 and 1974, however, the current account deteriorated rapidly. In 1974, the current account deficit was £3.8 billion, or almost 5 percent of national income. Sterling had been floated in June 1972, but the current account deficits persisted despite a 20 percent decrease in the value of sterling by the end of 1974. Finally falling reserves and a sharply depreciating exchange rate led the authorities to adopt restrictive monetary and fiscal policies in 1976, despite high unemployment. The policies adopted led successfully to a current account surplus and also eventually to an appreciating currency. The current account moved into surplus in 1977 and 1978.

Unemployment has more recently become a problem in the United Kingdom. Between 1964 and 1970, unemployment averaged 2.0 percent in Britain. Although international comparisons are difficult because of reporting differences, the rate was comparable or below that experienced by the other industrial countries. In the 1970s, unemployment began to assert itself as a policy problem. Unemployment increased from 2.6 percent in 1970 to 3.9 percent in 1975 to 5.4 percent in 1979. In mid-November 1980, adult unemployment reached 2.03 million or 8.4 percent of the workforce.

The Policies

Policies to deal with these problems have changed from government to government. Until Mrs. Thatcher, however, they generally consisted of aggregate demand management policies aimed at short run stabilization of output, employment, and the balance of payments, frequently combined with an incomes policy to control inflation. The role of monetary policy has changed substantially over the last two decades, with the emphasis changing from concern about the structure of interest rates to control of the monetary aggregates. Over this period, various selective credit controls have also been used. In addition to the management of aggregate demand, various attempts have been made to institute policies aimed at improving the rate of economic growth over the medium run by promoting investment and increased productivity. These policies have ranged from investment tax incentives to medium term planning arrangements.

From the 1950s to the mid-1960s, the management of the economy has been characterized as 'stop-go.' Alternating policies of contraction and expansion of aggregate demand were adopted to deal respectively with balance of payments crises and increasing unemployment. Periods of rapid growth and declining unemployment brought on by expansionary policy would lead to increased imports and current account deficits, given the fixed exchange rate regime. Contractionary policies would then be adopted, leading to declining deficits and increasing unemployment. Eventually, expansionary policies would be adopted again, starting the cycle over.

In 1964, the Government attempted to deal with the balance of payments problem without deflating. Instead, it imposed a surcharge on many imports and restricted capital outflows. However, by the middle of 1966, it was obvious that deflation was also necessary and severely restrictive policies were adopted. By 1967, it became apparent that even high unemployment was not preventing the balance of payments from deteriorating and sterling, which had been fixed at $2.80 since 1949, was devalued in November to $2.40. The devaluation was intended to alleviate the balance of payments problems by decreasing imports and stimulating exports.

Because the expected improvement in the balance of payments would add to demand, the 1967 devaluation was supported by fiscal deflation in 1968 and restrictive monetary and fiscal policy in 1969. These policies finally resulted in current account surpluses in 1970 and 1971. The devaluation of sterling had not, however, removed the conflict between balance of payments equilibrium on one hand and strong growth plus low levels of unemployment on the other. Throughout this period unemployment increased, particularly in 1971, as a result of the policies pursued to ensure a current account surplus. Thus, in 1971 and 1972, the unemployment objective again became dominant. Unemployment had increased severely in 1971. In addition, the slowdown appeared to be having insignificant effects on inflation. Mildly reflationary fiscal measures in 1971 were followed by a massively reflationary budget in 1972. The public sector deficit moved from a surplus of +.7 billion in 1970 to deficits of +1.6 billion in 1972 and +2.7 billion in 1973. Monetary policy was also relaxed, partly in response to the new Competition and Credit Control policies of 1971, which removed quantitative restrictions on bank lending. Bank lending to the private sector increased from +1.9 billion in 1971 to +6.4 billion in 1972 while M3 increased by more than 25 percent in both 1972 and 1973.

The combined effect of these monetary and fiscal policies was a rapid increase in demand, particularly private consumption. Output increased sharply in 1972 and 1973 and unemployment began to decline. Once again, the balance of payments deteriorated as imports rose rapidly. The Government announced, however, that the expansion would not be abandoned to defend sterling. Instead, the exchange rate was floated in June 1972.

Starting in 1973, the U.K. economy weakened, in terms of output and productivity growth, unemployment, and inflation. These problems were aggravated by the commodity price boom of 1973 and the quadrupling of oil prices in December 1973. Between 1971 and 1974, there had also been a very sharp increase in the average propensity to save from about 8½ percent to 14½ percent. This and the oil price increase imposed deflationary pressures on the economy.

When Wilson's Labour government came to power in 1974, these deflationary effects were partly offset by expansionary fiscal policy. In addition, real wages increased in 1974, further increasing demand. As a result, the United Kingdom was expanding relative to other countries, which were not pursuing policies to offset the deflationary effects of the oil price increases. Increased balance of payments problems resulted. Up to 1975, however, the country's exchange rate remained relatively stable, mainly because large amounts of OPEC's increased earnings flowed into London's financial markets.

By mid-1975, it became increasingly obvious that the policy of offsetting the deflationary effects of the oil price increase could not continue. Inflation and balance of payments problems worsened. The balance of payments on current account had moved from a deficit of approximately +1 billion in 1973 to +3.6 billion in 1974. The annual percentage change in retail prices increased from 9.2 percent in 1973 to 24.2 percent in 1975. In 1975 strongly deflationary policies were adopted, and the economy moved into recession. In response, real incomes, consumption, and private investment, all declined.

Despite the recession, repeated exchange rate crises arose in 1976. The exchange rate depreciated rapidly in April 1976 and again in October 1976. Balance of payments problems and lack of foreign confidence in sterling became the immediate priorities of the Government. Fears arose that the falling exchange rate would intereact with money wage rises and domestic inflation and result in a 'vicious' cycle of a depreciating exchange rate and accelerating inflation. A series of restrictive measures were introduced to ease the pressure on the exchange rate. Quantitative credit controls were imposed and the Minimum Lending Rate, which is the rate at which the Bank of England lends to the banking sector, was increased from 9 percent in April to 15 percent in October.

In December 1976, the Government under Prime Minister Callaghan adopted a set of measures, which had been worked out with the IMF for a $3.9 billion loan to further deal with the exchange rate crises. The major causes of sterling's weakness were the high rate of inflation and a large public sector deficit. Although monetary and fiscal policy had both been relatively restrictive in 1976, the IMF conditions included both further cuts in public expenditure – designed to decrease the PSBR – and targets for Domestic Credit Expansion. 'DCE' is a measure of the change in the domestic money stock including an adjustment for changes in the money supply caused by external surpluses or deficits. The Letter of Intent to the IMF included planned reductions in the PSBR. A target of +8.7 billion was set for 1977/78 and of +8.6 billion for 1978/79. Expenditure cuts of +1½ billion in 1977/78 and +2 billion in 1978/79 were to be made to help achieve these targets. DCE was to decrease from£9 billion in 1976/77 to£7.7 billion in 1977/78 to£6 billion in 1978/79.

The results of these policies included a sharp recovery in the exchange rate and later a decrease in interest rates. The successful negotiations with the IMF increased confidence in the financial markets and the government was able to sell large quantities of debt to the non-bank public. As a result, in the second half of 1977/78, DCE was negative and the growth rate of sterling M£was below the stated target range.

In the second half of 1977, fiscal policies were relaxed. Inflation had slowed and the current account had moved into surplus. DCE, the PSBR, and monetary growth were all less than originally planned. At the same time, the unemployment rate was considered high.

In 1978, the main objective of economic policy was to increase demand to promote recovery while holding down inflation. The 1978/9 Budget called for a decrease in personal income taxes and an increase in public expenditure. In an attempt to keep the PSBR below its target of 8½ billion, the Government's National Insurance Surcharge on employers was raised by 1½ to 2½ percent. Overall, the fiscal stance in 1978/9 was slightly expansionary.

The role played by monetary policy in aggregate demand management has changed dramatically over the last two decades. Until 1971, monetary policy did not play a major role in the control of aggregate demand. Neither the Bank of England nor the Treasury were particularly interested in controlling the money supply. Instead, the interest rate structure was the authorities' major concern. The Report of the Treasury Committee on the Working of the Monetary System of 1959, known as the Radcliffe Report (HMSO, Cmnd 827, August 1959) expressed the view that

> The authorities. . .have to regard the structure of interest rates rather than the supply of money as the center-piece of the monetary mechanism. This does not mean that the supply of money is unimportant, but that its control is incidental to interest rate policy.

As late as 1969, the Bank of England reiterated this view (Bank of England, 1969).

The concentration on interest rates was partly motivated by the Government's concern with financing the Government debt. There was a conflict between managing the debt and undertaking an active monetary policy to control the level of aggregate demand. Controlling the money supply, particularly preventing the monetization of government debt by the banking system, required increased interest rates. The authorities were reluctant, however, to raise interest rates. As managers of the government debt, their concerns included minimizing the interest burden of financing the government debt, preserving conditions for the Government to finance its continuing borrowing requirement, and ensuring that existing debt continued to be held. The authorities believed that financing the government debt required stable interest rates and, therefore, stable prices. It was assumed that rising interest rates would create expectations of falling bond prices and make it difficult for the authorities to sell bonds, as investors sought to avoid capital losses. The authorities, therefore, followed a monetary policy based on gradual adjustments to the structure of interest rates.

The authorities' concern about the structure of interest rates meant that aggregate demand management was dominated by fiscal policy. They realized, however, that control of domestic credit conditions could contribute to the management of demand. Given the government's interest rate policy, this led the authorities to administrative controls over the volume of lending by banks and other financial institutions and through controls over the terms of hire purchase credit. Between the 1950s and 1971, when credit reforms were instituted, there was a gradual increase in direct administrative intervention in financial markets until it became the major technique of monetary control.

Starting in 1951, when wartime controls were ended, monetary and credit policies became more important. In 1951, the clearing banks were requested to observe minimum ratios between both cash and liquid assets and deposit liabilities. Before 1951, only a cash ratio had existed. The new liquidity ratio included both cash and short-term assets such as Treasury bills, commercial bills, and money lent short term to the London Discount Market. The Discount Market consists of 11 discount houses and certain firms carrying on similar business. The discount houses borrow their funds primarily 'at call' from banks, chiefly the London Clearing Banks, and other financial institutions. They invest the borrowed money primarily in Government stocks and Treasury bills, local authority securities, and certificates of deposit. The Bank of England acts as lender-of-last-resort only to the discount market. The Bank will always lend whatever quantity is requested by the discount houses, but reserves the right to dictate the terms on which it will lend. This guarantees that the banks will always be able to 'call' the money placed with the discount houses. The discount houses also always cover the weekly tender for Treasury bills. Until 1971, this was done at a single price, agreed upon by the discount houses in advance.

The policy instruments used by the Bank of England included the Bank Rate and open market operations. The Bank Rate was the rate at which the Bank of England would lend to the banking sector through the discount houses. To increase interest rates, the Bank of England would increase the Bank Rate and 'make it effective' by selling government debt in the open market. Open market sales would decrease banks' balances. To adjust, banks would call in their loans to the discount houses. If open market sales were large enough to create an over-all shortage of cash in the money markets, the discount houses would be forced to borrow from the Bank of England at the increased Bank Rate. They would raise their lending rates in response, setting off a general increase in interest rates. Between 1951 and 1971, the banks would change borrowing and lending rates in response to a change in the Bank Rate, rather than waiting for the Bank to 'make it effective.' The new requirements of 1951 meant that the authorities could deprive the banks of cash by selling Treasury bills, or deprive them of 'liquid-assets' by selling bonds, which were outside the definition of 'liquid assets.'

The government's management of the gilt-edged market was determined by the desire to maximize investors' desire to hold British government debt. This followed from the government's need to finance both its current borrowing requirement and replace maturing debt.(1) Until the 1970s, the only quantitative goal of monetary policy was to limit bank lending to the domestic private sector. Bank lending to the public sector, therefore, did not directly affect the government's monetary policy objectives.

By the late 1950s, the authorities began to realize that these instruments were not adequate to control the credit available in the economy. The government's policy towards interest rates was largely responsible for this. If banks were being constrained by the liquid assets ratio, they would sell bonds rather than decrease advances. The authorities would purchase these bonds as a way of maintaining 'orderly markets.' In particular, the authorities would buy bank bonds nearing maturity. This both smoothed the markets and encouraged bond holding by making short bonds very liquid. It also, however, decreased the effectiveness of open market operations.

To increase the authorities' control over the credit available in the economy, the "Special Deposits" scheme was introduced in 1960. Under this scheme, the authorities could require the clearing and that the Scottish banks place Special Deposits, set in terms of some percentage of eligible liabilities, with the Bank of England. These deposits would bear interest,(2) but not count toward the required 'liquid assets' ratio. A call for special deposits was meant to force the banks to decrease loans to the private sector, without having to rely on increased interest rates. This attempt to minimize the effects on interest rates failed almost from the start. Rather than decreasing loans, the banks would meet calls for special deposits by selling maturing bonds.

This resulted increasingly in the Bank of England resorting to direct controls or 'moral suasion.' In the mid-1950s, controls included 'requests' by the Bank of England on both the quantity and direction of bank credit. In the 1960s, 'advice' was extended in addition to hire-purchase companies. This supplemented the Department of Trade and Industry's control of initial downpayments and repayment periods. Explicit quantitative loan ceilings were used first in 1961, and were included in all the budgets between 1965 and 1971. In 1961, the Bank of England's requests to limit advances applied not only to deposit banks but to other banks and a variety of other financial institutions. In 1965, these limits were extended to the finance houses. By the late 1960s, the Bank of England was sending copies of its loan ceiling requests to other institutions, such as pension funds and building societies, asking them to take into consideration the Bank's policies, although these institutions were not subject to ceilings.

The quantitative controls were directed at controlling credit while minimizing the effects of monetary control on interest rates and debt management. The side effects, however, were a decrease in competition and efficiency in the banking sector and disintermediation to uncontrolled financial institutions. During the 1960s, other banks and financial institutions not subject to quantitative controls increased their lending at the expense of the clearing banks. In 1967, the Bank of England attempted to remedy this by establishing a Cash Deposits Scheme for non-clearing banks, comparable to the Special Deposits scheme. This scheme was never used and expired in September 1971 with the institution of Competition and Credit Control to be discussed below. The pattern of development over these years was toward increasing controls due to bank evasion of existing regulations.

Other Bank of England instruments included foreign exchange controls and operation of the Exchange Equalization Account. Both could be used to influence domestic credit conditions. Hire purchase controls, under the authority of the Department of Trade and Industry, were also used to control credit.

Toward the end of the 1960s it became increasingly obvious that this approach to credit control was not working. The economy deteriorated throughout the 1960s, and repeated balance of payments crises led eventually to the devaluation of sterling in 1967. In 1968 and 1969, the Bank of England and the Treasury began to consider changing their monetary and credit policies. In May 1969, external pressures furthered this process. As a condition for IMF aid, the Treasury was required to limit Domestic Credit Expansion. This implied a shift away from control of interest rates and towards the monetary aggregates. By the spring of 1971, existing arrangements were announced to be inadequate and suggestions for change were invited from interested parties. In May 1971, the authorities enumerated the major limitations of the existing system to be the following: 1) Restrictive policies through controls on bank lending were proving ineffective because of disintermediation; 2) Quantitative controls limited competition between the banks and therefore decreased the efficiency of the banking sector; 3) The burdens of control were not shared equally among the financial institutions, with the larger banks acting as the major channel of restraint (Treasury and Bank of England, 1980, p. 17).

Toward the end of 1971, reforms were instituted under Competition and Credit Control which reflected these dissatisfactions with the existing system. The reforms were disigned to develop 'new techniques of monetary policy, with the objective of combining an effective measure of control over credit conditions with a greater scope for competition and innovation.' The reforms reflected a desire to rely more on prices to control domestic credit than on quantity controls, and to place greater emphasis on the control of the money supply as a policy objective.

The reforms included the following:

1) All ceilings on bank lending were removed.

2) The Reserve Asset Requirement (RAR) was instituted. This requires the banks to hold on a daily basis a minimum reserve ratio of 12½ percent of 'eligible liabilities'. Eligible reserve assets include the following:

a. Balances with the Bank of England (excluding Special Deposits);
b. Money-at-call with listed discount market institutions and brokers;
c. Treasury Bills issued by the British and Northern Irish Governments;
d. British Government marketable securities with less than one year to maturity;
e. UK local authority bills eligible for rediscount at the Bank;
f. Commercial bills eligible for rediscount at the Bank (to a maximum of 2 percent of eligible liabilities).

3) The Special Deposits scheme was extended. When called, the deposits were to be a uniform proportion for all banks subject to the new Reserve Asset Requirement and a similar requirement was applied to Finance Houses. The interest paid on such deposits was to be the Treasury bill rate.

4) The London and Scottish clearing banks ended their collective agreements on interest rates.

5) The Discount Market continued to have exclusive access to the Bank of England's lender-of-last-resort facilities. It was agreed that the

discount houses would continue to apply for the weekly Treasury bill issue, but not at an agreed price. In addition, they must also hold 50 percent of their funds in agreed government debt. Finally, call money lent to the discount houses was to count as required reserve assets.

6) The government's policy of unqualified support for the gilt-edged market was ended. Rather than supporting bond prices by buying bonds near maturity, bond prices and therefore interest rates were to be allowed to fluctuate. This reflected increased concern with the money supply rather than the structure of interest rates.

7) The London clearing banks agreed to hold 1½ percent of their eligible liabilities in the form of non-interest-bearing balances at the Bank of England. The requirement for any month relates to the level of eligible liabilities on the make-up day in the previous month. It is not necessary to maintain the ratio on a daily basis: instead daily deviations can be averaged over the month.

These reforms, therefore, moved in the direction of permitting an effective monetary policy at the expense of managing interest rates and the national debt. There was some ambiguity, however, because the retention of Special Deposits and the widening of assets eligible as reserves reflected continuing concern over the level of interest rates. Special Deposits could act like open market operations but have less effect on interest rates. By including certain government securities in the definition of reserve assets, the desirability of these assets was increased relative to others, implying lower interest rates. Despite these ambiguities, the reforms reflected the increased desire to control the money supply rather than interest rates.

Although these reforms gave the authorities the ability, via interest rates, to control the money supply, they were not used for this purpose in the early 1970s. Both fiscal and monetary policy were expansionary starting in late 1971. A rapid increase in the money supply occurred between 1971 and 1973 as a result of increases in domestic credit as well as inflows of foreign capital. M3 grew at 11.3 percent in 1971, 20.2 percent in 1972, and 20.6 percent in 1973. Because of the government's intentionally expansionary monetary policy, a conflict between interest rates and control of the money supply did not arise.

In 1973, the conflict between controlling the money supply and interest rates reasserted itself. In response to excessive money supply growth and 'round-tripping' during 1973, the Supplementary Special Deposits (SSD) scheme, or 'corset', was instituted. 'Round-tripping' involves borrowing from a bank, sometimes through overdraft facilities, and lending or redepositing the borrowed funds with the same or another bank at higher interest rates and thus directly contributing to the growth rate of the money supply. It results when relative interest rates are skewed in a way that makes such behavior become profitable. It was believed that roundtripping was contributing 1 percent a month to M3 during the summer of 1973. The 'corset' called for the banks to place non-interest bearing deposits at the Bank of England if the growth rate of interest-bearing-eligible liabilities (IBELs) exceeded certain limits. The scale of supplementary deposits increased with the excess growth rate over that allowable. The rate of call increased from 5 percent, for an excess of 3 percent or less, to 50 percent for an excess of more than 5 percent. By limiting competition for interest-bearing deposits, an immediate objective of the corset was to change relative interest rates in such a way as to remove the incentive for round-tripping.

The imposition of the 'corset,' rather than continued adherence to the market-oriented philosophy of the Competition and Credit Control reform, marked a return to quantitative controls. As mentioned in the Green Paper on Monetary Control the 'main purpose for introducing such controls. . .has been to reduce the need to raise interest rates, at least in the short term, by causing banks to ration their lending (Treasury and Bank of England, 1980, 3). The corset differed from the quantitative controls of the 1960s in that it applied directly to the liabilities' side of banks' balance sheets, rather than the assets side. Controls in the 1960s had applied to the growth of bank advances on lending, rather than to deposits.

Although the 'corset' was a movement away from market-oriented control techniques and was used repeatedly until the spring of 1980, monetary policy and particularly control of the money supply became increasingly important throughout the remainder of the 1970s. Under Callaghan's government in 1976, monetary policy became distinctly more 'monetarist,' partly in response to IMF pressures. As mentioned above, IMF conditionality included targets for both DCE and the PSBR. Shortly after the IMF agreement was concluded, the government announced a target for the growth rate of £M3 of 9-13 percent. In response to the monetary explosion of 1972-1973, control of the money supply had become an internal objective of the Bank of England in 1974, but explicit targets were not announced until December 1976. Since then, the authorities have continued to announce explicit targets for the growth rate of M3 on an annual basis. Instruments available to control the growth rates of the monetary aggregates did not change with the adoption of monetary targeting and continued to include changes in interest rates, the size of the government deficit and its financing, plus the Supplementary Special Deposits scheme. These instruments will be discussed in greater detail below.

Prime Minister Callaghan's Government was moderately successful at achieving its monetary targets. The March 1977 Budget established a target range of 9-13 percent for the rate of growth of sterling M3 for 1977/78. Monetary growth was moderate in the first half of the year, but accelerated later in the year. This was due primarily to the external sector. Foreign exchange reserves increased as the Bank intervened to maintain the exchange rate at about $1.72. This pressure on the money supply and sterlization proved increasingly difficult. The decision was made that it was more important to achieve the monetary targets than to hold down the exchange rate. The exchange rate was allowed to appreciate to remove the pressure on the money supply from foreign inflows. The money supply, in any case, exceeded its target because of an unexpectedly large increase in the PSBR.

In the April 1978 Budget, the target for the growth rate of sterling M3 was decreased to 8-12 percent. It was also announced that monetary targets would be reassessed every six months rather than once a year. Facing evidence of increasing bank lending and doubts that the PSBR limit would be met in 1978-79, the Government announced a set of restrictive measures on June 8, 1978. These included introduction of the National Insurance Surcharge to reduce the PSBR, an increase in the MLR from 9 percent to 10 percent, and the reintroduction of the SSD scheme. The corset had previously been in effect from November 1976 to August 1977. In November 1978, monetary conditions were further tightened. The MLR was increased from 10 to 12½ percent. In addition, the target range for £M3 was held at 8-12 percent, but a change in the base figure from April to October 1978 implied a more restrictive monetary stance. The MLR was further increased to 14 percent on February 8, 1979. In the years to mid-April 1979 the growth of M3 was about 11 percent, within the 8-12 percent range set in the previous April. In the first 6 months to mid-April 1979, M3 grew at a 12 percent annual rate, within the 8-12 percent target range which had been rolled forward to October 1979. In the first half of 1979, however, demand for bank credit was strong and sterling bank lending to the private sector grew at an annual rate of 28 percent. It was also clear that the 'corset' was causing disintermediation in the form of bank acceptances held outside the banking sector, which implied that the money supply figures were becoming increasingly distorted and not a good measure of the monetary position of the economy. It was under these monetary conditions that Mrs. Thatcher took office in the spring of 1979.

Although explicit monetary targets were first used under Mr. Callaghan's government, they were part of a larger policy program based on the management of aggregate demand, combined with other policies aimed at restraining wage and price inflation and promoting industrial development. Monetary targets, although important and stressed, were not accorded priority over all other government objectives. This differs dramatically from the role assigned monetary policy under Mrs. Thatcher, as will be discussed below.

While the evolution in monetary control was taking place in the United Kingdom, selective credit controls were also used to varying degrees over the last two decades. As opposed to controlling the aggregate quantity of credit, selective credit controls seek to influence the composition of credit extended by the banks. Sometimes selective controls were imposed intentionally; other times selective effects resulted from various attempts to control the aggregate quantities. Selective policies were used both to influence the short-run impact of aggregate demand policies on different sectors of the economy and to influence the direction of credit over the longer term as a means of promoting desired structural change.

Some form of pay policy has been used by both parties in Britain for most of the last two decades. This reflects a belief that wage and price decisions contribute to the inflationary proces and therefore, must be modified if inflation is to be successfully controlled.

Incomes policies were used by Edward Heath's Tory Government between 1971 and 1974 despite initial pronouncements against such policies. The 1970s started with high pay increases and inflation, partly because the conservative government ended the previous Labour government's incomes policies upon taking office in 1970. The new government had declared its intention to avoid formal price and pay policies and rely instead on market forces. During the first six months in office, hourly wage rates increased at an annual rate of 16.2 percent. In response, the Government tried to encourage voluntary de-escalation in pay settlements. The "N-1" policy called for a step-by-step decrease in pay settlements to 8 percent by the end of 1971, with the public sector setting an example. During 1971, there was some evidence that this approach was working. However, 250,000 coal miners initiated a strike which resulted in a Court of Inquiry declaration that the miners were a "special case" granting them a settlement of 20 percent. This discredited the Government's "N-1" approach to pay and settlements escalated.

The Government attempted to negotiate a voluntary pay policy with the Trade Union Congress and the Confederation of British Industry, but was unsuccessful partly because of contention with the unions over the Industrial Reorganization Act. As a result, a statutory 90-day standstill on prices, wages, and dividends was instituted on November 6, 1972. This was followed by 'Stage Two,' adopted in April 1973, which called for a statutory pay norm of £1 plus 4 percent. This implied a weighted average increase in earnings of about 7.5 percent. A ceiling of £250 was also imposed on pay increases. 'Stage Three' established a statutory norm of 7 percent or £2.25, whichever was highest, and a ceiling of 350. Exceptions were allowed for productivity improvements up to 3.5 percent, change in pay structure up to £1 percent, staged movements toward equal pay, compensation for 'unsocial hours,' and extra holidays. The average pay bill, including exceptions, was expected to increase 10-11 percent. Threshold agreements were also instituted under Stage Three. From a base of October 1973, an increase in the retail price index of 7 percent would trigger a payment of 40 pence per week. For every percentage point above 7 percent, an additional 40 pence would be paid.

In March 1974, the Conservative Government was replaced by Harold Wilson's Labour Government after a miners' strike which called for settlements in violation of Stage Three. The Labour Government was committed to ending statutory pay policy and Stage Three controls were removed in July 1974, when the appropriate legislation was finally repealed. The threshold provisions, however, continued to apply. The large increase in the cost of living following the oil price increases triggered the threshold payments more than was expected and resulted in inflationary wage settlements. With the ending of the statutory pay policy, the Labour Government adopted a policy of voluntary cooperation with the unions, embodied in the Social Contract. It was based on proposals discussed in a TUC-Labour Party document published in February 1973. This policy was not successful during 1975, partly as a result of the increases in the cost of living which led to large wage settlements. For 1975/76, the Government concluded a tighter agreement with the TUC. A 6 a week maximum was called for in addition to a 12 month rule. Although not completely successful in holding average earnings on target, the rate of earnings increase declined. The policy was voluntary, but TUC support was won in return for specific government commitments on prices and industrial policy. In 1976/77, the agreement between the TUC and the Government was renewed. A 5 percent norm was established, with a minimum of £2.50 and £4 maximum. The policy again was not completely observed, but the increase in earnings came below double digits by October 1977. In general, therefore, the Social Contract was successful during 1976 and 1977. Cooperation between the TUC and the Government led to a moderation in the rate of increase of wage settlements.

In 1977/78, no comparable agreement between the TUC and the Government could be reached. The Government set a 10 percent target for increases in earnings without TUC approval. The actual increase during the year, was closer to 15 percent, an increase of 7 percentage points over the preceeding year. In 1978/79, the Labour Government set guidelines of 5 percent for pay settlements. Neither the TUC or the Labour Party, however, supported the Government's pay policy. Initially the guidelines were to be backed by sanctions, but the use of sanctions was defeated in parliament in December 1978. Despite the lack of explicit cooperation from the trade unions, toward the end of 1978 it looked as if pay settlements were moderating. At the end of 1978, however, several high settlements were reached. In early 1979, the Govenment's pay guidelines were further challenged. Truck drivers secured a 22 percent settlement and the local authority manual workers, after a disruptive strike, won a pay increase of 9 percent plus one with a guaranteed staged comparability exercise. In general, the 1978/79 pay round was marked by industrial disruption and an increase rather than a decrease in the rate of settlements. In April 1979, just before the May 3rd election, civil service unions held a one-day strike and rejected a generous government offer in line with public sector pay deals that had been made over the winter.

In addition to aggregate demand management and incomes policies, both parties have also relied on a number of specific 'industrial policies' to promote increased productivity and economic growth. These policies have been specifically aimed at the United Kingdom's deteriorating industrial performance, evidenced by its diminshing share of world trade in manufactures and increasing import penetration. The use of these policies has reflected concern about whether other policies adopted, specifically aggregate demand management, were sufficient to ensure the investment and improved industrial efficiency needed to keep the United Kingdom's economic performance from falling further behind.

MRS. THATCHER

Mrs. Thatcher came to office in the wake of Callaghan's unsuccessful attempt to use aggregate demand management and an incomes policy to deal with the problems of the British economy. She espoused an economic program based on 'monetarist' theories and belief in a freely operating market economy. In these respects, Mrs. Thatcher's program marked a major change in policy in the United Kingdom. The Government stated its medium-term objectives to be the reduction of inflation and the improvement of the 'supply side of the economy.' Short-term stabilization policies were rejected in favor of policies considered necessary for creating 'the conditions for a sustainable growth of output and employment in the longer-term.' The cornerstone of the anti-inflation policy was to be a reduction in the growth rate of the money supply. Improvement in the supply side was expected to result both from reduced inflation and increased reliance on the free functioning of the market economy.

In accordance with its anti-inflation policy, the Conservative Government has consistently pursued a decrease in the growth rate of sterling M3 since it came to power. In the budget speech in 1979 shortly after taking office, the Chancellor of the Exchequer Geoffrey Howe announced the Government's intention to progressively decrease the growth rate of the money supply over the immediate future. A money supply target of 7-11 percent at an annual rate for the ten months to mid April 1980 was announced as a first step.

The Government reiterated its monetary policy objectives in 1980 in its Medium-Term Financial Strategy, included in the Financial Statement and Budget Report for 1980-1981. A target range of 7-11 percent had been announced for sterling M3 for 1980-81. In addition, the Government announced its intention to reduce the annual growth of the money supply to about 6 percent by 1983-84. Toward this goal, the Government announced a progressive deceleration of the target range over the period as follows:

Ranges for Growth of the Money Stock (£M3)
(Chancellor of the Exchequer, 1980, p. 16.)

	1980-81	1981-82	1982-83	1983-84
Percentage change during year............	7-11%	6-10%	5-9%	4-8%

In Mrs. Thatcher's third budget, the 1981-82 band of 6-10 percent was reconfirmed, despite a large overshoot of the 1980-81 target.

The current government's justifications of its monetary policies appear to be based on both the work of Milton Friedman and various "rational expectations" authors, in particular William Fellner. First, it is believed that a reduction in the growth rate of the money stock is necessary and sufficient for a permanent reduction in inflation.

> There is a clear relationship between the growth rate of the money stock and the rate of inflation in the medium term. This is the foundation of the Government's strategy for reducing inflation by means of monetary control. The mechanisms by which changes in the money stock are transmitted to the price level may be different in different countries and different periods in history. They may depend on the methods of monetary control adopted, and they will probably change over time as the private sector's perception of policy changes. But the proposition that prices must ultimately respond to monetary control holds whatever the adjustment process in the shorter term may be (Treasury, 1979-80, 11-12).

In addition, it is believed that the Government cannot determine the level of employment. There is no long run trade off between inflation and unemployment. Policies which attempt to decrease unemployment will in the end only increase inflation. Given this, the Government does not set targets for the ultimate objectives of the inflation rate and nominal GDP, because they are not within its direct control. Instead, it sets targets for an intermediate target, the growth rate of the money supply, which is more responsive to policy instruments and therefore more directly under its influence.

The Government believes that the best way to formulate its monetary policy is to set targets for the growth of one of the monetary aggregates. Sterling M3 has been chosen as the appropriate aggregate for targeting, both by this government and previously by Mr. Callaghan's. It is realized that no one aggregate is adequate to measure the monetary conditions in the economy, and therefore several other aggregates are monitored in addition to sterling M3. On the other hand, the authorities argue in favor of setting targets in terms of one aggregate because this facilitates the public's appraisal of the Government's policies. In the short run, the various monetary aggregates can diverge substantially. Targeting several aggregates, therefore, might imply apparently inconsistent policy measures in the short run and would make appraisal of the Government's policies difficult. The desire to maximize the public's understanding of the Government's policies also explains why monetary targets are explicitly announced and published.

The authorities justify the choice of sterling M3 for the target as follows:

> It is well understood in the markets. It indicates links with the other policies – fiscal policy, debt marketing policies, policies to restrain bank credit and exchange market management – and gives a general assurance that the macro-economics policies available to the Government will be used in a way which mutually support each other in the reduction of inflation. It is also relatively easy to define in terms of the banking system (Treasury and the Bank of England, 1980, iv).

The choice of an intermediate target should be predicated on its relationship to ultimate policy objectives. The opinion of the authorities appears to be that, although the various monetary aggregates can move in divergent directions in the short run, over longer periods they are more closely related. Policies directed at controlling one of the aggregates will tend also to control one of the others. Therefore, the choice between the various monetary aggregates is not discussed in terms of which is most closely related to inflation or nominal GNP. This is considered a second order issue since generally the various monetary aggregates will move together. The authorities do reserve the right to change the specific target chosen in the face of structural change. This could cause more permanent divergences in the monetary aggregates, in which case the choice of the particular aggregate would be more important. In the absence of such changes, however, the above institutional considerations have contributed to sterling M3 being chosen over the other aggregates as the intermediate target variable.

In addition to the belief that restraint in the growth rate of the money supply will lead to declining inflation in the medium term, the Government appears to be appealing to 'rational expectations' theories to argue that the loss of output in the short run depends on how quickly behavior takes into account the monetary commitments of the Government. If earnings growth comes quickly into line with the growth of the money supply, the costs of bringing down the inflation rate in terms of lost output and employment will be minimized. The Government expressed its hope that monetary targets would have a direct effect on wages through effects on price expectations. The Government has argued in favor of its announced firm commitment to a progressive decrease in the growth rate of the money supply as a means of beneficially influencing expectations. Private sector behavior will lead more quickly to the attainment of a decrease in inflation, if Government policy is understood and not expected to change. As mentioned, published monetary targets in terms of a single aggregate are considered the means by which the Government's determination is made clear to the private sector. More flexible policies of the 'feedback' type would lack credibility and therefore would not have as beneficial an effect on expectations. The Government's policies, in particular, the Medium-Term Financial Strategy reflect this belief in the importance of the expectations effect.

The Government recognized, however, that its policies would probably involve transitional costs in terms of lost output and employment. The Government believes however, that such losses need have no long run effect on future growth potential. At the same time, the authorities argue that any adverse effects of excess capacity on investment from their policies will be offset by the beneficial effects of a reduction in inflation and the resulting decrease in uncertainty and risk. This presupposes that inflation will be reduced and attaches an implicit cost to the short-term transitional effects – less than the benefits from the reduction in inflation. This suggest an ambiguity about whether the authorities believe there are no long-term costs associated with their policies or whether the costs are outweighed by the benefits.

The main instruments available to the authorities to control the money supply are fiscal policy and interest rates. The authorities make a distinction between control of the money supply over the medium term to bring down the trend and control over shorter periods of time of fluctuations around the trend. The Government feels that the available instruments are adequate to achieve its medium-term monetary objectives, but would like to see improvement in monetary control over shorter periods (Treasury and the Bank of England, 1980).

The Government attempts to control the money supply by employing a combination of policy instruments which affect the main components of sterling M3. To see this, it is useful to examine the following accounting identity of the asset side of the banking system balance sheet, or the credit counterparts of the money stock.

Increase in sterling M3 = Public Sector Borrowing Requirement

- sales of public sector debt to the non-bank public
+ increase in banklending to private and overseas sectors
+ net external inflow to private sector

It should be noted that the components on the right hand side of the above identity are not independent; any policy action which affects one component will induce changes in the others and the net effect on the money supply will not be one for one. On the other hand, the signs on the components on the right hand side are generally presumed to be correct.

Fiscal policy, through its effect on the PSBR, is seen as one of the main policy instruments available to the authorities to influence monetary conditions. Fiscal instruments include tax and expenditure policies. A consistent fiscal policy is seen as essential to monetary control and the authorities have continually reaffirmed their intentions to decrease the PSBR as a proportion of GNP in support of the Government's monetary objectives.

The authorities recognize that there is not a fixed relationship between the PSBR and changes in sterling M3, and that alternative combinations of the PSBR and interest rates are consistent with the achievement of a given target for the growth rate of the money supply. An increase in the PSBR implies higher interest rates for a given money supply growth rate. The effect of the increase in the PSBR on sterling M3 is offset by the effect of increased interest rates on bank lending and the purchase of gilts by the non-bank public, two other counterparts of a change in sterling M3.

It is not clear whether the authorities believe that fiscal policy affects aggregate demand independently of its contribution to monetary conditions. The Bank of England (Bank of England, 1979-80) argues that the PSBR should be allowed to vary cyclically and operate as a built-in stabilizer. This implies that the PSBR can have real effects in the short run, whether financed by sales of gilts to the bank or non-bank sector, or alternatively whether the debt is monetized or funded. On the other hand, the Treasury in the Memoranda on Monetary Policy is unclear whether it believes that 'crowding-out,' which occurs when public sector "activity displaces private sector activity," is complete or not.

> An increase in the PSBR (as a percentage of GDP) is not necessarily an expansionary policy if it is associated with unchanged monetary targets. The increased interest rates necessary to maintain monetary control will have a contractionary effect tending to offset any stimulus to demand from tax cuts or from increased public spending.
>
> The scale of these offsetting effects is very uncertain and the econometric evidence in this area is not easy to interpret (Treasury, 1979-80:10).

For complete crowding out, whatever the state of the economy, an increase in the PSBR would have to result in increased interest rates which had a totally offsetting contractionary effect on private expenditure. This is most plausible in an economy at full employment. In an economy at less than full capacity utilization, it is less likely. An expansionary fiscal policy may actually increase private investment via an accelerator-type mechanism, whatever the interest rate effects. Whatever the effect of fiscal policy in the short run the authorities recognize that it may be difficult to avoid an increase in the PSBR in response to an unanticipated recession.

Another main instrument of monetary control is short-term interest rates. Although an increase in interest rates will have differing effects on all the counterparts of a change in sterling M3, the general presumption is that an increase in interest rates will decrease the growth rate of the money supply. This results from two effects which are considered to dominate any others which might work in the opposite direction. A rise in interest rates tends to both increase gilt sales and decrease bank lending. The sale of gilts to the non-bank private sector allows the Government to finance the PSBR without directly increasing the money supply: the public debt is funded as opposed to monetized. Changes in interest rates have often been aimed at slowing money growth by reviving sales of gilts to the non-bank private sector. If an increase in interest rates creates the expectation that rates will fall in the future, the demand for gilts will increase in the expectation of future capital gains. Therefore, interest rates have been used to affect the public's speculative demand for money. The authorities also attempt to affect bank lending through changes in interest rates. The authorities realize that bank lending is influenced by other factors besides interest rates, including the financial position of the company sector. In general, the authorities realize that interest rates will affect bank lending only slowly and that "it is not feasible. . .to exercise an exact control over bank lending through interest rates in the short run" (Treasury and the Bank of England, 1980).

The Bank of England varies short-term interest rates by altering the MLR and making it effective through money market operations conducted through the discount market. There exist two requirements on the banks, the Reserve Assets Ratio and the associated power to call for Special Deposits, and the Cash Requirement on the London Clearing Banks. Joint use of the RAR and the Special Deposits scheme was initially regarded as a means of controlling short-term interest rates. It became apparent quickly, however, that such joint use was not workable. In response to a shortage of reserves caused by a call for Special Deposits, banks would bid for increased liabilities with which to obtain more reserve assets rather than decrease their total assets. This would cause perverse movements in both interest rates and sterling M3. The Treasury bill rate would fall relative to the inter-bank rate. As the interbank rate rose relative to other rates, bank deposits, certificates of deposits and, therefore, sterling M3, would increase. Consequently, the authorities have reviewed the operation of the RAR and do not consider it necessary for influencing short term interest rates. It has been recommended, therefore, that it be replaced by a prudential liquidity requirement. The Cash Requirement is, therefore, the fulcrum on which the Bank of England operates through its money market operations to affect short term interest rates.

As mentioned above, the financing of the Government debt is interrelated with the PSBR and interest rates. When the PSBR is financed outside the banking system, it does not contribute directly to the growth of the money supply. The demand for gilt-edged securities depends on both the level of interest rates and expectations about future movements in interest rates. As mentioned, administered changes in interest rates and the Bank of England's money market operations are often intended to affect expectations in addition to influencing the cost of money to the discount market. The extent to which the government succeeds in funding the debt, however, is at the expense of interest rates. A large PSBR complicates monetary control by putting pressure on the authorities to undertake greater funding, while the demand for gilt-edged stocks can be quite erratic. This can result in short run volatility of the monetary aggregates. During periods of uncertainty, the interruption of sales of gilt-edged stocks to the non-bank public leads directly to short run increases in sterling M3. To avoid this problem, some changes in the technique of debt sales have already been adopted and others have been suggested to achieve a smoother pattern of gilt sales. Toward this end, various tender systems have been proposed which would allow larger changes in the prices and yields on gilts. A partial tender technique with a minimum tender price was instituted in March 1979. The minimum price, however, means that the tender technique is not being used to ensure the sale of a given volume of gilt-edged stocks. Some type of marketable index-linked security has also been suggested as a means of decreasing short-term fluctuations in government funding. The government would also like to broaden the market for short-term government debt to ease the pressure on long dated yields. Lower long-term interest rates would contribute to a revival of the capital market. This would allow companies to obtain finance in ways that do not directly contribute to the money supply; i.e., in ways other than borrowing from the banks.

In addition to fiscal policy and changes in short-term interest rates, until quite recently, quantitative controls in the form of the corset have also been used by the authorities to influence monetary conditions. As discussed above, it sets guidelines for the growth of banks' interest-bearing eligible liabilities in an attempt to slow bank lending without directly increasing interest rates.

The Thatcher Government has used a combination of these instruments – fiscal policy, interest rates, gilt sales, and quantitative controls – in attempting to achieve its monetary targets. As mentioned, the Thatcher Government has repeatedly stressed the importance of a decrease in the PSBR to help achieve its monetary objectives without relying excessively on interest rates.

The main reductions in government expenditure called for over the period were in industry, energy, trade and employment programs, housing and education, and in the total net borrowing requirement of the nationalized industries. At the same time, provision for defense and law and order expenditure increased.

In addition to attempting to decrease the deficit, the Government has relied on high interest rates and large sales of 'gilt-edged' government securities to control the growth rate of sterling M3. Until June 1980, quantitative control of bank lending, in the form of the Supplementary Special Deposits Scheme or 'corset,' was also used.

Thatcher's policies to improve the supply side of the economy generally involve attempts to decrease the interference of the government in the economy and to promote the free operation of markets. Upon taking office, as a means of increasing incentives and rewarding initiative, the June 1979 Budget decreased the direct tax burden on personal incomes.

Personal income tax allowances were increased and the basic income tax rate was decreased 3 percent to 30 percent. The top rates on earned income were reduced from 83 percent to 60 percent and on unearned income from 98 percent to 75 percent.

Corporate income taxation was also changed. The basic rate of corporation tax is 52 percent. A preferential "small companies" rate of corporation tax of 42 percent applies to profits up to a certain limit. Between this and a higher limit, increasingly higher rates apply on profits until the 52 percent rate becomes effective. These limits were increased from £50,000 and £85,000 to £60,000 and £100,000. In 1980, these limits were further increased and the "small companies" rate was decreased to 40 percent.

To offset the loss of revenue from these direct tax changes, indirect taxes were increased. Value Added Tax (VAT) was increased from 8 percent and 12-½ percent to 15 percent. In addition, excise duties on oil and the Petroleum Revenue Tax (PRT) were also increased.

The government also came to office intending to limit its intervention in the price and income determination process. Although clearly committed to 'free collective bargaining,' the Conservative Government was ambiguous on what this meant for public sector pay settlements. It was not clear whether the commitment was to be 'what the taxpayer can afford' or the "comparability." The preceeding government had been committed to the latter. In March 1979, the Clegg Commission was set up to undertake comparability studies of pay in the private and public sectors in an attempt to avoid damaging public sector pay strikes. The Tories came to power and continued to refer claims to Clegg. In addition, the Government had made commitments to protect both the police and armed forces' pay from inflation.

After a year in office, the Conservative policy on pay in the public sector has become less ambiguous. It was decided public sector pay had to be restrained, both because of anger in the private sector about the disparity between public and private sector settlements and because high public sector settlements were contributing to excessive public sector expenditure. On August 4th, the Clegg commission was abolished in the interest of bringing public sector pay down. The Government also decided to suspend for this year the comparability-based agreement covering 550,000 white collar civil servants. In early November 1980, a 6 percent pay limit was imposed on local authority employees. It was then confirmed that the Government intended to hold all public sector pay increases to 6 percent.

Other policies adopted involved further attempts to decrease the role of the government in the economy. Mrs. Thatcher has declared that public expenditure as a percent of GDP should decline over the medium term. Public sector holdings in industry have been sold and financial assistance both to industry and regional development programs have been reduced. Foreign exchange controls have been lifted and quantitative credit controls have been removed. The exchange rate has been allowed to appreciate without government interference.

During the first two years in office, the Conservative Government found it difficult to carry out simultaneously all of the elements of its economic policy program. Most notoriously and damagingly for the overall economic policy package, Mrs. Thatcher has not been able to control the growth rate of the money supply. Between June 1979 and July 1980, sterling M3 grew at an annual rate of 15.9 percent, compared to a target of 7-11 percent. The growth rate accelerated over the summer, increasing 5 percent in the month from mid-June to mid-July alone. Between February, the start of the 1980-81 target period, and October 1980, sterling M3 grew at an annual rate of 24 percent. In November 1980, the Chancellor of the Exchequer acknowledged that the growth of sterling M3 would exceed the range set through April 1981.

The Government's inability to hit its targets in its second year in office can be partly explained by the removal of the Supplementary Special Deposits Scheme in June 1980. Its removal was motivated by recognition that it was causing disintermediation and undermining the usefulness of the monetary aggregate targets. A major source of this disintermediation was the 'bill leak.' This involved increased holdings outside of the banks of bank accepted commercial bills. Some reintermediation, and therefore an increase in sterling M3, was expected with the removal of the 'corset.' The size and speed of the reintermediation that actually occurred, and therefore the effect of the money supply, was not expected.

The excessive growth rate of sterling M3 could not all be explained by the unwinding of the corset, however. On October 27, 1980, the Chancellor announced that the underlying growth rate of sterling M3 was 18 percent to 19 percent and recognized that the excessive growth rate of the money supply during the summer months could not all be attributed to the corset. This suggested more basic problems with control of the growth rate of the money supply. The main methods of control, interest rates and the PSBR, were proving inadequate.

The major contributing factor to the excessive growth rate of the money supply has been the Government's inability to restrain the PSBR. The Government projected a PSBR of ±8.5 billion for 1980/81. On November 24, 1980 the Chancellor of the Exchequer announced that the PSBR in 1980/81 would amount to ±11.5 billion, or ±3 billion more than targeted. Explanations for the PSBR's overshoot included a larger than expected recession which has increased some expenditures, such as social security payments, the nationalized industries' borrowing requirement, and decreased revenues, such as income taxes and national insurance contributions; large public sector pay settlements; and higher than expected defense spending in the first months of the year.

In anticipation of the PSBR overshoot, the Cabinet conducted several public expenditure reviews. One such review was undertaken in October and November 1980. Aiming to keep expenditure in 1981-1982 near the level proposed in March 1980, the Treasury recommended public spending cuts of ±2 billion for 1981-82. The Treasury, however, met much resistance in the Cabinet, and the November 1980 actions announced by the Chancellor of the Exchequer called for tax increases of ±2 billion and curbs on public expenditure of ±1 billion to offset the pressures on the PSBR in 1981-1982. The tax increases included an increase in employees' National Insurance Contributions, from which expenditures on most contributory social security benefits are made, and a supplementary tax to be paid by the oil companies in addition to the Petroleum Revenue Tax. The increase in National Insurance Contributions can be seen as a partial reversal of the income tax cuts instituted in June 1979.

Further increases in taxes were called for in the Government's third budget; taxes on gasoline, alcohol, and tobacco were all increased, and the personal income tax brackets were not adjusted for inflation.

Because of the large PSBR, the Government has relied on high interest rates and large sales of its debt to the non-bank public to control the growth rate of the money supply. The MLR, similar to the discount rate, was increased to a record 17 percent in November 1979, reduced to 16 percent in June 1980, and kept there until November 24, 1980. High interest rates, however, failed to decrease demand for credit by the private sector and there were pressures on the Government to bring down interest rates.

On November 24, 1980 the MLR was lowered from 16 percent to 14 percent, reflecting the Government's desire not to rely excessively on interest rates, but to bring down the PSBR to control sterling M3. The decision to cut MLR was in anticipation of a slowdown both in bank lending and in the growth rate of the monetary aggregates as a result of the increasing recession. The Bank of England announced that given expectations about a slowdown in monetary growth and the Government's newly announced fiscal policies, it has been decided that nominal short-term interest rates can now be moderately reduced without undermining the firm monetary discipline that policy must continue to exert. The Government had been under pressure to decrease interest rates from many directions, including such Conservative Supporters as the Confederation of British Industry, which had called for a 4 percentage point decrease in the MLR a month earlier. The decrease in the MLR along with the plans for the PSBR reflect the Government's desire and political need to lighten the burden of its policies on the private sector. In March 1981, the MLR was reduced a further two percentage points.

During the Conservative Government's first year in office, both earnings and inflation increased. In the 1979/80 pay round, average earnings rose by 22 percent compared to about 16 percent for the 1978/79 wage round. Earnings rose much more rapidly in the public sector than in the private sector. Within the public sector, earnings increased more rapidly in sectors that had been referred to the Clegg Commission. Wage settlements declined in the 1980/81 pay round. Competitive pressures in the tradeable goods sector have been a major contributing factor. In the public sector, the end of comparability awards contributed toward decreased wage settlements. In addition, in November 1980, the Government announced its intentions to hold down public sector pay increases to 6 percent.

Inflation, as well as wage settlements, accelerated during the Government's first year in office but subsequently, inflation slowed. The year-on-year increase in retail prices was almost 22 percent to May 1980, whereas in the 1978/79 financial year, under Mr. Callaghan, the retail price index increased by 10.1 percent at an annual rate. Much of the increase to May 1980 was accounted for by special factors. Oil prices increased sharply in 1979 and contributed approximately 3 to 4 percentage points to the retail price index. The June 1979 Budget increased VAT to 15 percent to replace the revenue lost from decreased income taxes. This added another 3 to 4 percentage points to the RPI. Finally, increased mortgage rates added a further percentage point. In addition to these special factors, the underlying rate of inflation increased. By August 1980, the year-on-year increase in retail prices fell to 16-¼ percent. This fall largely resulted from the effects of the indirect tax increases in the June 1979 Budget dropping out of the index. Monthly increases, however, had also lessened. Over the six months to December 1980 retail prices only increased 4.3 percent.

The successes on wage and price inflation that the Government experienced in its second year resulted more from increases in the unemployment rate and the appreciation of sterling than from a slowdown in the growth rate of the money supply, which had not occurred. Unemployment rose in the month to mid-November 1980 to a new post-war peak of 2.16 million, or about 8.4 percent of the work force, while vacancies decreased for the seventeenth month in a row. Throughout, sterling remained strong, partly as a result of the high interest rates associated with the Government's monetary policies. The high level of interest rates and sterling contributed to a slackening of the economy despite the fact that sterling M3 grew faster than targeted.

Interpretations and Alternatives

One interpretation or explanation of the Conservative Government's inability to carry out its economic policy program in the first two years in office is that the Thatcher Government came to power with too many objectives. Mrs. Thatcher was committed to cutting inflation, reducing government spending and borrowing, decreasing personal taxation, and increasing defense expenditure. In addition to these commitments, in terms of objectives, upon taking office the Government adopted a monetary policy which was presented in an inflexible form. Targets for the growth rate of sterling M3 were set, along with projections for the PSBR, which were announced to be the centerstone of the government's economic policies. The strong commitment to its monetary policies were made in the belief that this would have beneficial expectational effects which would lower the cost of the policy in terms of lost output and employment. It is not clear, however, that the Government's monetary policies were initially consistent with its other commitments in terms of the tolerable short run effects on the economy. After several unanticipated events in 1979, including the increase in oil prices and the level of public sector pay settlements, the consistency of the government's policies in these terms worsened. This argument implies that there were constraints on the authorities in terms of the short run real effects of their policies. Although the government has argued that the level of unemployment should not be a policy objective, all concern about employment has not been abandoned. Indeed, the fact that a gradual reduction in the money supply is being sought reflects the recognition that tight monetary policy has effects on unemployment and that these effects are undesirable. This explanation, then, of the government's inability to control the money supply is that the costs in terms of the real short run effects on the economy of attaining simultaneously all of the government's objectives were too high. Given this conflict, the objective that was sacrificed was the money supply target.

Others argue that the Government's inability to control the money supply has not resulted from incompatible policies, but from ineffective instruments. In particular, it is argued that controlling the money supply by manipulating interest rates has been unsucessful. Proposals to change to monetary base control arise out of this line of argument. It is suggested that a switch from the current system of control which relies on the relationship between interest rates and the demand for money to monetary base control, which would rely on the more stable relationship between reserve assets and banks' liabilities, would increase the control over the money supply in the short run and, thereby, contribute to more effective long-term control.

An argument in favor of reserves over interest rates as a short-term operating instrument is that under an interest rates policy, the short-term operating instrument will not be changed adequately to achieve a monetary aggregate target because interest rate changes – increases in particular – inherently have political implications. This will prevent the short-term interest rate policy from being used effectively. Monetary base control is more likely to be successful because it lessens governmental discretion in interest rate determination.

It can be argued, however, that there is no reason why the authorities would be more willing to tolerate high interest rates under a monetary base system than they are under the current system. If the reserve rule adopted led to unacceptable consequences in terms of interest rates and the short run real effects on the economy, the rule would be abandoned rather than the results passively tolerated. The authorities in a joint Treasury-Bank of England consultative document on 'Monetary Control' argued in favor of a monetary base indicator system with override possibilities. This called for interest rate changes to be triggered by deviations of the growth rate of the monetary base from some target path. The override possibility would allow the authorities to let the reserve target be exceeded in cases where interest rate changes were considered unacceptable.

As discussed earlier, in the United Kingdom, alternative combinations of the PSBR and interest rates are consistent with given money supply targets. It can be argued, therefore, that the overshooting of the PSBR in the first two years of Mrs. Thatcher's government, given the Government's money supply targets, has implied unacceptably high interest rates and that this problem would not disappear with a move to monetary base control. In this case, a rigid system of base control would only be more effective in controlling the money supply if it prevented the authorities from deciding that the interest rates implied by such a policy were unacceptably high and from abandoning the money supply targets. The use of a monetary base control technique, therefore, does not diminish the need for a consistent fiscal policy. In particular, if the consequences of such a technique are to be acceptable it must be combined with policies consistent with the monetary targets over the medium term.

The above arguments center on whether there is not an alternative to the form of "monetarism" adopted by Mrs. Thatcher. Other, more fundamental, critics argue that there are alternatives to monetarism that would be more effective at attaining what should be the objectives of the Government, both in the short run and over the longer term. These alternatives generally criticize and propose alternatives to the same aspects of the Government's policies and the theories underlying these policies. Primary among these criticisms is the overriding priority given to the reduction of inflation by the current Government without justification in terms of the costs of inflation. This results in both the short run and long run effects of these policies on the real economy being inadequately taken into consideration.

The Government argues that the short run consequences of its policies on real economic activity need not adversely affect the growth potential of the economy over the longer run. The economy is seen as self-stabilizing, tending to full employment and non-inflationary growth. Improvement in the poor growth and productivity performance in the U.K. can only be solved, therefore, by improving the supply side of the economy, which is independent of the macroeconomic policies adopted. In particular, the expansion of aggregate demand can only have short run effects on economic activity. By discounting the short term effects of the Government's policies on real variables, the 'overriding priority' given to inflation is indirectly validated. This line of argument has been criticized by those in favor of less 'monetarist' alternatives on several grounds. First, the effects of the policies on real economic activity in the short term can affect the longer run potential of the economy by lowering investment and, therefore, the future available captial stock. Similarly, unemployment today may affect the quality of the labor stock available in future periods and thereby the long run potential of the economy.

The Government's argument on the short run effects of its policies is also criticized on the grounds that whatever the implications of the policies for the long run potential of the economy, the effects of these policies in the short run on unemployment and output are real costs that must be balanced against the gains in terms of reduced inflation over future periods. The Government's monetarist and supply side policies are considered to be nothing but disguised restrictive aggregate demand policies which aim to reduce inflation by increasing unemployment. These critics then argue that the benefits of the reduced inflation do not offset the increased unemployment and its effects on the future industrial base of the economy.

Closely related are the issues of whether the economy will automatically recover after a deflationary policy and whether inflation will reappear when the economy recovers. Critics of the government argue not only that the costs for the real economy of the Government's policies will be large, but that it is not clear that the benefits gained in terms of decreased inflation will be permanent.

Another aspect of the Government's economic policy program which has come under attack is its espousal of an 'expectations effect' of its money supply targets on wage settlements based on 'rational expectations' models of the economy. These models in general, and their application to the U.K. economy in particular, have been criticized on the grounds that it is not clear that it is irrational for wage earners to negotiate for wage settlements in excess of the money supply targets, contrary to the predictions of these models. Given the disaggregated nature of the bargaining process, the costs in terms of unemployment and wage increases in excess of the targeted growth rate of the money supply can be passed on to others, both within firms and across industries. Labor does not bargain as one unit and then share the costs and benefits of the outcome.

The rational expectations models assume an aggregate wage equation in which price expectations depend on the growth rate of the money supply. It is not clear that individual wage bargainers' behavior makes such an aggregate equation appropriate. Individuals will expect prices to follow money supply targets only if they expect other workers to moderate wage demands in line with money supply targets as well. In the absence of wage and price policies, there is no reason to expect wage bargainers to behave in this way. If they do not, the costs of the Government's policies in terms of unemployment and lost output will be greater.

The Government's 'hands-off' policy toward the exchange rate is a final aspect of Mrs. Thatcher's economic program that is frequently criticized. The authorities' position is that the exchange rate should be allowed to float freely, given the monetary policy adopted by the government. The Government's restrictive policies through high interest rates have contributed to the appreciation of the exchange rate. The higher exchange rate may have beneficial effects on domestic inflation by decreasing the price of imports, putting pressure on the traded goods sector to price competitively, and indirectly moderating wage demands. The Government has recognized that thre may be a temporary loss of competitiveness if prices and wages do not moderate. In the longer term, however, it is assumed that the level of the exchange rate will have no effect on either competitiveness or unemployment. Critics of the government's policies question how temporary the effects of such a policy are and suggest alternative policies regarding the level of the exchange rate and its effects on the domestic traded goods sector.

There exists dichotomy between the alternative strategies proposed between those that argue in favor of reflation in the short term and those that see the need for deflationary policies, but not of the type adopted by the current government. Both schools give high priority to reducing inflation, but not 'overriding' priority as does the current Government. The latter critics of the Government consider the monetary targets included in the Medium-Term Financial Strategy excessively rigid and propose more flexible deflationary policies. The authorities recognize that the policies adopted reduce flexibility, but have argued that a strong commitment to monetary targets increase the likelihood that "expectations and behavior will respond favorably" (Bank of England, 1979-80). Critics argue that since there is little evidence that the expectations affect works, the costs of such a policy in terms of lost flexibility become excessive. Fixed monetary targets remove both the level of aggregate demand and the monetary-fiscal mix from government control and prevent the Government from responding to unexpected changes in the economic environment. This alternative strategy is often combined with proposals for an incomes policy. This reflects both disbelief in the 'expectations effects' or any quick response of wage behavior to disinflation and belief that the effects of disinflation on the real economy are costs that should be minimized if possible. Given that it is not clear that the wage setting structure adjusts in response to a disinflation, the costs in terms of lost output, employment, and investment could be high, particularly if it is not certain whether the success in terms of inflation is lasting. An incomes policy would be a means of communicating the policies of the authorities to the labor market, on whose behavior the costs of the policy depends. If the problem is that the labor market is disaggregated and it is not clear that it is rational for individuals to lower wage demands given uncertainty about other people's behavior, an incomes policy has a role to play as a complement, not a substitute, to aggregate demand management policy.

Those in favor of reflation rather than deflation as an alternative policy strategy criticize the current Government's policies on basically the same issues. Restrictive aggregate demand, however, is rejected as either ineffective at reducing inflation or actually counterproductive. Proposals differ primarily regarding treatment of the exchange rate; some argue in favor of devaluation while others believe that import controls are necessary to protect British production.

SUMMARY AND CONCLUSION

Mrs. Thatcher has embarked on an economic program that is a major change in approach from policies adopted by previous governments of both parties. It is justified by the "over-riding" priority given to the reduction of inflation. Although inflation control had been considered an important policy objective by previous governments, it was only one of several objectives. In addition, although monetary policy had become increasingly important throughout the 1970s, with explicit monetary targets being adopted in 1976, control of the money supply was not considered sufficient to deal with inflation. Incomes policies, in addition, were used by both parties before Mrs. Thatcher's elevation. Such policies have now been rejected as unnecessary and ineffective for reducing inflation and counterproductive by interfering with the free functioning of the market economy.

It is difficult to reach any conslusions on the effectiveness of Mrs. Thatcher's policies, because they have not been successfully implemented. Sterling M3 has been growing at more than twice the target range of 7-11 percent and excessive growth cannot all be attributed to the ending of the Supplementary Special Deposits scheme. The PSBR will also overshoot the government's target both in 1980-81 and 1981-82. Despite this, the economy has come under pressure. Nominal interest rates reached record levels, sterling has continued strong, unemployment has increased, and real GDP has decreased. In response, price inflation and wage settlements have been coming down. It is unclear, however, how permanent these gains will be, or what the costs of the government's policies will be, or what the costs of the government's policies will be in terms of lost output and unemployment. It is equally difficult to determine the effects on the economy of the Government's supply side policies because the performance of the private sector, particularly manufacturing, has been dominated by the effects of the Government's monetary policies. Critics argue that it is very difficult to distinguish Mrs. Thatcher's policies from simple restrictive aggregate demand management policies.

NOTES

(1) Toward this end, the Bank would deal in gilt-edged stocks of all maturities at prices close to those in the market as a way of increasing the desirability of gifts.

(2) The interest rate paid on Special Deposits would be 1/16 percent nearest to the average Treasury Bill rate at the weekly tender of the previous week. Bank of England Quarterly Bulletin, December 1960.

REFERENCES

Bank of England, Quarterly Bulletin, volume 9, no. 4, December 1969.

______, Memorandum on Monetary Policy, Treasury and Civil Service Committee, House of Commons, Session 1979-80, HC 720.

Chancellor of the Exchequer, "Medium-Term Financial Strategy," Financial Statement and Budget Report, 1980-81, March 26, 1981.

Dornbusch, Rudger and Stanley Fischer, "Sterling and the External Balance," in Britain's Economic Performance, Richard E. Caves and Lawrence B. Krause, eds., (The Brookings Institution, Washington, D.C., 1980).

Treasury, Memorandum on Monetary Policy, Treasury and Civil Service Committee, House of Commons, Session 1979-80, HC 720.

Treasury and the Bank of England, Monetary Control, joint consultive document, Cmnd 7858, March 1980.

8 The Political Causes and Effects of Argentine Inflation

John T. Pothier

> Give to people, especially the workers, all that is possible. When it seems to you that you are giving them too much, give them more. You will see the results. Everyone will try to scare you with the spectre of an economic collapse. But all of this is a lie. There is nothing more elastic than the economy which everyone fears because no one understands it.
>
> - President Juan Peron, 1953.(1)

> First we kill all the subversives; then we will kill their collaborators; then their sympathizers; then those who are indifferent; and finally, we will kill all those who are timid.
>
> - General Iberico Saint Jean, Governor of Buenos Aires province, 1976.(2)

> (A)n economy can be run, in a fairly normal manner, despite high inflation indices. (Recent developments) might suggest that Argentina functions better with three digit inflation than with two-digit inflation.
>
> - Editorial, Argentine newsmagazine, 1980.(3)

These epigraphs provide an intriguing overview of the politics of Argentine inflation. The first represents Peron's advice to a Chilean president and constitutes a certain recipe for inflation. The second quote (denied by the general after it appeared in a New York Times editorial) conveys the extreme passion resulting from a social breakdown caused by hyper-inflation and civil violence. The final quotation flows from the belief that although triple-digit inflation may be odious, it sometimes may be more desirable than attempts to wrench an economy to a low (or lower) inflation range. The quotes document the reciprocal link between politics and inflation. Perón's quote foreshadows how politics can create inflation; the latter two demonstrate how inflation can effect politics – e.g., repression and resignation.

The sentiment of resignation is quite understandable. From 1937 to 1980 (see fig 8.1), inflation averaged over 35 percent a year and prices increased by a factor of one million. Figure 8.1 in fact understates inflation during 1975 and 1976. From May 1975 to May 1976, consumer prices increased almost ninefold – an average rate of over 4 percent a week. By the first quarter of 1976, prices were rising over 6 percent a week; by March 1976, over 8 percent a week. That month's increases, if sustained, would have produced annual inflation rates of 4,500 percent and 17,800 percent for consumer and wholesale prices, respectively.(4) However, military officers (many of whom were more restrained – at least in their utterances – than General Saint Jean) deposed Perón's widow and took charge of Argentina.

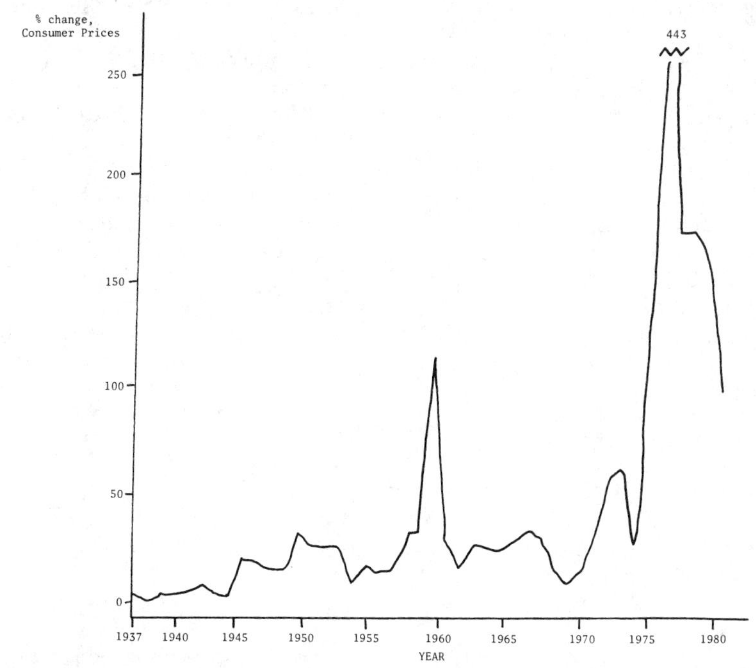

Fig. 8.1. Argentine inflation.

This chapter focuses on inflation during the almost five years since the March 1976 coup, with an emphasis on the political causes and effects of inflation: what control does the political system have over inflation, and what are the effects of inflation (or attempts to control it) on the polity? The first two sections of the essay discuss the political/economic background and the Argentine inflation context. The subsequent two sections analyze the attempts by the current government to control inflation and the effects that such policies (as well as inflation per se) have on Argentinian politics. A concluding section evaluates the political economy of Argentine inflation.

POLITICAL AND ECONOMIC BACKGROUND

In the late 19th century, the expression "as rich as an Argentine" became common in Europe (Witsonski, 1978, 15). Economic developments have conspired to belie that designation. In 1920, Argentina had the sixth highest per capita income in the world; it now ranks 36th (Wynia, 1980,1). During the 1930s, it was the second largest wheat exporter and supplied 50 percent and 80 percent of the world trade in beef and corn, respectively; by 1976, it captured only 8 percent of the world grain market (NYT, March 23, 1977, D-14). In 1940, its GNP was 6 percent of that of the U.S., one-third more than Brazil's, and four times Mexico's; by 1977, Argentina's GNP was 2 percent of that of the U.S., one-third of Brazil's, and less than Mexico's (RRP, January 31, 1978, 119). Figure 8.2 charts the stagnation and stop-go growth pattern that have led Paul Samuelson to cite "the miracle of Argentine underdevelopment" (de Onis, 1976, 60).

Argentina's advantages over most less develped coutries (LDCs) make Samuelson's perplexity especially understandable. It is the only LDC ranking with the United States, Canada, and Australia as major food exporters and (along with Mexico) is one of the few non-OPEC LDCs that approaches energy self-sufficiency. Its one percent annual poplulation growth rate spares it from the problems of rapid growth plaguing most LDCs and its 28 million people are highly sophisticated, with a literacy rate exceeding 90 percent. Finally, Argentina is one of the few Latin nations with a small "peripheral" sector (7) and its economy is well developed and balanced (at least by LDC standards), with

Sector[8]	% of GDP	% of Labor Force
Commerce/Services	44.6	45
Industrial	40.6	35
Agricultural	14.7	20

vigorous service and industrial sectors and a close congruence between sectoral GDP and labor force shares. Development economists would maintain that these advantages should have resulted in a substantially more dynamic economic performance. Argentina's underdevelopment thus seems even more miraculous.

The explanation for the stagnation may well be political rather than economic. Scholars of Argentina often refer to the lack of a sense of community in Argentina – this theme appears in the sociological literature; analysis of survey research (Kirkpatrick, 1971, ch. 6); and even in the writings of a former Peronist cabinet minister when he claims that the country is both decadent and forgetful (Zinn, 1979, ch. 1). This absence of a strong national identity flows from a history of group conflict. The first half-century or so of Argentine independence (1810-1862) saw regional conflicts and civil wars pitting the interior provinces against Buenos Aires over the issue of federalism. A second historical phase, the "gilded age" from 1862-1916, witnessed a tenous compromise between regional interests, domination by an agricultural elite of cattle barons, a vast influx of European capital and immigrants, and impressive economic growth. The third, and current, phase began in 1916 and has been characterized by class conflict, spearheaded first by the middle class and then by the workers.

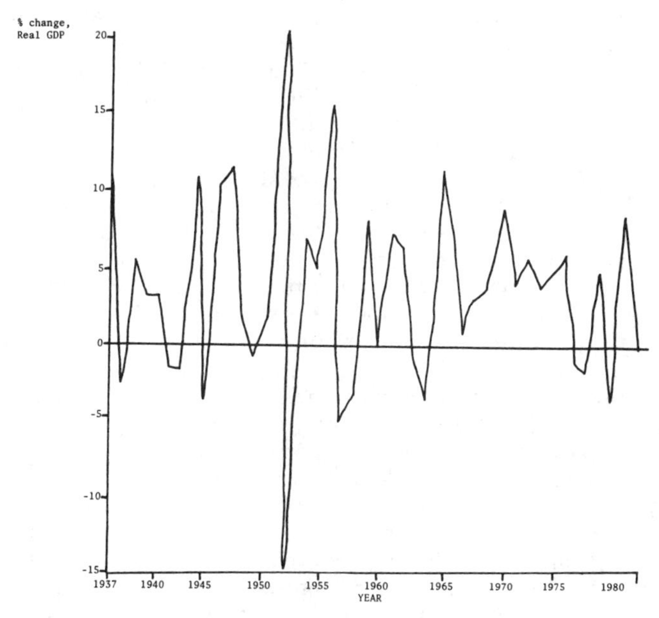

Fig. 8.2. Argentine economic growth

This period of class conflict, waged through electoral and more latent means, is both a cause and effect of the current economic malaise. Conflict began when the 1916 election (the first held after extension of the suffrage to all male citizens) was won by the Radical party, serving as the vehicle of the urban middle class. The Radicals were reelected several times but were deposed in the 1930 coup and frozen. The 1943 coup originally engineered by nationalist officers reacting to foreign penetration of the economy, evolved into a regime that established the labor unions as a major political force. Politics since the 1940s has been marked by overt and covert tensions between – and shifting alliances of – the workers, the middle classes, and the agricultural/exporting interests.

This unresolved conflict, and the resulting lack of social consensus, is a key factor in Argentine economic performance. No simple economic explanation can account for either the economic stagnation cited earlier or the chronic inflation – politics, instead, deserves much of the blame for arrested growth and surging price increases. At the broadest level, the political conflicts have made it difficult for Argentina to plan its development, apportion economic gains and losses, and shape economic changes. At the more concrete level, the conflict is responsible for three features – populism, a rigid interest group structure, and political instability – which are crucial elements in the political economy of Argentinian inflation.

The populist strain in Argentine politics – and the start of the inflationary era – is traceable to Juan Domingo Perón, President from 1946 to 1955 and (after 18 years in exile) again in 1973 and 1974. Perón's ideology (a bizarre mix of socialism, fascism, and nationalism) was less important than his political skills and populist tactics, which enabled him to rise from an Army Colonel in 1943 to several cabinet posts and – on the basis of a powerful union/urban poor political base built while Minister of Labor – to election as president in 1946 and reelection in 1951.(10) His presidency saw the enactment of major social welfare legislation, an 81 percent increase in real wages from 1943 to 1949 (Epstein, 1975, 619), and (due to efforts by Perón and his wife, Eva) a strong sense of pride and self-respect among the poorer segments of society. Their gains – political, economic, and social – came at the expense of the agricultural elites, whose profits Peron expropriated (11) in at attempt to transform Argentina from an agricultural to an industrial nation. However, his populist program failed on several fronts. The industrialization effort would be difficult even without the economic naivete exemplfied in the first epigraph to the essay as Wynia (1980, 5) notes, its failure meant that by 1955, Argentina was neither a primary product exporting nation nor an industrialized one. Perón's policies, rhetoric, and escalating authoritarianism also alienated important forces in Argentina (farmer, foreign investors, the Church (12), etc.) and accelerated social disintegration. Finally, his populist legacy remains a part of the political landscape. It has led to an emphasis on consumption over investment and to a struggle by societal groups for a larger share of the national pie.

The rigid interest group structure spawned primarily by Perónist populism has also been an indirect cause of Argentine inflation. As in other Latin American societies, the political actors in Argentina include business, foreign investors, the military, etc. However, three interest groups are unique in their coverage and/or power:

- agriculture Unlike most of Latin America, Argentina has a small rural peasantry – the sector has instead been dominated by the large cattle ranches that produce most of the nation's export earnings. The main political vehicle of the cattlemen has been the Argentine Rural Society (SRA), whose 2500 members supplied 5 of the 9 presidents, 4 of 7 Vice-presidents, 12 of 14 agriculture ministers, and 27 of the other 79 cabinet posts from 1940 to 1943 (Smith, 1969, 48-50). Although sometimes in conflict with small farmers and other agricultural interests, the SRA and others have united to oppose Perón and others whose policies threatened their status.

- unions, Organized labor and Perónism grew together – industrial unions achieved power under Perón and gave power to him. Membership quadrupled from 1945 to 1954 (Epstein, 1979, 449) and around 40 percent of the labor force – as opposed to less than 25 percent in the U.S. – is unionized (Ayres, 1976, 477). The importance of the General Confederation of Labor (CGT) has been diminished by its "intervention" (being taken over by the military) and later dissolution by the current military government, but labor remains an important, albeit sub rosa, participant in Argentine politics.

- bureaucrats. As a result both of Perónist nationalizations and a general Latin American proclivity for a large "parastatal" (state-run enterprise) sector, Argentina has developed a large and politically potent government bureaucracy. Its 2.5 million-plus civilian government employees translates into one bureaucrat for every 10 Argentines, as opposed to one per 90 citizens in France, 100 in the U.S. 180 in Italy, and 213 in Spain (RRP; January 21, 1977, 647).

The importance of these groups is noted by Diaz-Alejandro (1970, 122) when he asserts that the 1948-1955 inflation

> could be viewed as resulting from the struggle among urban workers, urban entrepreneurs, the public sector, and the rural sector to maintain the gains or recover the losses in real income sustained during the 1946-48 boom.

Their influence, and their skill in waging struggles, has probably increased since the 1940s; their desire to maintain gains or recover losses has probably not diminished. This distributional struggle, combined with the absence of either a social consensus on distribution or government authority strong enough to impose its consensus, makes inflation inevitable (Hirsch, 1978, 276).

Political instability has been the final major element in the political economy of Argentine inflation. Since 1940, Argentina has been led by 18 chief executives – two died in office, one resigned, and fifteen gained or lost power in military coups (Snow, 1979, 54). The 1955 coup against Perón was followed by 2½ years of military rule; a civilian government under Frondizi (1958-1962); an interlude of military rule; civilian administration under Illia (1963-1966); seven more years of military control under three different regimes; a second Perónist era (1973-1976); and a military junta since March 1976. The effects of this chaos are not surprising. From 1946 to 1976, the nation had 35 ministers of economy (Time, 1980,59). The economy went through boom and bust periods – the 38 years since the 1943 coup have seen 10 years of exceptional growth (8 percent-plus increases in real GDP) and 13 years of no growth or decline. Finally, inflation crept upward despite stabilization plans launched in 1952, 1957, 1959, 1962, 1967, and 1973.

By 1973, the 18 years of chaos had made the return of Perónism acceptable to the military. The March election was the first in ten years (and the first in 22 years that allowed participation by Perónists, although not by Perón) and was won by Hector Campora, campaigning on the slogan "Campora to the Presidency, Perón to power." However, many factions of Perónism had developed in 18 years and it soon became clear that only Perón, and not a surrogate, could govern. Campora's resignation after 50 days in office paved the way for Perón, now 78, to be elected president with 62 percent of the vote in September. The economy immediately improved and inflation decelerated, probably more as a result of a world boom in agricultural prices (13) than of his "Social Pact" with the CGT and a small business confederation.(14) However, Perón died of cancer in July 1974 (well before his economic policies had run their course) and was succeeded by the Vice-President – his wife Isabel.(15)

It is questionable whether Perón could have controlled inflationary pressures for long and even less likely that any female president could be effective, given Argentine attitudes. It was thus almost certain that Isabel Perón, a woman in her early 40s with little education or political experience, could handle Argentina's problems. She could not keep a stable Cabinet – at least 35 people held the eight cabinet posts during her 20 months in office and six held the Economy portfolio alone (Di Tella, 1978).(16) She was plagued by indecision, reversing her stance on wage increases several times, resulting in a loss of both credibility and union support. She chose questionable advisers, including her erstwhile Social Welfare Minister, a former traffic cop whose flirtations with voodoo led to a reputation as Isabel's Rasputin. Finally, her inability to reconcile the demands of the Perónist factions, and her growing identification with the right wing of the movement, led to a surge in civil violence to the point where, in early 1976, left and right wing terrorists were claiming a life every 5 hours (LA; March 26, 1976; 104).

The maladministered populism of Mrs. Perón was clearly leading the nation toward hyper inflation. By late 1975, a 300 percent inflation rate and 60 percent interest on savings deposits produced an enormous incentive for consumption and further fueled inflation (Newsweek, 1975, 44).(17) Excessive government spending produced a 1975 budget deficit of more than 12 percent of GDP and a fourth quarter where the deficit was 16.4 percent of GDP and expenditures were more than five times revenues (Di Tella, 1978, 222). The nation was experiencing its second straight year of recession, stagnating trade, massive capital flight, and near bankruptcy of the Central Bank. Members of strong unions were the only ones whose income nearly kept pace with inflation, resulting in disparities such as restaurant waiters making more than the President of the Supreme Court (de Onis, 1976, 54).

The crisis came to a head in mid-March 1976. Terrorism mounted. Mrs. Perón made it clear that she would not resign, declaring defiantly "If I have to become the woman with the whip, I will do it for the fatherland" (LA, May 21, 1976, 155). The opposition party leader effectively eliminated the possibility of a new civilian government by announcing on nationwide television "people ask me if I have a solution – and I have none" (RRP, February 9, 1978; 185). Finally, the annualized increases in wholesale prices surged from December 1975 to March 1976 – 198 percent, 736 percent, 1,948 percent, and 17,835 percent, respectively. The military deposed the government on the night of March 23-24. This essay will analyze the anti-inflation policies pursued during the five-year tenure of the military after turning to a brief discussion of important inflation issues.

THE INFLATION CONTEXT

Objective analysis of inflation is hindered by the sensationalism in newspaper headlines and, even worse, in scholarly works. It has been called the "cruellest tax,"(18), a "hydra-headed monster," and, in a recent book by Buchanan and Wagner (1978), a factor behind sexual promiscuity. This section of the chapter will attempt to provide a more analytical perspective by dealing with four issues of special import: causes of inflation (i.e., monetarist-structuralist debates), alternative ways to conceive of inflation, winners and losers in inflation, and stabilization costs.

Monetarist-Structuralist Debate

Economists in developed countries have long debated "demand-pull" and "cost-push" theories of inflation. Development economists, recognizing the potential uniqueness of LDCs, have re-oriented the debate and produced a rich literature on "monetarist" and "structuralist" causes of inflation.(19)

The monetarist perspective, often associated with Milton Friedman's "Chicago School" and with the IMF, is probably familiar to most readers. Although it entails sophisticated mechanisms and assumptions on the velocity of circulation, rational expectations, etc., the monetarists' basic tenet is that inflation is caused by "too much money chasing too few goods." Their remedies for inflation rely on constricting the growth of the money supply and (especially the LDCs, where the imperative may be producing more goods for the money to chase) using fiscal policy to stimulate production.

The structuralist perspective, sometimes credited to the Economic Commission on Latin America (ECLA), asserts that monetary expansion is more passive and merely finances the inflation resulting from structural problems in LDC economies. It claims that LDCs exist in a non-Keynesian world where growth is constrained more by supply than by demand and that they suffer from imperfectly functioning markets, slow response to price signals, and low factor mobility. Some structuralists claim that long-term supply curves in LDCs are less elastic than in developed countries – i.e., that a given increase in output is associated with a larger price increase. Examples of sectoral maladies include:

- agriculture. Bottlenecks and supply inelasticities in the rural sector (often caused by inefficient land tenure and labor systems) result in growth in food output lagging behind general economic growth and the increased demand for food. The result is increased food prices, which in turn produce higher wage demands and the higher labor costs that start a classic "cost-push" spiral.

- foreign trade. The heavy trade dependence of many LDCs make them especially vulnerable to exogenous shocks ("imported inflation"), general deterioration in trade terms, and foreign exchange bottlenecks. Currency devaluation will provide scant relief, since a large proportion of the higher-priced imports are intermediate goods for monopolistic firms who will generally maintain import levels and pass on the hgher prices to consumers.

- government finance. The generally regressive nature of taxation schemes in many LDCs results in output increases producing a less than porportionate increase in government revenues. This in turn increases the government deficit and the retained purchasing power of consumers, both of which can fuel inflation.

Finally, Diaz-Alejandro (1970, 121) makes a more general structuralist point, based on the assumption that price-setters in LDCs are reluctant to ever lower nominal prices, even when efficiency and productivity gains so dictate. Because of this "downward price flexibility," changes in relative prices (ratios between prices of different commodities) require higher general prices.

The disputes between these two schools are not merely moot academic debates, but instead carry important political ramifications. Disagreements over causes (e.g., money supply growth as an active or passive force) produce disagreements over solutions and their political side-effects. The monetarist-IMF remedy of austerity in monetary policy is attacked by structuralists as being ineffective and producing unemployment and great burdens on poorer segments in society. The structuralist-ECLA cure of eliminating structural causes (e.g., adopting progressive tax schemes) or accepting inflation as a means of promoting growth is criticized by monetarists as being both ineffective and dangerous, since acceptance of inflation creates the psychological/expectational effects that lead to more inflation.

Unfortunately, Argentine policy-makers can gain little insight on the debate from empirical studies of their economy. Maynard and van Ryckeghem (1975) and Diaz-Alejandro (1970) find support for the structuralist hypotheses; Wachter (1975) and Diz (summarized in Diaz-Alejandro and Mallon, 1975) present evidence that strengthens the monetarist perspective; and replication of these analyses using more recent data would be hampered by data inaccuracies and biases produced by the highly inflationary period of the mid-1970s.(20) Perhaps it is best to accept Mallon's (1975, 126) compromise conclusion: structuralist factors are the cause of Argentine inflation, but the actual rate (for any constellation of structural maladies) is determined by monetarist mechanisms. In any case, there is a decided pluralism both of potential remedies for inflation and of resultant political and economic effects.

Alternative Conceptions of Inflation

Inflation is usually measured by the rate of increase in (or the first difference of) a price index. However, at least three other measures should be used to portray the inflationary status of an economy.

The first is the acceleration or deceleration of inflation, or the second difference of a price index. Acceleration of inflation (regardless of the level) wreaks more havoc with business, consumers, and the government than does a stable rate of inflation. (Deceleration can also create problems, but all but the most rapid deceleration yields compensating social and/or economic benefits.) Figure 8.3 charts Argentine inflation over the last seven years and shows periods of continuous acceleration (May 1974-May 1976) and deceleration (May 1976-May 1977). Inflation was clearly less of a problem in June 1980 than it was in June 1975, despite an almost identical inflation rate of 110 percent over the previous 12 months.

A second important measure is the predictability of inflation, since the unanticipated is far worse than the anticipated. Tobin (1972, 15) notes that

> the ultimate social cost of anticipated inflation is the wasteful use of resources to economize holdings of currency . . . I suspect that intelligent laymen would be utterly astounded if they realized that <u>this</u> is the great evil economists are talking about. They have imagined a much more devastating cataclysm, with Vesuvius vengefully punishing the sinners below. Extra trips between savings banks and commercial banks? What an anti-climax!

Of course, Tobin's sanguinity would probably be tempered if he was discussing triple-digit inflation rather than single- and low double-digit levels (people can only move so quickly between banks) and would certainly change if, as in Argentina, price and/or wage controls prevent

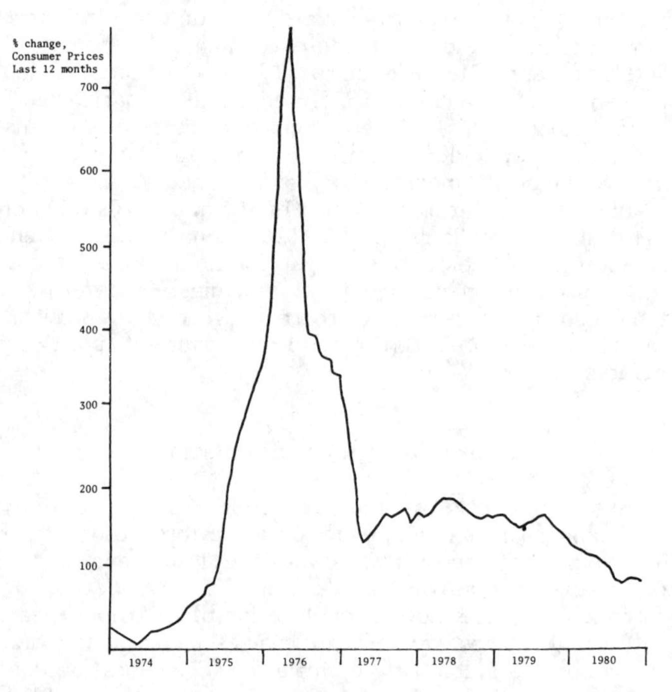

Fig. 8.3. Argentine Inflation 1974-1980

the free operation of markets.(22) But his basic point remains valid – anticipated inflation has consequences that are far from catastrophic. Determining the degree of anticipaiton or predictability, however, is a tricky enterprise. In some cases, there is a seasonal component – in the 1960s, inflation tended to accelerate in the fourth quarter and decelerate in the first quarter of each year, undoubtedly because of the influence the Southern Hemisphere's summer (December-March) and harvest cycles have on food prices. In other cases, secular trends such as the relatively smooth decline over the last 15 months (see fig. 8.3) make inflation more predictable. The importance of anticipating inflation is emphasized in a Conference Board study (Green, 1977) which notes the resources companies devote to attempting to forecast inflation. Of course, these forecasts are sometimes self-fulfilling, since price-leaders will raise their prices to the expected level of inflation.

A final alternative measure is the evenness of inflationary effects. Differential inflation rates have distinct political and social consequences. If consumer prices rise faster than wholesale prices, or food price increases outpace those of other consumer goods, for a sustained period of time, consumers lose to businessmen and the poor lose to the rest of society, respectively. Although these issues will be elaborated later in the essay, an extreme example is rent control in Buenos Aires which resulted in food prices increasing more than 20 times more than rents from the late 1930s to the early 1960s (Diaz-Alejandro, 1970, 366). While some change in relative prices is to be expected and is in fact healthy for an economy, changes of this magnitude represent a major redistribution of income away from rentiers – an event made possible by their virtual political disfranchisement during the first Perónist era.

These alternative measures of inflation (as well as the monetarist-structuralist debate) have important political ramifications. The acceleration and deceleration of inflation can result in coups, election defeats, etc. The degree of predictability of inflation affects the regime support by key groups, notably the business community and foreign investors. Finally, the inevitably uneven performance of different inflation indices (since prices never rise completely in tandem) has immediate and occasionally major effects on the distribution of income and power among various societal groups. As noted in the third epigraph, it is not triple-digit inflation per se that is destabilizing, but the characteristics of that inflation.

Winners and Losers in Inflation

Although excessive inflation certainly has negative effects on the economy as a whole, some individuals benefit, and some lose, from inflation, at least in relative terms. A commonly cited example is that of debtors (who gain) and creditors (who lose) when real interest rates are negative. In countries with inflation as high as Argentina's, the demarcation between winners and losers – as well as the magnitude of gains/losses – is greater.

An example is the "inflation subsidy" (Davis, 1963) to businesses who borrow at highly negative real interest rates. This subsidy resulted in the financial departments of many Argentine corporations becoming important profit centers in late 1975 when inflation surged to more than five times the interest rate (Green, 1977, 32). The subsidy can also exist when real interest rates are positive if exchange rates do not fully reflect differential inflation rates between nations. For example, the Wall Street Journal (July 16, 1979, 6) describes how Argentines with access to $500,000 can make a guaranteed real annual profit of over 20 percent merely by playing the exchange and bond markets. The Davis analysis of Chilean inflation (1963) suggests that a major cause of inflation has been political pressure from business interests unwilling to forego the inflation subsidy.

Diaz-Alejandro (1970, 379) provides other examples of the historical effects in Argentina of major distortions of relative prices. The steady losers have been the owners of rent-controlled property, small savers, and pensioners. A mixed record was maintained by the unions (which gained when negotiated wage kept pace with inflation) and agriculture (which gained when inflation forced a currency devaluation that increased their export earnings). Finally, the sectors heavily dependent on financing sources and/or expensive technology – housing, transportation, mining, telecommunications, etc. – have been badly squeezed.

The identity of winners and losers can change from year to year. Jackson, et. al. (1972, 37) distinguish between two types of inflation:

> In equilibrium inflationary economies, social and industrial conflict is mostly about the distribution of the yearly (marginal) additions to the national product. . . (I)n the strato-inflations, social conflict centers on the basic distribution of income itself.

In other words, the struggle between groups trying to defend their living standards at all costs leads to a shifting pattern of winners and losers – only the most sophisticated (or lucky) financial experts and speculators can consistently come out ahead.

Of course, the ranks of losers dwarfs those of winners when an economy becomes hyper-inflationary. Hirsch describes the pell-mell rush of groups trying to make up for ground lost since their last wage or price adjustment.

> In the end, all may lose from the higher inflation and/or unemployment that result from the chain of such leapfrogging, but at any point in the chain, a participant will lose more by standing still while others leapfrog over him (1978, 279).

In short, the problem is one of collective goods, where individual rationality translates into group irrationality. Political struggle creates the inflation that in turn alters the nature of political struggle.

Costs of Stabilization

Although the post-1976 stabilization effort will be explored in the next section of the essay, it is important to note that just as inflation has social costs, attempts to control inflation have other, different costs. Hirsch aptly notes (1978, 270) that it is "difficult to stop inflation in a distributionally neutral way, so that even groups that do not gain from inflation itself are none the less fearful of measures to counter it." An especially severe obstacle is the need to maintain a stabilization policy for a relatively long period and to resist the temptation to relax the austerity measures at the first indication of a dampening of inflation. The 1966 coup ushered in a "bureaucratic-authoritarian"(23) regime (O'Donnell, 1978 and 1979) that began a long-term stabilization program. However, the plan was abandoned in 1969 when the rise in beef prices – a structuralist malady arising from simultaneous inelasticities in supply and demand – squeezed real wages and led to worker riots (Maynard and van Ryckeghem, 1975, 200).

Two features of the Argentine economy create special headaches for economic managers. The first, as Mallon (1968, 177-179) notes, is the link between inflation and balance of payments crises. Periods of high inflation generally bring on an external payments crunch, which forces a currency devaluation. The resultant increase in exports (mostly domestic wage goods – e.g., food, textile fibers, leather, etc.) diverts supplies away from internal markets and creates shortages and inflation. As noted in the earlier discussion of structuralism, import levels drop only slightly and higher prices are passed on to industrial and private consumers. As a result, the economy suffers more inflation – both export and import induced – as a result of an attempt to counter a problem (the payments crunch) originally caused by inflation. If policymakers are particularly unlucky, the current account situation will not have improved enough to overcome the payments crunch, and they will have to start a new cycle of devaluation and inflation.

A second and related, problem is the perverse relationship between economic growth and inflation. Table 8.1 shows that when a period of growth is halted by a recession, inflation has either ratcheted up significantly or (as in 1952 and 1978) stayed about the same. Recessions are supposed to dampen inflationary pressures (24) and the double whammy of economic decline and accelerating inflation places heavy burdens on those who lose their jobs, especially since Argentina has no official unemployment compensation scheme and workers' savings (if there were any) had already been depleted by negative real interest rates.

The difficulties associated with stabilization programs lend credence to Epstein's (1978, 219) observations that they "can only be successful if the government responsible for it has sufficient force available to it to coerce those who will be asked to pay its costs" and that those who aren't represented in the government are those who end up shouldering most of the burden. The next two sections of the chapter provide evidence to buttress these observations.

POLITICAL CONTROL OF INFLATION

The military junta that began the "Process of National Reorganization" in March 1976 has surely recognized the reciprocal link between politics and inflation. Moreover, they have proven to be more realistic in understanding the limits of political control than the Argentine army colonel who, following his assignment to San Juan province during the 1943 coup, posted a general order "From 1200 hours, class struggle is strictly prohibited throughout the province" (LA, April 2, 1976, 105). This section of the essay is devoted to a discussion of the personnel, principles, implementation, and management problems associated with the post-1976 policy. The subsequent section reverses the causal linkage from the political control of inflation to the political effects of inflation. Although figure 8.3 documents the progress made since 1976 in reducing inflation, the analytical perspectives on inflation developed in the previous section must be kept in mind.

Personnel

The structure of government since 1976 has been both simple and relatively constant. The President of the Republic (Jorge Videla since March 1976; Roberto Viola after March 1981) is chosen by a 3-member junta of the chiefs of staff of the Army, Navy, and Air Force.(25) The executive branch is administered by a cabinet whose membership has been primarily military; legislation is promulgated by a legislative commission (CAL) composed exclusively of active and retired officers. However, most of these officials have devoted their energies to the campaign against terrorism, leaving economic policy primarily in the domain of the economy ministry, headed by José Martínez de Hoz.

Table 8.1. Growth and Inflation(26)

Annual % Change

Periods of Growth	Real GDP	Consumer Price Index	Periods of Recession
1946-48	7.6	14.8	
	-.8	31.0	1949
1950-51	10.7	25.7	
	-14.1	24.3	1952
1953-55	9.2	12.3	
	-4.3	22.7	1956-57
1958	8.1	31.6	
	0	114.0	1959
1960-61	7.2	20.2	
	-2.3	26.0	1962-63
1964-74	5.6	28.8	
	-1.4	291.7	1975-76
1977	4.9	176.2	
	-3.7	175.4	1978

Martínez de Hoz is an ideal symbol of the thrust of the junta's economic policies. He previously was president of the largest private steel company in Argentina and is, therefore, quite familiar with the industrialist perspective. His family background (including a father who was president of the Argentine Rural Society) provides ties with the old agricultural elites. His political background and public relations skills have enabled him to maintain a generally positive public image (at least given the severity of his policies). He was even tagged with the nickname of the "wizard of Hoz." Finally, his connections in academia allowed him to quickly assemble a team of bright, young, and generally monetarist economists for sub-ministerial posts. The combination of Martínez de Hoz' background and personal appeal has helped Argentina regain the confidence of the international community – David Rockefeller declared in March 1978 (when inflation was around 170 percent) his "great satisfaction at the conduct of the ministry of economy under Martínez de Hoz" (LAER, April 14, 1978, 105).

Principles

The basic strategy of the Martínez de Hoz program has been to stimulate investment over production and production over consumption (LAER, January 27, 1978, 28). He notes how the reversal of these priorities under Perónism

> created a tremendous distortion in the economy, which became unbalanced, with the different sectors fighting amongst each other for a larger share of the national pie (Euromoney, 1978, 2).

He further notes the dislocation caused by his economic policies.

> You cannot achieve change without hurting someone. . . . You can't make an omelette without breaking eggs, so we are breaking many eggs and the omelette is gradually taking shape (ibid., 6).

Many eggs indeed would have to be broken to transform Argentina from a speculative to a productive economy.

Four sets of anti-inflation measures have been prominent in economic policy since 1976. The first set has been undertaken in the hope of reducing long-term inflationary pressures, despite pronounced short-term inflationary effects. Examples include borrowing on international markets (designed to re-establish solvency after the 1975-76 debacle), incentives for domestic and foreign investment (geared toward increasing productivity), and the lifting of price controls (aimed at increasing competition). The goals of solvency, productivity, and competition as anti-inflation weapons have also been prominent in a second set of measures dealing with trade policy. After the agro-exporting sector had been reconstructed, the government slashed import tariffs and maintained an overvalued peso, resulting in the Argentine market being flooded with cheap foreign goods and domestic producers being forced toward increased efficiency and productivity to remain competitive. Reform of the financial system has been the third set of measures and has resulted in the virtual elimination of the "inflation subsidy" and in tight controls on money supply expansion, including bank reserve requirements exceeding 40 percent. Finally, government deficits have been substantially reduced by improved tax collection, slashing public employment by 15 percent from 1976 to 1978 (Organization of

American States, 1979, 14), and selling off almost half of the state-owned companies (BW, July 21, 1980, 83).

However, the most important anti-inflation measure has been tight government control over wages. The market, trade, banking, and government finance policies cited above are textbook examples of solutions with minor redistributive impacts and great advantages – beyond that of reducing inflation – for the economy as a whole. The wage policy, on the other hand has been far from neutral – a former Economics Minister claims that a basic principle of the policy has been that "workers participation in national income should fall in order to increase profits and investment and to help fight inflation" (Ferrer, 1980, 137). The mechanisms of this wage policy have included government decree of wage levels (adjusted every few months); a ceiling on flexibility above basic wage levels, payments above which are not tax-deductible; and requirements that wage hikes be tied to productivity gains. The effects as will be documented in the next section of the chapter, has been a major redistribution of income away from workers. Of couse, Martínez de Hoz would undoubtedly claim that wages were artificially high in 1976 and that low real wages are responsible for reductions in unemployment – from 5 percent in the greater Buenos Aires area in April 1976 to around 2 percent in late 1980.

A final key principle in the campaign against inflation has been that of psychology. Maintaining a "proper" perspective on inflation creates a tricky dilemma for the economics team. On the one hand, they must project the impression that the economy is recovered and inflation is under control in order to maintain the confidence of the business and international financial communities. In short, they must downplay the dangers of inflation.(27) However, acceptance of triple-digit inflation as normal – or, at least, as not dysfunctional in a major way – can produce what Martínez de Hoz calls the "mental indexation" that recycles inflation (Euromoney, 1978, 4). In fact, the criticism the Economics Minister has received for underplaying vs. overplaying inflation (or for going too fast vs. too slow, or for depressing real wages vs. draconian monetary controls, etc.) has led Martínez de Hoz to remark that the proof that he has the right program is that everybody is against it (RRP, April 20, 1979, 539).

Implementation

Although economic policy has generally adhered to these principles and broad goals, implementation has been sensitive to economic conditions. Four distinct phases can be noted.(28)

The first, running from the March 1976 coup to early 1977, was focused on attempts to end the economic chaos of the Perónist years. Martínez de Hoz borrowed $1.2 billion on international markets in 1976 (NYT, March 25, 1977, 8) to replenish national reserves. Trade unions were "intervened" and wages were adjusted by governmental decree. A 40 percent tax on agricultural exports was abolished to stimulate the rural sector (BW, July 21, 1980, 79). The Perónist price controls were lifted and decontrol of rents was begun cautiously. Finally, the regime jawboned industry – the Secretary of Commerce urged businessmen to moderate their price increases so that Argentine youth would not have to choose between "vegetation, emigration, or grabbing a machine gun" (BLA, May 12, 1976, 152).

A second phase (in effect for most of 1977) saw a failed experiment with price controls. This retreat from free market principles was inspired both by an acceleration of inflation at the end of 1976 and by the junta's fears that declining real wages would create dangerous conflict. The Air Force member of the junta declared in February that "businessmen must make a sacrifice in proportion to that made by wage earners" (RRP, February 28, 1977, 251). Martínez de Hoz, sensing the sentiments of his military masters, picked up this theme in his March 1977 call for business responsibility.

> We know that the State that attempts to use the police to control prices is ineffective, that is why we are not going to suggest it. . . . But we should know how to judge and deal with those who are not big enough to deal with circumstances and who believe they can carry on as if they were islands (RRP, March 11, 1977, 303).

Just in case business did not understand the implied threat, Martínez de Hoz imposed a 120-day price "truce" the next day. (Many firms apparently anticipated the action and posted preemptive price increases before the Minister acted – see QER, 1977, 3rd Quarter.) The regime also resorted to symbolic anti-inflation measures over this period, such as the highly-publicized military takeover of 23 produce distribution centers in Buenos Aires, based on the assertion that middlemen were responsible for high fruit and vegetable prices (NYT, April 13, 1977, 6). However, the price "truce" (entailing strict controls on price increases by the largest firms) reduced the inflation rate only slightly, and the lifting of the truce reopened the price wars.

In the third phase (late 1977 to late 1978), economic policymakers were faced with their worst nightmare – persistently high inflation and a brutal recession. The regime was forced to ease the most draconian measures and make some concessions, especially to the working class, when unemployment reached 4 percent – high by Argentine standarda and particularly onerous with inflation near 200 percent and no unemployment compensation. However, the economics team tenaciously adhered to basic principles. They categorically refused to formally index wages (even after a series of work stoppages and unofficial strikes in October 1977) and announced that, starting in January 1978, the Central Bank would no longer print money to finance the government deficit.

The final phase of the anti-inflation program (late 1978 to the present) has seen a dramatic return to the structural targets announced in April 1976. By August 1978, Argentina completed payment of all IMF debts. In 1979, it began publishing monthly schedules for wage adjustments and peso devaluations in an attempt to ease the process of forecasting – and, thus, anticipating – inflation. The junta put the final nail in the organized labor coffin by promulgating a restrictive trade union law in late 1979, just at the time they opened the political dialog to civilians ready to "play the game – according to the rules" (QER, 1980, 2nd Quarter). Import tariffs were dropped still further, foreign investment rules were liberalized to make them even more attractive to external capital than the incentives enacted in March 1977, the devaluation of the peso was accelerated to meet the objections of farmers and other exporters (WSJ, September 18, 1980, 35), and the tax structure was changed in a way that even a business periodical concluded "apppears to favor producers over consumers" (BLA, July 16, 1980, 225). In short, the economic/political authorities have engaged in a major effort to fight inflation and stabilize economic performance by "reallocating among comparative advantage" (Ferrer, 1980), preventing wages from rising at the rate of inflation, and "rationalizing" the structure of financial markets and government finance.

Management Problems

Although the government has generally adhered to the guiding principles described earlier, and has implemented the program with great technical skill and the willingness to be somewhat sensitive to macroeconomic conditions, they have suffered major setbacks in their attempts to "finetune" an economy with triple-digit inflation. Three examples of the pitfalls of political control of inflation are illustrative.

The first is the problem of simultaneously attacking high inflation, stop-go growth, and low public confidence. The government responded to public fears of runaway inflation by declaring a 120-day price truce in March 1977. When controls were lifted in July, a predictable – and ostensibly temporary – spurt in prices produced both a preemptive inventory buildup by business and a spate of purchases of durables by consumers, both fearing continued high inflation. These economic responses proved self-fulfilling by producing an artificial stimulus to growth – August inflation was 250 percent and third quarter real GDP rose 9 percent, both on an annualized basis. The Central Bank interpreted the simultaneous surges in inflation and GDP as evidence of a premature heatup (rather than as a short-term response to the lifting of controls) and clamped down on money supply expansion. The result was a liquidity crisis, a pronounced rise in interest rates (savers could receive over 250 percent a year; borrowers had to pay close to 400 percent – see Organization of American States, 1979, 29 and LAPR, October 28, 1977, 334), and inevitably, a recession that had only had minor dampening effects on inflation. In short, by trying to simultaneously solve the three problems of inflation, stop-go growth, and low public confidence, the planners made all three worse.

A second management problem is the incredible persistence of high inflation – comprehensive programs will reduce it, but only by a little and only over the long term. To a certain extent, inflationary momentum is beyond the control of the government. The economics ministry has told the Organization of American States (1979, 38) that international price increases have been especially traumatic to the Argentine economy – according to one study, they explain over half of the rate of inflation. (The OAS was openly skeptical of this claim.) Other components of inflation can be traced to psychological defensiveness by price setters. A 1978 government study of price increases by 500 firms found over 41 percent to be non-cost related – e.g., due to mental indexation – with 22 percent more due to tariff, exchange, tax, and interest rate policies, and only 11 percent due to increased wages and salaries, (RRP, January 19, 1979, 71). When external shocks, private sector defensiveness, etc. produce artificial surges in prices, the government is confronted with a difficult choice. It can increase the money supply to finance the inflation (and thereby lay the groundwork for future inflation) or it can maintain an austere monetary policy in the hope that a recession will purge the economy of "artificial" inflation. Argentine officials have leaned toward the first alternative, but have refused to fully finance the inflation by printing money.

A final management problem is coping with the disruptive effects that stabilization policies have on parts of the productive sector. A former Economics Minister (Ferrer, 1980) has attacked the anti-inflation program as having an anti-industrial bias and placing a heavy burden on small and medium size firms (i.e., those who cannot generate capital requirements internally). The large number of bankruptcies caused by the elimination of subsidies and most protectionist measures – and the defaults on loans by other firms strapped for cash – has in turn created a crisis for the banking system. The largest private bank collapsed in early 1980, three others followed shortly thereafter, and a second epidemic of financial failures jeopardized 15 more banks in late 1980 (World Business Weekly, 1981). Martínez de Hoz explicitly addresses the problem of business dislocation in a 1980 speech to the Buenos Aires Chamber of Commerce:

> We demand an effort which is sometimes painful, because in economy nothing is free, and what is taken away from some is given to others. . . . Those affected by this situation must not demand a return to the past. . . . We must distinguish between the defense of a particular sectorial interest and those which represent the general interest it is the government's duty to promote (EIA, March 1980, 7).

The government's political control of inflation by post-coup policies has been relatively successful. The regime has made major steps toward meeting its goals of freeing the economy and reducing the state's role in economic decision making. They have implemented their anti-inflation policies with untiring persistence and impressive technocratic skills.

They have not been deterred by the management obstacles they have faced and they seem to have learned from their mistakes – the Central Bank is not as paranoid about short-term overheating of the economy as it was in mid-1977. Finally, they have managed to bring the inflation rate down to double-digit levels (see fig. 8.3) with the deceleration being predictable enough to avoid the problems caused by unanticipated – or, in the post-1976 case, over-anticipated – inflation. But only half of the story has been told. We now turn to an analysis of the effects of this inflation and the anti-inflation program on Argentine society and politics.

POLITICAL EFFECTS OF INFLATION

Three and one-half months after the 1976 coup, the military commander in Tucuman province lamented that for every guerilla killed by his security forces, "the economic policies of Martınez de Hoz create five more" (LA, August 6, 1976, 242). The minister, if he was allowed a response, might well claim that it is the killing itself that creates more guerillas or that a more intense effort at economic reconstruction – similar to the post-Allende Chilean model, which forced unemployment to record levels – would create an even more unfavorable ratio for the general. In any case, the general's lament constitutes an extreme example of the effect that economic policy can have on politics. This section of the chapter explores four more general political effects of inflation and anti-inflation policies: changes in the decision making structure, income redistribution, an altered profile of winners and losers from inflation, and general social malaise.

The most obvious political ramification of the inflation and civil violence of the mid-1970s is that Argentina is no longer a democracy. The nation that was the first in Latin America to win freedom from Spain (1810) and to elect a president by nearly universal (male) suffrage (1916) is just completing five years of a brutal military dictatorship. Based on the announced plans of the junta, (29) the nation will experience military rule for a period longer than any other in modern Argentine history.

The repression of the military regime (which they claim is the only effective antidote to terrorism) is great, even by Latin American standards. A variety of sources place the number killed by government forces in the 5,000-10,000 range – analogous, on a per capita basis, to 40,000-80,000 deaths in the U.S. Arrests and detentions are even more common, with one source (Stuart, 1978, 16) claiming that less than one-sixth of the inmates in Argentina's prisons have been convicted of non-political crimes. Finally, there are few indications that authoritarian measures will be relaxed. Hardliners in the military still exercise power, despite the selection of moderate Gen. Roberto Viola as the next President. Sporadic terrorist attacks (including three seperate assaults on high economic officials in late 1979) provide a rationale for continued repression. And the siege mentality of the junta – exemplified by a government poster showing Argentina as a beefsteak about to be consumed with a knife and fork and urging, "Let's unite and we will not become a morsel for subversion" (Stuart, 1978, 14) – makes liberalization especially unlikely.

The policies of the junta are likely to have more lasting effects on the polity than those adopted during previous interludes of military control. First, the junta has attempted to eliminate the aspects of the political climate, cited in the first section of this chapter, that have contributed to inflationary pressures. Perónist populism is seriously wounded and is unlikely to recover without the personalist appeal of a Perón; the interest group structure has been emasculated by the abolition of the CGT (and by other anti-union policies) and the dismantling of parts of the federal bureaucracy; and political stability (at least in the narrow sense of predictability of government control) has been maintained by carefully planned transitions and successions.(30) Second, the gradual re-democratization will almost certainly be from the bottom up (i.e., municipal and provincial governments first) so that the armed forces, retaining control of the national government, can monitor – and if they feel the need, reverse – the process with little political cost. They certainly do not want to repeat previous experiences of national elections (1958, 1963, and 1973) being quickly followed by a return to military rule (1962, 1966, and 1976). Finally, the military is especially wary of what the prestigious Review of the River Plate has called "The Return of Populism" in a lead editorial. The Review claims that, paradoxically, economic success by the junta makes a populist restoral more likely – "Demagogy will recover its former virulence all the better for having an economy that has recovered sufficiently for the malign effects of populism not to make themselves felt immediately" (January 31, 1978, 119). The military waited 18 years between deposing Perón and allowing him back; this time, they will be even less hasty in allowing the re-establishment of the status quo ante.

A second political effect of inflation and the anti-inflation program has been a major redistribution of income away from workers, mostly as a result of tight government control over wages. Ferrer (1980, 147) notes a substantial increase in "conspicuous consumption" by the wealthy; others are less anecdotal and base their claims on the real earnings of workers. Government statisticians generally assert that real wages have remained constant or increased slightly since the military takeover, while other observers and studies have claimed drops of between 10 percent and 50 percent. To a large extent, these discrepancies are a function of the choice of base period from which to measure changes in real wages and the use of different deflators to convert nominal wages into real wages. Real earnings also come out higher if overtime payments and wages from a second job are factored in and if the 1977 increase in the basic work week from 35 to 42 hours (Wynia, 1978a, 230) is factored out. Although the studies finding major declines in real wages appear to employ the best methodology and to result in better summary measures of worker welfare, two conclusions are certain. First, since all agree that real wages dropped by well over one third in the last anarchic months of Mrs. Perón's rule and that these losses have not nearly been recouped since March 1976 (despite an increase in total national income), income has been redistributed from workers to the rest of Argentine society. Second, the developments of the last five years constitute an acceleration of a 25-year trend: in 1954, wages and salaries were 54 percent of national income; during the second Perónist era, they were about 40 percent; by late 1977, they had dropped to 31 percent, the lowest level since 1935 (Wynia, 1978a, 211 and 230).

Perhaps a more precise indicator of the redistribution of income is the data displayed in Table 8.2. In a well-balanced economy, consumer and wholesale prices tend to rise in tandem, subject to lags and other minor perturbations.(31) If the increases in the indices diverge for a long period, then income is being redistributed between retailers and consumers. The period since 1976 has been the one with the largest advantage for retailers (i.e., retail prices rising more rapidly, producing wider profit margins), as well as the longest period of major disparity between indices. (The Ongania regime – another military government attempting an austere stabilization effort – was the second best period for retailers over the last twenty-plus years.)

The reasons for the gap between the two indices are straightforward – government control of wages keeps labor costs (more important in the wholesale than in the retail index) low and the lifting of price controls allows retailers unlimited markups. The effects of this gap are somewhat more complex than a mere expansion of retail profits. Two features associated with the gap – the composition of the workers' "market basket" and the process of adjusting wages – make it especially onerous for workers.

The breakdown of consumer purchases is crucial to assessing the effects of differential inflation on workers. Just as retail price increases may diverge from wholesale price increases, the increases of the various components of the "market basket" comprising the retail index may vary. An example is food prices, whose increases over 1976 and 1977 outpaced those of the other components of the index.(33) The higher inflation rate of food prices in the first two years of military rule was especially painful, since real wages registered their greatest drop over this period, and food is both a necessity and a good for which purchases cannot be deferred (unlike, for example, clothing). At the beginning of 1976, food was already 59 percent of the average working-class family's budget (LAER, January 9, 1976, 8). The greater than average increase in food costs, and the less than average increase in wages, undoubtedly increased this already high percentage. These differential rates of inflation meant that by April 1978, only 10 percent of workers received wages that allowed them to purchase the "market basket" of basic goods and services the government used in calculating the retail price index (LAER, April 7, 1978, 104). Moreover, the concentration of the most rapid price increases in those goods and services for which workers spend a disproportionately large share of their income results in a higher effective inflation rate for the poor than for the rich.(34)

TABLE 8.2
Retail VS. Wholesale Prices(32).

Administration	Dates	% increase in retail prices	% increase in wholesale prices	Net Beneficiary	%Advantage
Frondizi	1958-1962,I	242.0	217.0	Retailers	11.5
Illia	1963,IV-1966,II	82.2	65.8	Retailers	24.9
Ongania	1966,III-1970,II	76.0	56.5	Retailers	34.5
Lanusse	1971,II-1973,I	139.2	155.3	Consumers	11.6
Peron*	1973,II-1976,I	834.7	955.8	Consumers	14.5
Videla	1976,III-1980 Nov.	4327.0	2666.3	Retailers	62.3

*includes the presidencies of H. Campora, J. Perón, and I. Perón

The wage adjustment process also has an important effect on income redistribution. Although it may seem that the length of time between wage adjustments is immaterial as long as the increases reflect the rate of inflation since the last change, the lag can be enormously important if inflation is high, since real purchasing power can be maintained only by monthly (or even more common) adjustments. For example, if inflation is running a steady 8 percent a month (152% a year), then wage increases every 2, 4, or 12 months produce annual drops in real wages of 3.7 percent, 10.6 percent, and 32.2 percent, respectively, even if each increase is fully indexed to intervening inflation. If, as in the Argentine case, the increases do not match the retail price inflation, the decline in real income will be still greater.(35) Thus, the decision by the junta in mid-1977 to adjust wages every 4, rather than every 2 months (LAER, July 8, 1977, 204) accelerated the process of income redistribution. Moreover, as Jackson, et. al. (1972, 39) notes, workers in strato-inflationary economies tend to view their wage right after an increase as being the "just" one, perceiving that they are underpaid as each month until the next increase cumulatively erodes their purchasing power. The longer the lag between adjustments, the greater is this sense of deprivation.

The economic rationale behind tolerating these results rests on the theory that excessive inflation can end only when sectors of society are forced to bear a sacrifice. Only when some receive less real income for their product (in this case, workers for their labor) can others using that product lower the prices for their product and thereby decelerate inflation. The Review of the River Plate makes this point via an analogy –

> increases in nominal wages as a method of increasing real earnings is the same as speeding up a merry-go-round in the hope that the children at the back will catch up with those in front of them (December 13, 1978, 915).

However, economic actors in inflationary periods, unlike children seated on a merry-go-round, do not maintain their relative position. In fact, those at the "back" of the Argentine economic merry-go-round have fallen further behind both when the merry-go-round speeds up and when it slows down – i.e., during both the acceleration of inflation in 1975 and early 1976 and the deceleration since 1976. While a policy of temporary impoverishment of workers – or, for that matter, of businessmen or farmers or rentiers – may be justified on economic grounds, a decline lasting well over five years is difficult to justify especially when it occurs as a result of government action.

A third general effect that inflation and anti-inflation policies have had on Argentine politics is an altered profile of winners and losers. While less extreme than the redistribution of income away from the working class, the general reallocation of political and economic resources between societal groups has been great. The greatest winners by far have been those in the international sector – especially the agricultural exporters and multinational corporations. A major loser has been much of Argentina's domestic industry. A mixed record has been maintained by the financial and services sectors.

Agricultural interests have benefitted from the reestablishment of what Wynia (1978a, 21) calls the "export orthodoxy" as a central tenet of national dogma. The rural sector quickly recovered their losses from the Perónist years – from the first half of 1976 to the first half of 1977 (a period during which real wages dropped significantly), real farm income rose 29 percent (EIA, January 1978, 37). They continued to register gains through most of 1977 and 1978 and were largely responsible for healthy positive balance of trade figures. Starting in mid-1979, farmers suffered from the government's policy of slow devaluation of the peso, since their inflation-driven peso costs were squeezing their dollar receipts from exports. In September 1980, after extensive lobbying, the junta reversed their policy and accelerated the readjustment of the peso's value (WSJ, September 18, 1980, 35), just in time to benefit farm profits from the 1980-81 harvest season. Farmers have also benefited from the junta's refusal to join the U.S. led grain embargo against the Soviet Union.

Foreign business interests have also registered great gains. In the 3½ years since the March 1977 easing of foreign investment rules, more than $2 billion in new foreign direct investment entered the country, with over half originating from the United States (RRP, July 31, 1980, 131). This marked switch from the disinvestment under Mrs. Perón's rule was accomplished through a series of incentives, including the March 1977 guarantee of equal treatment for foreign and domestic investors and 1978 legislation preventing taxation of the "paper profits" that derive from inflation. The result has been a massive increase in the net profit of multinationals operating in Argentina, especially those with sophistication in hedging and other tactics with foreign exchange markets. The average annual rate of return on investment for U.S. affiliates went from 5.2 percent during the 1973-75 period (the lowest in Latin America) to 19.2 percent over 1976-79 (the highest in the region), at the same time that the regional average stayed at about 16 percent.(36)

Domestic business interests have had a more uneven record. They have benefitted from the same incentives as those offered foreign investors, but have been hurt by a general reduction in the levels of protective tariffs and by the elimination of many government subsidies. As a result, the firms that are competitive with foreign affiliates and with imports have done reasonably well; other industries have fared badly. Aldo Ferrer (1950) alleges that the current government is attempting to reverse the process started by Perón in the 1940s and to transform Argentina back into a pre-industrial state. Although the criticism is a bit overstated, it seems clear that segments of domestic industry have been losers under the anti-inflation policy. Their relative losses may well be the result of the closing of the CGE – the business association that served as the analog of the CGT in the labor field. The reduced potency of business as an interest group stands in contrast to the agricultural sector (whose interest groups remain politically active) and the multinationals (whose financial support and confidence was crucial to the post-1976 recovery).

The fate of the banking and financial services industry has also been a mixed one. They did extremely well in the first few years of the post-1976 program. Deregulation in 1977 gave them a buffer against continued inflation, since they could raise interest rates at will, ensuring that they could maintain positive real interest rates or (more importantly) preserve a wide spread between the interest rate paid savers and that charged borrowers. This flexibility has made the banking sector one of the most competitive in Argentina – more than 80 percent of deposits are in 30-day certificates (LAER, September 21, 1979, 294) and savers have become quite sophisticated and are constantly shopping for higher interest rates. The competitiveness in turn allows (or forces) more flexibility by the banks. One official has described his bank's operations –

> Each day we look at our loan demand. If we need more capital, we just push the savings (interest) rate up a bit. If the other banks don't counter us, within two days you see people begin switching over to us. (WSJ, July 16, 1979, 1).

However, the mutually-reinforcing elements of flexibility and competition proved to be mixed blessings in the economic slowdown of early 1980. As noted earlier, bankruptcies and loan defaults by domestic borrowers (exacerbated by cash-flow problems caused by 30-day roll-overs and the need to post competitive rates) led to a series of bank crises and failures, including the collapse of the nation's largest private bank. To prevent the crises from reaching epidemic proportions, the government was forced to take on the new (and unaccustomed, given the junta's generally laissez-faire predisposition) role of bank receivership and/or ultimate guarantor of private deposits.

In short, the roster of winners and losers since 1976 does not represent a new pattern for Argentine politics. The old agricultural exporting elites and the foreign sector have been the unqualified winners; the working class has been the major loser; and Argentine industry and the financial system have posted both gains and losses. The relative predictability of inflation since 1976 means that there have been few windfall – as opposed to sustained – gains or losses resulting from unanticipated inflation. This situation, of course, constitutes an improvement over the hyper-inflation under Mrs. Perón. However, the very fact that inflation is so predictable (and so high) results in its final important political effect – general social malaise.

One source of the malaise is the limitation placed on social mobility by the anti-inflation policy. Following the 1955 anti-Perón coup, a military officer reportedly told a trade union delegation that the coup occurred "so that in this country the son of the janitor will die a janitor" (Epstein, 1975, 629). While there are fewer roadblocks on the avenues of mobility today (and a greater reluctance on the part of government officials to point them out to union members), the contraints are nonetheless present. Although reliable data is not available, it seems that the gain from the decline of real wages cited earlier has accrued to the wealthiest strata, rather than serving as the fuel to propel the white collar workers and the middle class up the socio-economic ladder. Previous bouts with triple-digit inflation have shown this trend – for example, the 114 percent inflation of 1959 was largely responsible for the wealthiest five percent increasing their share of national income from its 27.3 percent level in 1953 to 32.1 percent 1959 – an increase of 17.6 percent.(37) The gains of the top 10 percent of society were purchased at the expense of the other 90 percent and it is unlikely that the pattern of the last few years would be vastly different.

Income Percentile	% change in share of national income, 1953-59
(highest) 95-99	+17.6
90-94	+5.2
71-90	-5.7
21-70	-9.8
(lowest) 1-20	-9.3

If the income shift has not proved a sufficient obstacle to mobility, a shrinking labor market has. According to Ferrer (1980), marginal workers – females and the very young and old – have been discouraged by both job and pay prospects and have either left the labor force or (along with many of their laboring colleagues) turned to self-employment – 27 percent of the labor force was self-employed in late 1980, as opposed to 8 percent in 1976 (RRP, December 11, 1980, 867 and LARR, October 10, 1980, 3). In many countries, such a massive shift to self-employment would be taken as evidence of a growing entrepreneurial class exemplifying a pattern of social mobility. In Argentina, however, the change is more likely due to members of the middle and working classes resigning themselves to being strapped by inflation and declining real wages and turning to self-employment in the hope of eking out a living comparable to that enjoyed in the past.

A series of other indicators of a demoralized people can be enumerated. The constant introduction of new currency denominations undoubtedly has a numbing effect – the 500,000 peso note was premiered in July 1980 and , given that its dollar value dropped below $200 in early 1981 and is still falling (38), a million peso note will probably soon follow. The short-term perspective of many Argentines (exemplified by the earlier data on the concentration of savings deposits in 30-day instruments) produces a self-image of hand-to-mouth survival, rather than one of stability and normality. Even many small retailers view their stores more as a real estate investment yielding a safe (but low) return on investment than as a place of business and consequently don't mind if sales are meager.(39) (WSJ, July 16, 1979, 26) These are not the symptoms of a thriving, prosperous people.

Finally, there is little optimism about the future or expectations of growth and dynamism. Just as the increase in a price index is merely a symptom of underlying inflation, many Argentines fear that the inflation is merely a symptom of underlying economic decline. In short, few Argentines are bullish on Argentina. An industrialist I interviewed in late 1978 claims that Argentines suffer from what he calls the "British disease" – the sense that the nation has passed its peak and is in the midst of a slow decline into national poverty.(40) (A major difference, of course, is that Britain did experience a period of economic and political preeminence; Argentina, although a candidate for such greatness in the early parts of this century, never quite made it.) Rather than having the unfulfilled expectations of the nationals of most LDCs, Argentines have inured themselves to a prolonged process of continually lowering their expectations. Perhaps no other political effect of inflation and/or anti-inflation programs is more important than producing this sense of national resignation.

CONCLUSION

Evaluation of the anti-inflation program of Argentina's military government is a difficult task. A superficial look at the inflation rate shows that they have made enormous progress. A more analytical perspective shows a mixed record, with the drop in inflation purchased at the expense of major social costs – costs, however, that are less than those paid by Chile (more repression and impoverishment) in its post-Allende campaign against inflation. Should the Videla regime be congratulated for reducing the inflation rate from the 4- or 5-digit range to 2-digit levels or for protecting workers from high unemployment? Or should it be excoriated for not bringing inflation down fast enough and/or for basing its program on repression, regressive income distribution, and the reenshrinement of old elites?

Other crucial questions flow from the difficulty in segregating the effects of particular actions or policies – or anicipating the effects other actions or policies would have had. Has the level of repression (leaving aside questions of moral justification) helped the anti-inflation program by limiting the disruptive effect of terrorism or by frightening the labor movement into acquiescence? Or has it hindered attainment of inflation goals by diverting productive resources toward a campaign of violence and by engendering more terrorism? Would a draconian monetarist solution of clamping down on the money supply and pushing the nation into a deep recession have the cathartic effect of purging Argentines of inflationary expectations? Or would the post-recession inflation soon return to pre-recession levels or, still worse, repeat the 1978 experience of an inflation rate insensitive to an economic decline? After inflation was first stabilized in the 100 percent-200 percent range, would indexing wages to near the retail price index increases allow workers to maintain a nearly constant real wage? Or would such indexing speed up the Review of the River Plate's merry-go-round and start a new cycle of hyper-inflation? Inability to answer these "what if?" questions disappoint the outside observer and, more importantly, frustrate the policymakers and implementers.

Several firm conclusions can be ventured, though. The inflation rate is far below what it was in 1976 (41), but the change was accomplished through an enforced sacrifice by the working class. Inflation has undergone a more or less steady deceleration over the last five years, yet still maintains a stubborn downward stickiness, exemplified by the problems crossing the plateau from triple to double-digit levels that were hinted at in the last epigraph to this essay. Unanticipated inflation is minor enough to have minimal social costs, but the inflation that everyone anticipates is one characterized by differential rates of price increases that hurt the poor more than the rich, consumers more than retailers, and domestic small business more than the multinationals and the cattle barons. Finally, the reallocation of power and redistribution of income resulting from inflation and the anti-inflation program has only surpressed, and has done nothing to resolve, the conflicts between economic classes that has plagued Argentina since 1916.

Free market inflation can often serve as a vehicle for pursuing the distributional struggle resulting from such conflict. As Tobin notes

> Inflation lets this struggle proceed and blindly, impartially, impersonally, and non-politically scales down all its outcomes. There are worse methods of resolving group rivalries and social conflict (Tobin, 1972, 13).

Inflation's role as an arena of social conflict and as peaceful arbiter of course disappears when the government tampers with the ground rules – e.g., by lifting all price, and maintaining all wage, controls. Still, the 1981 situation can be regarded as an improvement over 1975-76. Maier (1978, 71) restricts Tobin's claim by stating that "beyond a certain rate, inflation cannot play this role as social lubricant and instead aggravates the very distributional conflicts it helped assuage." This threshold was passed in 1975-76, when almost all Argentines suffered the ill effects – economic and psychological – of runaway inflation. The post-1976 solution has been an economic policy designed to prevent all from suffering by forcing selected groups to suffer.

It is certainly true that excessive attention to tallying up – and reacting to – minor gains and losses from inflation is itself inflationary. However, it is also true that policies forcing groups to experience extreme losses (or gains) over a prolonged period must be called into question (42), especially when such policies result from explicit and intentional government action rather than government inaction in the face of market movements. For example, since there is no intrinsically correct level for labor's share of national income, the validity of policies reducing it from 40 percent to 30 percent in just a few years is a question of values and politics, rather than economics.

Such policies must also be judged on pragmatic grounds. Wynia (1978a, 16) claims that effective solultions to Argentina's economic problems depend less on the form of government that implements policy or even on the economic strategy chosen than it does on building popular support for the chosen policy. In other words, even a "bureaucratic-authoritarian" regime faithfully implementing a text-book-perfect stabilization plan will not succeed unless it can create the social consensus that Argentina sorely lacks. It is unlikely that five years of military rule has imposed this consensus or that the lifting of military rule will not lead to the same sort of populism, rigid interest groups, and political instability that have led Argentina down the inflationary path in the past.

The earlier quotation by Tobin notes that distributional conflicts are natural – and if waged through inflation, sometimes even healthy – for a society. Hirsch (1978, 270-276) qualifies this assertion by noting that this conflict is at most a necessary condition for high inflation. A necessary and sufficient condition is that this conflict take place in the absence of either a social consensus or authority strong enough to impose its consensus.(43) Argentina has always lacked the former; the presence of the latter over the last half-decade is no guarantee that the conflict, once unleashed, will not again lead to inflation. The imperative for government policy in the next five years is forging the consensus and building the popular support that Wynia claims is a prerequisite to success.

The 1976 economic situation wa clearly intolerable. The results of policies that have brought Argentina to a more tolerable situation in 1981 are also unpalatable and may not prevent recurrence of the 1975-76 debacle. In 1980, Martínez de Hoz explained how the absence of open politics, and the adoption of a long-term perspective, will allow his program to succeed

> In the past 30 years, no economic program until now had been applied for more than two years without a change in approach. . . . We have done what an elective government with an election next year can't do – we have accepted short-term negative effects for long-term progress. Ours is a medium-term program that has to go on for at least five years to see results (BW, July 21, 1980, 78).

The verdict is still out on the results, not because of failures of economic policy in creating some successes, but because the next phase of economic policy must reverse the development that made the first phase possible – that is, it must become political. The long-term progress that the Minister awaits can only occur by consolidating economic gains through an inclusionary political process that will channel conflict into consensus. Without any doubt, excessive inflation is bad; however, society must be convinced that the remedy is better.

NOTES

(1) Quoted in Witonski; 1978, 14.

(2) Quoted in, inter alia, Latin America Political Report; April 25, 1977, 125.

(3) Review of the River Plate; November 20, 1980, 754-756.

(4) Three methods are used in this paper to express the inflation rate. The first is to extrapolate (or annualize) an increase in a price index as if the increase of a given month or quarter were to continue. As noted in the text, a monthly price increase of 54 percent translates into a 17,000 percent-plus annual rate. A second method is to calculate a point-to-point (e.g., December-to-December) increase in a price index. Figure 3, which depicts the increases in consumer prices over the previous 12 months, is an example. Finally, inflation can be measured on an average-to-average basis – i.e., the change in prices from the average level in one period to the average level in the next. Figure 1, which charts the increases in average price levels from year to year, exemplifies this last method.

(5) The data on which the 1937-1979 inflation rates are based come from the International Monetary Fund's monthly, International Financial Statistics – henceforth cited as IMF, IFS. The 1980 inflation rate is based on January-July data from IMF, IFS; August-November figures representing the Argentine government index (as reported in the Review of the River Plate); and December data from the Review's own index.

(6) 1937-1945 GDP data are adapted from Diaz-Alejandro, 1970, Statistical Appendix. 1946-1979 data are from IMF, IFS. The 1980 estimate of zero growth is from the Economics Ministry, as reported in the New York Times; January 19, 1981, D-9.

(7) Defined as less than 10 percent of the population in 1970 having annual incomes of less than $100 (O'Donnell, 1979, 23).

(8) GDP data (which refer to 1978) are adopted from Organization of American States, 1979, 3. Labor force data appears in Snow, 1979, 4-5.

(9) The governor of Buenos Aires province at the time coined the term "patriotic fraud" to refer to the electoral abuses by conservative interests (O'Donnell, 1979, 126).

(10) He captured 56 percent of the vote in 1946 and 63 percent in 1951. Analyses of Peron's electoral appeal can be found in Schoultz, 1977 and Kirkpatrick, 1971.

(11) Agricultural production declined 42 percent and food exports (in constant dollars) dropped 67 percent from the late 1930s to the early 1950s (Edel, 1969, 7).

(12) The proximate cause for Perón's overthrow in September 1955 was probably his excommunication two months before for having legalized divorce and prostitution.

(13) This was the second instance of Perón beginning his presidential tenure as the beneficiary of international economic developments. In 1946 and 1947, the Argentine economy grew in response to the post-war surge in demand for agricultural commodities and Perón had the economic buffer of large gold and foreign exchange reserves.

(14) Some have argued that the Social Pact artifically surpressed inflation and produced scarcities and a black market. See Ayres (1976) for an intriguing treatment of the economic and political ramifications of the pact.

(15) Perón's selection of Isabel as his Vice-President on the election ticket had originally been viewed as a shrewd political move. Choosing anyone else would have forced him to also choose which of the many Perónist factions were following the "true" path. However, his mortality brings the wisdom of his choice into question.

(16) A probably apocryphal story holds that the Cabinet waited several hours for a meeting since the President was with her seamstress and refused to dismiss her since (due to inflation) she could not afford to delay her dress order (Newsweek, 1975, 44).

(17) The Newsweek article also notes how the inflation (and the resultant undervaluing of the peso and high demand for hard currency) produced a bonanza for tourists. A luxury hotel room could be purchased for $3 a day, a first class meal for $1, and a fifth of brand name gin for 45¢!

(18) One cannot help but wonder if the sales tax on coffins charged by some U.S. states is not crueler.

(19) English-language treatments of this debate include (in descending order of recency) Wachter, 1976; Hunger and Foley, 1975; Mallon, 1975; Maynard and van Ryckeghem, 1975; Trevithick and Mulvey, 1975; Diaz-Alejandro, 1970; Krieger, 1965; and Harberger, 1963.

(20) The classic study of hyperinflation is Cagan's (1956), which uses a monetarist perspective. However, econometric techniques cannot prove or disprove hypotheses; they can only quantify them.

(21) Sources: IMF, IFS for data through July 1979; other data collected as in footnote 5.

(22) In fairness to Tobin, it should be noted that his article – a 1972 Presidential speech to the American Economics Association – was composed before the onset of "stagflation" – simultaneous states of economic stagnation and inflation.

(23) O'Donnell distinguishes the bureaucratic breed of authoritarianism from the "populist" variety (presumbly Perón's) and the "traditional" breed (presumably that of the 19th century caudillos.) The former are characterized by attempts to exclude the urban popular sector from power; the latter two are marked, respectively, by attempts to incorporate or ignore this sector.

(24) Some might claim that inflation causes recessions, rather than recessions causing reduced inflation. While this claim might have some merit when applied to 1959 or to 1975-76 in Argentina or to economies where inflation accelerates from 2-4 percent to double-digit levels, there is no compelling reason why increases in double-digit inflation should have this effect. The period from 1960 to 1963 is a case in point – the acceleration of inflation from 20 percent to 26 percent should not have led to two years of booming growth being followed by two years of harsh contraction. In fact, a recent study (Hanson, 1980) of five Latin countries – Argentina was not included – concluded that each 10 percentage points of unanticipated inflation has tended to produce an extra percentage point of GDP growth.

(25) Sources are the same as in footnotes 5 and 6.

(26) Both Videla and Viola had served as Army Chiefs of Staff (and thus, junta members) before assuming the Presidency. Videla held both positions for the first two years after the coup.

(27) A cartoon in an Argentine weekly shows a dragon (inflation) carrying Martínez de Hoz in its teeth as he proclaims, "Don't worry; it's really quite tame." Cited in RRP; October 20, 1978; 605.

(28) The scheme is developed, with adaptations, from Ferrer, 1980.

(29) The previously longest stretch of military control (1966-73) lasted slightly under 7 years. President Viola's term expires in 1984 (8 years after the coup) and government officials cite estimates that a return to democracy is 5 to 10 years into the future.

(30) Although Martínez de Hoz will apparently not stay on as Economics Minister in the Viola Administration, the basic principles and policies of his tenure will almost certainly be maintained.

(31) These lags and perturbations tend to average out over the long term. For example, from 1975 to November 1980, U.S. consumer and wholesale prices both rose 59.2 percent.

(32) Source: IMF, IFS. The dates for presidential administrations are based on the assumption that a regime's policies do not begin to have an effect until the first full quarter after assuming power and that the effect continues into the last quarter of a presidential term.

(33) The cited data series is an unofficial Buenos Aires cost-of-living index calculated by the Review of the River Plate.

(34) A similar situation prevailed during the triple-digit inflation of 1959, according to an ECLA study based on analyzing market baskets at different income levels. The poorest (those with annual incomes equivalent to less than $1,000 in 1980 terms) experienced 131 percent inflation in the prices of their market basket; a middle category ($5,500 to $7,000) saw 114 percent inflation; and the wealthiest ($15,000 up) felt 100 percent inflation.

Over the 1950-63 period, the average annual rates of inflation for the poor, middle, and rich categories were 27.7 percent, 26.8 percent, and 25.0 percent, respectively.

Data adapted from United Nations, 1969, Table 36. Income levels in 1980 dollars based on the 1963 peso-to-dollar exchange rate and the U.S. consumer price index from 1963 to 1980, both obtained from IMF, IFS.

(35) An interesting effect of inflation on workers' real income is due to the Christmas bonus, the "thirteenth month" salary mandated by law during the first Perónist era. All employees receive a bonus equal to one-twelfth of their gross yearly wages, but – when inflation is high – the bonus is substantially less than the December paycheck, since it is based on nominal wages which (presumably) increase over the course of the year. If inflation is constant at 8 percent a month and wages are fully and simultaneously indexed, the bonus is less than two-thirds of the December paycheck.

(36) The average profit margins in other major Latin countries actually went down over this period – Mexico's went from 12.9 percent in 1973-75 to 12.5 percent in 1976-79, Brazil's dropped from 12.9 percent to 10.9 percent, and Venezuela's plummeted from 24.6 percent to 16.6 percent.

Data based on annual profitability reports appearing in Business Latin America.

(37) Data adapted from Table 1 of United Nations, 1969.

(38) The official exchange rate as of mid-February 1981 was 2300 pesos to the dollar, making 500,000 pesos equivalent to $217 on official

markets, However, given the continued overvaluation of the peso (30 percent according to BW; July 21, 1980, 78), the "real" dollar equivalent of half a million pesos is certainly less than $200.

(39) This sort of behavior – a seemingly rational response to inflation – can itself contribute to inflation. Retailers having a relatively minor concern with sales volume will tend to post higher prices. In addition, fragmentation of the retail trade creates the smaller economies of scale and occasional shortages that in turn can fuel inflation. (The Review of the River Plate has maintained on several occasions that Argentina has the highest retail outlet per capita ratio in the world.)

(40) The industrialist, a resident of Argentina since childhood, was noncommittal about his extent of agreement with the diagnosis. However, in January 1981, he travelled to the U.S. to explore opportunities for semi-retirement here.

(41) After four years as the nation with the highest inflation rate in the world, Argentina droppd to third place (after Israel and Turkey) in 1980 (NYT; January 5, 1981, D-1).

(42) The assertion is also applicable to other fragments of Argentine economic history – e.g., the depreivation suffered by owners of rent-controlled property from the first Perónist era to the late 1970s.

(43) Undoubtedly, this is a factor behind Fuller's observation: "Over the long run, the only societies with sustainable economies are apt to be fully participatory or utterly authoritarian" (1980, 38).

REFERENCES

Ayres, Robert L. "The 'Social Pact' as Anti-Inflationary Policy: The Argentine Experience Since 1973." World Politics. 28: 473-501, 1976.

BLA: Business Latin America, various issues.

Blejer, Mario I. "Money and the Nominal Interest Rate in an Inflationary Econmy: An Empircal Test." Journal of Political Economy. 86: 529-534, 1978.

Brittan, Samuel "Inflation and Democracy" in Hirsch and Goldthorpe, 1978.

Buchanan, James M. and Richard E. Wagner Democracy in Deficit. New York: Academic Press, 1977.

BW: Business Week, various issues.

Cagan, Phillip "The Monetary Dynamics of Hyper-Inflation" in Milton Friedman (editor). Studies in the Quantity Theory of Money. Chicago; University of Chicago Press, 1956.

Corden, W.M. Inflation, Exchange Rates, and the World Economy. Chicago: University of Chicago Press, 1977.

Crouch, Colin. "Inflation and the Political Organization" in Hirsch and Goldthorpe, 1978.

Davis, Tom E. "Eight Decades of Inflation in Chile, 1879-1959: A Political Interpretation," Journal of Political Economy. 71: 389-397, 1963.

de Onis, Juan. "Isabelita's Terrible Legacy." New York Times Magazine. March 21: 15+, 1976.

de Pablo, Juan Carlos. "Relative Prices, Income Distribution, and Stabilization Plans: The Argentine Experience, 1967-1970." Journal of Development Economics. 1: 167-189, 1974.

Diaz-Alejandro, Carlos F. Essays on the Economic History of the Argentine Republic. New Haven: Yale University Press, 1970.

di Tella, Guido. "The Economic Policies of Argentina's Labour-Based Government (1973-76)." in Rosemary Thorpe and Laurence Whitehead (editors). Inflation and Stabilization in Latin America. Macmillian: London, 1978.

Edel, Matthew. Food Supply and Inflation in Latin America. New York: Praeger, 1969.

EIA: Economic Information on Argentina (published by the Ministry of Economy). various issues.

Epstein, Edward C. "Politicization and Income Redistribution in Argentina: The Case of the Perónist Worker." Economic Development and Cultural Change. 23: 615-631, 1975.

_____. "Anti-Inflation Policies in Argentina and Chile: Or, Who Pays the Cost." Comparative Political Studies. 11: 211-230, 1978.

_____. "Control and Co-Optation of the Argentine Labor Movement." Economic Development and Cultural Change. 27: 445-465, 1979.

Euromoney - London. "How Argentina is Consolidating Success." December: supplement.

Ferrer, Aldo. "The Argentine Economy, 1976-1979." Journal of Inter-American Studies. 22: 131-162, 1980.

Forbes. "After the Coup, What?" April 15: 59-62, 1976.

Friedman, Milton. Monetary Correction. Westminster: Institute of Economic Affairs Occasional Paper 41, 1974.

Fuller, Robert. Inflation: The Rising Cost of Living on a Small Planet. Washington: Worldwatch Paper 34, 1980.

Goldthorpe, John H. "The Current Inflation: Towards a Sociological Account." in Hirsch and Goldthorpe, 1978.

Gordon, Robert J. "The Demand for and Supply of Inflation," Journal of Law and Economics. 18: 807-836, 1975.

Green, James. International Experiences in Managing Inflation. New York: The Conference Board, 1977.

Hanson, James A. "The Short-Run Relation between Growth and Inflation in Latin America: A Quasi-Rational or Consistent Expectations Approach," American Economic Review. 70: 972-989, 1980.

Harberger, Arnold C. "The Dynamics of Inflation in Chile" in Carl F. Christ, et. al. (editors). Measurement in Economics. Stanford: Stanford University Press, 1963.

Harvey, Robert. "Poor Little Rich Boy." Economist. 264: January 26, Special Supplement, 1980.

Hirsch, Fred. "The Ideological Underlay of Inflation" in Hirsch and Goldthorpe, 1978.

______. and John H. Goldthorpe. The Political Economy of Inflation. Cambridge; Harvard University Press, 1978.

Hunter, John M. and James W. Foley. Economic Problems of Latin America. Boston: Houghton Mifflin, 1975.

IMF, IFS: International Financial Statistics (published by the International Monetary Fund). various issues.

Jackson, Dudley, H. A. Turner, and Frank Wilkinson. Do Trade Unions Cause Inflation? Cambridge: Cambridge University Press, 1972.

James, Daniel. "Power and Politics in Perónist Trade Unions," Journal of Inter-American Studies and World Affairs. 20: 2-36, 1978.

Kirkpatrick, Jeane. Leader and Vanguard in Mass Society: A Study of Perónist Argentina. Cambridge: MIT Press, 1971.

Krieger, Ronald A. "Inflation Propagation in Argentina." Ph.D. Dissertation: University of Wisconsin, 1965.

LA: Latin America, various issues.

LAER: Latin America Economic Report, various issues.

LAPR: Latin America Political Report, various issues.

LARR: Latin America Regional Report, various issues.

LAWR: Latin America Weekly Report, various issues.

Maier, Charles S. "The Politics of Inflation in the 20th Century" in Hirsch and Goldthorpe, 1978.

Mallon, Richard D. "Exchange Policy – Argentina" in Gustave F. Papanek (editor). Development Policy – Theory and Practice. Cambridge: Harvard University Press.

______. in collaboration with Juan V. Sourroville. Economic Policy-making in a Conflict Society: the Argentine Case. Cambridge: Harvard University Press, 1975.

Maynard, Geoffrey and Willy van Ryjckeghem. "Stabilization Policy in an Inflationary Economy – Argentina" in Gustav F. Papanek (editor). Development Policy – Theory and Practice. Cambridge: Harvard University Press, 1968.

______ and ______. A World of Inflation. New York: Barnes and Noble, 1975.

Merkx, Gilbert W. "Argentina: Peronism and Power." Monthly Review. 27 (January): 38-51, 1976.

Newsweek. "Argentina: There's No Tomorrow." December 8: 44-47, 1975.

NYT: New York Times, various issues.

O'Donnell, Guillermo. "State and Alliance in Argentina, 1956-1976." Journal of Development Studies. 15: 3-33, 1978.

______. Modernization and Bureaucratic-Authoritarianism. Berkeley: Institute of International Studies, 1979.

Organization of American States. Short Term Economic Prospects: Volume VIII Argentina. OAS Document SG/Ser.G.41.11, 1979.

Pazos, Felipe. Chronic Inflation in Latin America. New York: Praeger, 1972.

Piachaud, David. "Inflation and Income Distribution;" in Hirsch and Goldthorpe, 1978.

QER: Quarterly Economic Review - Argentina (published by the Economist Intelligence Unit LTD), various issues.

Reid, Alastair. "Ar-gen-tina." New Yorker. 54 (August 7): 37-53, 1978.

RRP: Review of the River Plate, various issues.

Schoultz, Lars. "The Socio-Economic Determinants of Popular-Authoritarian Electoral Behavior: The Case of Peronism." American Political Science Review. 71: 1423-1446, 1977.

Smith, Peter H. Politics and Beef in Argentina. New York: Columbia University Press, 1969.

Snow, Peter G. Political Forces in Argentina. New York: Praeger, Revised Edition, 1979.

Stuart, Peter C. "The Cost of Life in Argentina." New Leader. 61 (April 24) 14-16, 1978.

Time "Dr. Joe's Miracle Cure." July 7:59, 1980.

Tobin, James. "Inflation and Unemployment." American Economic Review. 62: 1-18, 1972.

United Nations (Ecnomic Commission on Latin America) Economic Development and Income Redistribution in Argentina. U.N. Document E/CN.12/802, 1969.

Villanueva, Javier. "The Inflationary Process in Argentina, 1943-60." Mimeographed. 1964.

Wachter, Susan M. Latin American Inflation: The Structuralist-Monetarist Debate. Lexington, Mass: Lexington, 1976.

Whitehead, Laurence. "The Political Causes of Inflation." Political Studies. 27: 564-577, 1979.

Witonski, Peter. "The Legacy of Peron." New Republic. June 17: 13-17, 1978.

World Business Weekly. "A Time for Decision." January 19: 27-35, 1981.

WSJ: Wall Street Journal, various issues.

Wynia, Gary W. Argentina in the Postwar Era. Alburquerque: University of New Mexico Press, 1978a.

______. The Politics of Latin American Development. New York: Cambridge University Press, 1978b.

______. "The Political Economy of Argentina: Past, Present, and Future." Background material for a seminar sponsored by the Fund for Multinational Management Education and the Council of the Americas, 1980.

Yordan, Wesley J. "Inflation in Argentina: The Monetary Consequences of Social Conflict." Western Economic Journal. 4: 72-90, 1965.

Zinn, Ricardo. Argentina: A Nation at the Crossroads of Myth and Reality. New York: Speller, 1979.

9 Inflation and Democratic Transition in Spain

John F. Coverdale

The Spanish people have had exceptionally bad luck in the economic timing of their efforts to establish democratic regimes in the twentieth century. Their first attempt began in 1931, just as the world economy headed toward the trough of the Great Depression. Their current experiment in democratic politics began as the industrialized world initiated a painful adjustment to scarce and expensive energy, in an atmosphere of rapidly rising prices and falling growth rates. This essay will examine the effects of inflation and other economic problems on Spain's current transition to democracy as well as the ways in which the country's emerging democratic institutions have attempted to deal with inflation.(1)

The buoyant prosperity of the 1960s forms the background against which Spain's current economic and political problems must be seen. Thanks in large part to the prosperity of the rest of Western Europe, Spain's real gross internal product grew at a cumulative annual rate of 7.6 percent during the thirteen years 1960-1973. In the longer twenty-year period from 1955 to 1975, GIP grew at an annual rate of 5.8 percent (Banco de Bilbao, n.d., 34). This growth naturally brought with it profound changes in the structure of the Spanish economy. Industrial production tripled between 1960 and 1970. As late as 1950, 50 percent of Spain's active population was engaged in agriculture; by 1970 agriculture accounted for only 25 percent of the active population. During the same period industrial employment grew from 26 percent to 38 percent of the active population and services increased from 25 percent to 37 percent (Institute Naciónal de Estudística, 1977, 53).

Economic growth brought with it rapid urbanization as well. In 1950 only 18 percent of the population lived in cities of more than 100,000 inhabitants. By 1970 such cities accounted for 34 percent of the population (Fundación Foessa, 1976, 94).

The years of economic prosperity were years of high employment. Thanks in part to the temporary emigration of many Spanish workers to the countries of the Common Market, official statistics never showed more than 2 percent unemployment for any year between 1955 and 1971 (Banco de Bilbas, n.d., 30-1). Actual unemployment may have been somewhat higher than 2 percent, but it was certainly very low throughout the period. Statistics on wages are scattered and unreliable, but real wages clearly increased dramatically in the 1960s and early 1970s.

Even during the years of greatest prosperity, Spain experienced significantly more inflation than did the industrialized countries of Europe. Between 1963 and 1972, the consumer price index rose from 100 to 181 in Spain, while in industrialized Europe it rose from 100 to 150 (International Financial Statistics, 1974, 35, Bustelo and Casara, 1976). During the period of maximum economic growth and prosperity, then, Spanish prices increased almost 2/3 again as fast as prices in the industrialized countries of Europe (although not much faster than in other non-industrial countries). While the boom continued, neither the public nor the professional economists considered Spain's inflation a cause for serious concern.

1973 was the last truly good year for the Spanish economy. Real GNP rose 7.9 percent. Production and employment were near capacity. The peseta was strong and Spain's reserves rose some $2 billion to about $7 billion. The only real problem in 1973 was precisely inflation. The money supply grew at a blistering annual rate of 27.6 percent (International Financial Statistics, 1979, 35). Coupled with rapidly rising wages and the general economic boom, this led to the highest inflation rate in 26 years, 11.4 percent (International Financial Statistics, 1976, 34).

During 1973/74 oil price increases and the world recession severely shocked the Spanish economy, but the government failed to respond to the challenge posed by the new international environment. It would be more accurate to say that it chose not to respond. The assassination of Franco's heir-apparent, Admiral Carrero Blanco, had seriously weakened the government, and the cabinet formed by Prime Minister Carlos Arias Navarro in January 1974 had no intention of taking politically unpopular measures. As much out of political expediency as out of a failure to recognize that the period of easy growth fed by international prosperity and cheap energy had come to an end, the Arias government deliberately chose in 1974 and 1975 to maintain high levels of production and employment, even at the cost of more inflation. In 1974 consumer prices increased 15.6 percent, and in 1975, when most other European countries had managed to slow the rates of increase, the Spanish inflation rate rose again to 16.8 percent (International Financial Statistics, 1979 II, 45).

The policy of maintaining production and employment at all cost was temporarily successful in preventing the Spanish public from feeling the full effects of the new world economic situation. In the words of an OECD report, "By comparison with the experience of other member countries, the Spanish economy weathered both the oil crisis and the aftershock of the world recession reasonably well. In 1975 it was one of the few countries not to register a year-on-year fall in activity," although 1975 was "probably the worst year Spain had had, in terms of declining activity and rising unemployment, since 1959" (OECD, 1976, 5). This temporary and largely apparent success contributed to fomenting the illusion that Spain could successfully ignore the new economic realities of the larger world and pursue a policy of growth independently of world economic conditions. Specifically it suggested to Spanish workers that they could continue to increase their wages even in a period of stagnant productivity. This was accomplished by increasing the share of the national rent going to wages and benefits at the expense of the share going to profits. The share of wages and benefits increased from 60.28 percent in 1974 to 62.38 percent in 1975 while during the same period profits fell from 9.39 percent to 7.95 percent (Banco de Bilbao, 1979, 95).

During the final years of the Franco regime, then, Spain had already entered on the path of deliberate inflation in order to maintain employment and wages, thereby putting off to the future the painful adjustments needed to prepare the country for the new and less favorable economic climate created by higher energy prices.

At Franco's death in November 1975, King Juan Carlos chose to retain Franco's last prime minister, Carlos Arias Navarro. In Arias's new government, announced on December 12, 1975, partisans of liberalization-from-above held key positions and there were only three holdovers from the previous cabinet among its twenty members. The new government, however, had little to offer in the way of innovative policies.

Franco's death aroused many hopes of political, social, and economic reform. Spaniards who had been waiting for years and even decades for the dictator's demise expected sudden, radical change; but the government continued with a business-as-usual approach, prohibiting the Socialists from holding a press conference, using massive detachments of police to break up demonstrations in Madrid, and arresting leaders of the moderate left for illegal assembly.

The Arias government attempted in Spain what Marcello Caetano had attempted in Portugal: to maintain the fundamental structure of the regime after the death of the dictator, while making only those changes that seemed necessary to stay in power. It made some concessions to internal and international demands for liberalization and democratization, but tried to retain for the government the maximum possible measure of discretionary control and to preserve as much of the institutions of the Franco regime as possible.

On the economic front, the expectations raised by the dictator's demise, the erosion of purchasing power under the influence of inflation, and a generally deteriorating economic situation led to increased pressure for higher wages. In January 1976, Arias attempted to deal with this situation by decreeing a wage freeze. Workers responded with strikes that paralyzed the Madrid subway, the post office, and the railroads. The government struck back hard, using troops to run the subway and militarizing postal and railway workers. Thus the pressures caused by inflation contributed to forcing a government that would have liked to institute cautious mildly liberalizing reforms into applying the authoritarian measures that had characterized the Franco regime.

The first serious bloodshed under the new regime was also related to economic grievances. In Vitoria, the capital of the Basque province of Alava, a clash between police and citizens engaged in a 'day of struggle' in support of striking workers left five demonstrators dead and a hundred injured. The demonstrations in this case had clear political overtones and were closely related to demands for Basque autonomy but economic grievances played a significant role in their origin.

The only major measure taken by the Arias government to deal with the deteriorating economic situation, aside from the short-lived and ineffective wage freeze, was an unexpected ten percent devaluation of the peseta in February 1976. The devaluation was not accompanied by the complementary steps which would have been necessary to make it effective, and it became in fact one more source of inflationary pressure.

At a time when the industrialized countries of Europe were beginning to get their inflation under control, prices in Spain continued to rise virtually unchecked. By the end of the second quarter 1976, hourly wages stood 13 percent above their 1975 level (International Financial Statistics, 1977, 329). Unemployment was beginning to rise, investment was falling off alarmingly, and the balance of payments deficit was large and growing. The Arias government spoke of fiscal reform, but made no substantial progress toward implementing it nor toward monetary restraint. It failed both to take energetic short-term corrective measures and to make a serious effort to reform or create basic instruments of economic policy implementation.

The Arias government lasted a little over six months. During that period the press and Madrid's political leaders, both in the government and in the opposition, focused their attention almost exclusively on questions of political reform. Public opinion polls showed that most people were concerned principally about unemployment and inflation, while only a small minority ranked the political future as their chief concern. Yet the government and the opposition both seemed entirely absorbed in politics. Housewives and businessmen might worry about inflation and unemployment, but neither the government nor the opposition seemed to heed such mundane concerns.

By July 1976 Arias had demonstrated his inability or unwillingness to proceed with reform fast enough to disarm his critics and return some measure of peace and stability to Spain. Growing popular discontent threatened to undermine the stability of the monarchy itself. Accordingly, King Juan Carlos requested the Prime Minister's resignation and appointed in his place a 43-year-old politician, Adolfo Suárez González.

When Suárez took over from Arias, the Spanish economy was suffering from stagnation, inflation, unemployment, and a deteriorating balance of payments. Real GDP had increased only about one percent in 1975. In the first five months of 1976, prices had increased almost 12 percent, including a spectacular 4.6 percent rise in May.

According to official figures, unemployment had risen to over five percent, and thre was a growing pool of hard core unemployed. In 1975, imports had exceeded exports by $8.6 billion. The devaluation of the peseta in February 1976 did provide some temporary relief from balance of payments problems, but the trade deficit would still be $7.3 billion in 1976.

The new president of the government, like his predecessor and like almost all other Spanish politicians, was much more interested in politics than in economics. He felt a natural disinclination for economic issues, which he did not understand very well and which did not respond to his manipulative style of politics. In addition, Suárez felt, quite rightly, that his appointed government lacked the political authority necessary to impose a stern austerity policy and make it stick.

The economic measures taken by the Suárez government during its first year of life were, therefore, timid and inadequate. In October, the government announced an economic stability plan, calling for price controls on basic commodities and limiting wage increases to the rise in the cost of living, but it provided no mechanisms for enforcing these limits. It also increased income taxes by ten percent and attempted to control energy consumption and imports. In February 1977, a new economic program extended price controls, provided some export incentives, and called for holding the increase of the money supply to 21 percent in order to keep inflation below 17 percent. These measures may have had some slight beneficial effects, but they did nothing to solve the basic imbalances of the Spanish economy.

From an economic point of view, the entire three and a half years from 1973 to mid-1977 constitute a single period. Neither Franco's death nor Suárez's accession to power in place of Arias brought any fundamental economic changes. The last Franco government and the first two governments of the new monarchy all failed to undertake a serious fight against inflation. In consequence, the Spanish economy suffered from growing internal and external disequilibria. By summer 1977, they were producing critical problems in the form of slow growth, falling investment, rising unemployment, spiraling inflation, and a deficit of the current external balance.

If in the economic sphere the transition from Arias to Suárez brought with it no significant changes, in the political sphere the differences were dramatic. Like Arias, Suárez was closely connected to the Franco regime, within which he had made his career. He too insisted on maintaining government control over the process of political change, flatly rejecting all calls from the opposition for a sharp break with the past. Nonetheless, he did move forward quickly and decisively to give Spain an entirely new set of democratic institutions. In less than one year he held a successful referendum on the question of whether or not to reform the political system, legalized all the major political parties including the Spanish Communist Party, created a center-right party of his own, and held in June 1977 free elections for a legislative assembly which was to write a new constitution for Spain.

In retrospect it seems clear that Suárez was wise in postponing economic reform until after the elections. Demand for political reform was so strong and insistent that there could be no thought of putting it off until the economic climate improved. Suárez had to choose between concentrating on politics or trying to carry out economic and political reforms simultaneously. Political tensions would, however, have been vastly aggravated by stringent economic measures designed to bring inflation under control and initiate the structural changes needed to adapt the Spanish economy to the changed international situation. By concentrating on politics, the parties were able to find compromise solutions which enabled them to press forward with reform. Had the government attempted to implement a program of financial austerity at the same time as it presented its program of political reform, compromise would have been much more difficult and probably impossible.

In June 1977 Spanish voters gave Suárez and his Center Democratic Union (UCD) a narrow plurality. The UCD received 34.7 percent of the popular vote, followed by the Spanish Socialist Workers' Party with 29.2 percent, the Spanish Communist Party with 9.2 percent, and the right-wing Popular Alliance with 8.4 percent. Thanks to over-representation of the rural areas in which it was strongest and to an electoral law which favored large parties at the expense of small ones, the UCD won 165 of 350 seats in the lower house of the Spanish parliament. Although he lacked eleven seats for a majority in the Cortes and had won barely more than a third of the popular vote, Suárez emerged from the 1977 elections much strengthened. He had a clearly perceived popular mandate to continue his political reform program since most Socialist voters accepted its main lines.

Even after the June 1977, elections Suárez would probably have preferred to let the economy drift for another year while the newly elected parliament wrote a constitution for Spain; but the situation had become too critical to permit further delay. Suárez gave signs of his awareness of this problem in the construction of his new government. He reinstituted the position of Vice President for Economic Affairs, which had not even existed in his first government. To fill it, he chose a prestigious professor of public finance and fiscal law, Enrique Fuentes Quintana. Fuentes was a beiever in a free market economy, but he was also a forthright critic of the inequities of income distribution and of taxation in Spain. Suárez had offered him a portfolio in his first cabinet in July 1976, but at that time the new President of the Government had been unwilling or unable to promise Fuentes the free hand and vigorous support he demanded as a condition of joining the cabinet. Suárez's strengthened political position after the successful June 1977 elections and the pressing urgency of Spain's economic problems led him to guarantee his new Economic Vice President both freedom of action and solid political backing.

The second member of Suárez's new financial team was Francisco Fernandez Ordoñez, a lawyer and inspector of finance, who was the president of the Social Democratic Federation, one of the political groups that had fought the elections together as part of Suarez's coalition, the Center Democratic Union. Fernández Ordonez represented the center-left in Suárez's government. The other economic ministers were associated with the world of business and finance.

Suárez described his new government as center-left, but it was in fact far to the right of the original Italian government of centrosinistra and would be more accurately placed in the center-right segment of the European political spectrum. It contained no Socialists, and its Social Democrats were really men of the center rather than of the left. Several ministers had close personal ties to the powerful Spanish banks, and many were reformed servants of the Franco regime who would be considered either center-right or right in other European countries.

In the year since Suárez took over from Arias, the economic situation had grown far more difficult and was now worse than it had been at any time since the 1959 economic liberalization. Three and a half years of neglect and a policy of easy money had postponed adjustment to the new terms of trade and solution of Spain's domestic economic problems. The oil price hike had presented Spain a higher import bill at the same time as it indirectly reduced revenues from worker remittances, tourism, and investment. These problems had been compounded by inflation which led to an overvalued peseta with rising imports and falling exports.

By July 1977 the situation was critical. Spain was suffering from substantial unemployment, an unsustainable balance of payments deficit, and runaway inflation. According to official figures, unemployment stood at five to six percent of the active population, but the trade unions and many private economists placed their estimates considerably higher. In 1976, the deficit on current account had been $4.25 billion. During the first half of 1977 it was about $2.3 billion, and economists were predicting it would reach $5 billion by the end of 1977. In 1976 prices had risen 19 percent. During the first six months of 1977 the cost of living rose 13.2 percent and the pace was accelerating. During the month of July along prices increased another 3.7 percent (Instituto Nacional de Estadística, 1977 II). Experts warned of more than 30 percent inflation for 1977 unless urgent remedies were applied.

Of the many problems facing the Spanish economy, Fuentes Quintana was especially concerned about the balance of payments. The new economic team's first decision, a 19.6 percent devaluation of the peseta on July 12, 1977, aimed at reducing the deficit. Later in the month the government announced plans for further economic measures. It urged moderation in salary increases, suggesting a target of 17 percent for the year. In return for the sacrifices implied in accepting salary increases significantly smaller than the anticipated increase in the cost of living, it promised a thorough reform of Spain's archaic fiscal system to spread the burden of taxation more equitably. To facilitate collecting taxes, it promised to modify the law which had protected bank accounts behind a wall of secrecy since 1940. It also pledged to make more funds available for unemployment insurance and to give fiscal incentives for hiring new workers to relieve unemployment.

These proposals met with criticism from both the business community and the labor unions. Business leaders stressed the need for more incentives to invest and denounced the plan for ending bank secrecy. Labor spokesmen faulted the proposals for placing almost all of the burden on the workers. They complained that they were being asked to accept substantial losses of real wages in return for promises of future legislation that might never be implemented.

In August the government attempted to check the growth of the money supply and proposed emergency economic legislation including tax cuts for businesses that took on new employees, a tax on wealth, an income-tax surcharge, and luxury taxes. Despite the urgent tone of the government's declarations, this relatively mild package of emergency measures would not be finally approved for several months. Most of the proposals only took effect as part of the package of reforms included in the "Moncloa Pacts" in the fall.

The key to success of an anti-inflation program was the cooperation of the working class. Suárez met with union leaders in August and proposed the formation of mixed commissions to discuss economic plans, but this was far from sufficient to guarantee their collaboration. Recent European experience had demonstrated how difficult a social pact was to obtain, even for a left-wing government. The prospects for success by Suárez's center-right UCD government, which had received only about a third of the popular vote in June, seemed bleak.

By mid-September the government's lack of initiative had dissipated all the enthusiasm generated by the June elecions. It began to seem that the authority the government had derived from the first free elections in four decades would make no difference in economic policy. Spain appeared destined to drift into an ever deepening economic crisis characterized by inflation, unemployment, stagnation, and growing foreign deficits.

The implications of this economic situation, combined with serious political problems and violence in the streets, were ominous for Spain's still nascent democracy. On both the left and the right, voices of alarm were raised. The leader of the Communist-dominated Workers' Commissions, Marcelino Camacho, affirmed that "if a solution isn't found, we'll have a Pinochet." Basque industrialist Luis Olarra drew his analogy from Argentina: "If things continue like this, a Videla will come." Madrid was alive with talk of a government of national unity to take over from Suárez in this situation of general discontent and unrest.

THE MONCLOA PACT

On October 5, 1977, Suárez asked the leaders of all the main political parties to join him in the Moncloa Palace for a two-day meeting to draw up an "emergency plan" for solving the "grave difficulties" facing Spain. In his invitation, he said "the delicacy of the moment and the need to consolidate Spain's democracy have made it necessary to reach agreement between the political parties on how to solve some of the nation's basic political, economic and social problems." Reactions to the proposal varied, but no one refused the invitation to meet. On October 9, the various party leaders announced that they had reached a consensus on the broad outlines of an economic policy and of a program of political reform. By October 21, they had completed a 40-page text, which was signed on the 25th.

The economic part of the Moncloa Pact was essentially an austerity plan that offered social reforms and more parliamentary control over the economy in exchange for wage restraint. Workers were asked to accept a ceiling of 22 percent on wage increases in 1978. This would represent stagnation of real wages, but not their decline since monetary and fiscal policy would be designed to keep inflation at or below 22 percent. Government expenditures and outlays of the social security system would increase no more than 21.4 percent.

To guarantee that unions and private businesses would respect the 22 percent limit on wage increases, the pact stipulated that companies exceeding the limit by their own volition would be penalized by withdrawal of fiscal exemptions and of government credits. If unions imposed raises greater than those permitted, management would be permitted to reduce by five percent the size of the work force. Since Spanish labor laws – inherited from Franco – made it almost impossible to fire workers except in the case of a company about to go bankrupt, the provision about allowing businesses to dismiss five percent of their work force represented a real restraint on workers' wage demands.

In return for wage restraint, the government and the parties agreed to raise pensions 30 percent, increase unemployment benefits to the same level as the legal minimum wage, substitute progressive income taxes for indirect taxes, and undertake other fiscal reforms including new corporate taxes and a permanent tax on wealth. They pledged the creation of new classrooms for 700,000 more students in the public school system as part of a move toward completely gratuitous education. Programs of slum removal, control of urban land speculation, and construction of subsidized housing would be undertaken to help alleviate the housing shortage. Both government expenditures and the social security system (whose budget was larger than the combined budget of all the ministries) would be brought under closer parliamentary scrutiny and control. The pact also sketched out the basic principles of an agrarian reform program designed to convert renters into landowners and to put an end to sharecropping.

In addition to the economic reform plan, the Moncloa Pact contained a political agreement about short-term legislative measures "to adapt the law to the demands of the new democratic reality" of Spain. The measures involved covered a broad range of topics. During the following months, much of this legislation was passed or at least introduced in the Cortes.

The Moncloa agreements represent a milestone on the Spanish path to democracy. Without them the Spanish economic situation would probably have rapidly deteriorated. The resulting social tensions might well have blocked further progress toward democratization and even given rise to a return to authoritarian government, probably led by the right rather than by the still weak Spanish left.

The Moncloa agreements did not solve all the economic problems which had plagued Spain. What they did, as we shall see in more detail shortly, was to provide a temporary solution to the balance of payments problem and to bring inflation down to a level at which it could be tolerated. In this way, they provided Suárez with a one year breathing space in which economic conditions were good enough to permit, once again, concentrating on politics in order to write and approve a democratic, decentralized constitution for Spain.

If the Moncloa agreements were vital to the progress of democratization in Spain, it was also true that democratization made the agreements possible and made them work. In Fall 1977, both the government and the oppoisition realized that some form of social pact was essential if Spain's progress toward democracy was not to be cut short by economic difficulties and social tensions. Even more important, both the government and the opposition were sufficiently committed to democratization to make substantial concessions in order to achieve an understanding.

The concessions made by the government were less striking than those made by the opposition but, nonetheless, real. Fuentes Quintana had originally proposed fixing the wage ceiling at a level substantially lower than the expected 22 percent rate of inflation. There is some evidence that the Communist party went into the negotiations with the expectation that it would have to put up a fight to achieve an 18 percent wage ceiling and was astonished when Suarez offered the 22 percent figure. He did so to demonstrate his good faith and to win the support of Communists and Socialists for measures he considered vital to the survival not only of his government but of the entire project of democratization-from-above which it represented. In addition, the government promised measures of social and political reform to which it would have preferred not committing itself.

The difficulty of obtaining any sort of a social pact in other European countries highlights the extent of the concessions made by the Spanish working-class parties in signing the Moncloa agreements. It was especially difficult for them to tell their members and supporters, who had grown accustomed to a constantly improving standard of living under the Franco dictatorship, that they would have to renounce any real growth in their wages in a nascent democracy. Spanish workers had been led to believe that their economic lot would be improved by General Franco's demise, and it was politically difficult for their representatives to tell them they would have to renounce those dreams for the moment in order to consolidate the country's political freedom.

The willingness of the left-wing parties to accept the wage ceiling is a remarkable tribute to the maturity of the Spanish working class and to its sincere desire to contribute to the consolidation of democracy. It also reflects the special situation of the Spanish labor movement in fall 1977. Neither the Communists nor the Socialists had yet succeeded in achieving a powerful, well-organized national presence. The Communist Workers' Commissions and the Socialist General Workers' Union were still attempting to organize.

Workers were represented at the Moncloa negotiations exclusively by political parties, not by labor unions. The party leaders who went to the Moncloa to negotiate with Suárez were by temperament and position particularly sensitive to political issues and considerations. This made them more willing than union leaders might have been to make economic concessions in return for political gains. Furthermore, both the Socialists and the Communists were fully aware of the still precarious nature of their own position. The parties themselves had only been legalized a short time before, and the Communists especially could not ignore the fact that powerful elements in the army would like nothing better than an excuse to surpress them. This awareness of their own weakness contributed greatly to their willingness to reach an agreement (Menges, n.d,61-62).

The Spanish economy staged a remarkable turnaround in 1978. And this, despite the fact that Fuentes Quintana, the chief architect of Suárez's economic reforms, fell from power at the end of February 1978 and was replaced by a politician with little economic background, Fernando Abril Martorell. Between December 1977 and December 1978, consumer prices rose only 16.5 percent. The problem of inflation was still far from being resolved, but reducing the rate by ten percentage points during a year in which inflation rates remained high throughout Europe certainly represented a major accomplishment. Much remained to be done, but prices no longer appeared to be rising in an uncontrolled spiral. For all practical purposes Spain met the goal set in the Moncloa pacts of reducing inflation by the end of 1978 to 16 percent.

An even more dramatic change occurred in the balance of payments. Thanks to large tourist revenues, increasing foreign investments in Spain, falling imports and rising exports, and an improvement in the services account, Spain's balance of payments at the close of 1978 was favorable. During the year imports exceeded exports by $5.6 billion, but the balance on the current account was positive by $1.5 billion and the overall balance of payments showed a surplus of $4 billion. At the end of 1978, the country's reserves in gold and foreign currencies amounted to $10 billion, up from about $4 billion in June 1977 (Banco de Espana, 1979, 133; Banco de Bilbao, 1979, 146, 170, 173).

Excellent harvests, a booming tourist industry, and growing foreign demand for Spanish products accounted for a 2.8 percent increase in gross internal product during 1978, when the Moncloa Pact called for only a 1 percent increase. Thanks to exceptionally good agricultural conditions, growth in the primary sector of the economy was 7.5 percent. Industrial production increased by a modest 2.1 percent, and construction declined by 2.5 percent (Banco de Espana, 1979,38).

There were, however, negative factors as well. Spanish businessmen had not yet digested fully the double set of changes they simultaneously faced. They not only had to adjust to a much less favorable economic climate created by rising oil prices, they also faced a dramatic change in the conditions of the labor market as a result of the country's political transformation. The official _sindicatos_ had ceased to control labor years before Franco's death, and businessmen had learned to deal with the Communist-dominated Workers' Commissions, but within a political framework that favored employers and limited the options of the illegal labor unions. Suddenly the labor unions enjoyed full legal status, the right to strike, and political support from parties that held almost 40 percent of the seats in the Cortes.

Even without these dramatic changes in the environment of the labor market, investments would have been low because of the uncertain world economic outlook and because high salaries and low productivity had reduced profit margins. The new element of uncertainty introduced by the changes in the labor market led to a 6 percent drop in investment in 1978. This was the fourth consecutive year of declining investments. In real terms, 1978's level stood 15 percent below the level achieved in 1974 (Banco de España, 1979, 384).

The export sector was the only part of the economy to experience much growth after the Moncloa Pact. Internal demand increased by only 0.3 percent; inventories grew; and in most sectors, production declined. Under these circumstances, unemployment could only continue to increase. In the fourth quarter of 1978, there were 250,000 more people unemployed than in the fourth quarter of 1977. The 1.1 million unemployed represented 8 percent of the active population, up from 6.1 percent at the end of 1977 (Banco de España, 1979, 87).

In summary, thanks in part to fortuitous circumstances such as extraordinary good weather conditions, exceptionally high tourist receipts, and the relatively favorable evolution of energy prices, the Moncloa pacts permitted Spain to reduce the rate of inflation, improve its balance of payments, and increase its gross national product in 1978. The problem of unemployment, however, grew worse during the year.

AFTER THE MONCLOA PACTS

The Moncloa pacts were a one year agreement, made under extraordinary political and economic circumstances. By Fall 1978 both the political and economic circumstances had changed. On the political front, the text of the new democratic constitution had been approved by the lower house and was well on its way to final approval. With the drafting of the constitution behind them, neither the opposition parties nor the government felt the need to preserve the somewhat artificial environment of "concensus" which had enabled them to write a constitution acceptable to most Spaniards. In addition, a year's experience had greatly increased the self-confidence of the parties of the left which no longer saw themselves threatened with imminent repression by an army coup.

On the economic front, there was no longer the sense of impending crises which had forced the parties to work together. Everyone agreed that unemployment was a very serious problem, but there was no consensus on its solution. Business leaders and government officials insisted that inflation must be further reduced to stimulate investment and create new jobs. The labor unions demanded large public investments and programs designed to increase employment.

A new agreement to replace the Moncloa Pact would have to be negotiated by the labor unions and business organizations rather than by the political parties that had worked out the Moncloa Pact. The Communist dominated Worker's Commissions at first enthusiastically supported the idea of a new pact and talked of impending catastrophe if negotiations failed. But the Socialist UGT received the idea coldly and said that there would be no need for a policy of consensus after the constitutional referendum in December 1978.

The government showed little energy or enthusiasm in pushing forward with the negotiations. Abril Martorell held discussions with the unions in October but did not present concrete proposals until mid-November. By that time the Workers' Commissions had adopted a considerably tougher position, demanding 16 percent wage increases for the coming year, whereas the government was talking about a 12.5 percent ceiling on wages in order to reduce inflation to 10 percent. For its part the powerful Spanish Confederation of Business Organization called for a 10 percent ceiling on wage increases.

The government offered a plan calling for the creation of 150,000 new jobs, but the Workers' Commissions pointed out that 200,000 young persons would be entering the labor force and called for at least 300,000 new jobs. The Communists also demanded that the political parties participate in the negotiating of any agreement between unions and business organizations so as to foster the structural reforms promised in the Moncloa Pact, but not yet carried out. They especially insisted on democratization of publicly owned industries and worker participation in the running of the social security system.

As the constitutional referendum scheduled for December 1978 approached, no one appeared anxious to negotiate a sweeping new economic and social pact, at least until new elections were held, or until the formation of a new government with a solid majority in the Cortes clarified the political situation. As had happened repeatedly since Franco's death, political concerns pushed economic ones into the background. Even once the constitution had been approved by the public, the prospect of national and local elections in March and April 1979 kept attention focused on political issues.

Faced with the impossibility of achieving a new negotiated social pact, the government issued by decree in December 1978 a new set of wage and price guidelines for 1979. This economic program called for reducing inflation to 12-12.5 percent for the entire year and reaching a 10 percent rate by December 1979. Average salary increases would be kept under 12 percent and the growth of the money supply was targeted for 17.5 percent. Despite predicting that from 1979 to 1982 Spain would have to create 1 million new jobs outside of agriculture to compensate for a growing active population and the gradual shift of workers out of agriculture, the plan called for the creation of only 100,000-150,000 jobs in 1979 (El País, 1978).

The results of the national elections held in March 1979 varied little from those of the June 1977 ones. The UCD increased slightly its share of the popular vote and of the seats in the Cortes, but again failed to win an absolute majority of seats. The PSOE suffered a slight decline in its share of the popular vote.

The March 1979 elections were a bitter disappointment to Spanish Socialists who had hoped to improve their positions significantly and even to become the majority party. The radical sector of the party blamed this "defeat" on the excessively moderate stance adopted by the party's secretary, Felipe González. At the Party Congress in spring, González was defeated on a crucial ideological vote. This surprise defeat led to a bitter struggle between radicals and moderates for control of the party. Not until the special congress in fall 1979, where he was re-elected secretary, did González firmly re-establish his control over the PSOE.

The extent of González's victory only became fully apparent toward the end of 1979 when the Socialist labor union, the UGT, adopted a policy of cooperation with management and even chose to sign a sort of "private social pact" with the CEOE, the country's largest employers' organization. The UGT and the CEOE agreed on a general framework for new labor contracts in 1980 which called for wage increases of 13-16 percent, subject to revision in July 1980. In addition to this relatively moderate wage settlement, the UGT agreed to try to negotiate two year contracts rather than the one year ones which have been the norm in Spain. It also promised to moderate its demands when dealing with companies which were especially hard-hit by the economic crisis.

The UGT's decision to adopt this moderate and conciliatory attitude reflected the Socialist's generally favorable evaluation of Spain's political evolution since Franco's death. Spanish Socialists have recognized that they must collaborate with the government and with the business community to prevent a return to uncontrolled inflation accompanied by declining investment and rapidly rising unemployment which would be devastating to the working class. They have also concluded that Spain's new democratic institutions are worth safeguarding and that their still vulnerable character makes it essential to avoid overloading the system with unnecessary economic conflicts. The willingness of the leaders of Spain's second largest labor union to enter into a social pact with management is thus directly linked to the process of democratization.

The Spanish working class has responded favorably to the moderate position of the UGT's leadership. In the union elections held in Fall 1980, the UGT won almost as many contests as did the Communist-dominated Worker's Commissions. Two years earlier, in 1978, the Workers' Commissions had outdistanced the UGT by 12 percent. Now the two organizations each account for slightly less than one third of the organized labor-movement, with the Workers' Commission outdistancing the UGT by little more than one percent.

The significance of the 1979 elections was not limited to their effects on the Socialist party. They marked the end of Spain's prolonged transition from dictatorship to democracy. The chief problem was no longer to establish a democratic regime but to make it work. Consequently attention shifted away from the political problems of building institutions to the economic and social problems which had largely been postponed during the years after Franco's death. This meant that the major political groups and parties were now more free to pursue their own policies.

The government's new short and medium-term economic plan, announced on August 14, 1979, reflected the commitment of the UCD as a center-right party to a market economy (Cinco Días, 1979). It renewed the government's promise to reform Spain's rigid labor laws and announced its intention of gradually phasing out most price controls. It promised businesses aid in making structural changes and new tax incentives to invest. Workers were offered expanded programs to ease the problems of unemployment and limited measures to stimulate the demand for labor. As part of this program of liberalization, the government announced in October 1979 that it would not impose a wage ceiling on the private sector for 1980 (El Pias, 1979).

Spain's economic performance in 1979 was mixed. The government's plan for reducing inflation significantly from its 1978 level of 16.5 percent failed. Prices rose 15.7 percent rather than the 10 percent the government had projected. On the other hand, Spain's inflation rate did not climb in a year in which repeated OPEC price hikes triggered sharp increases in many European countries. This minor success in inflation-fighting was purchased, however, at the cost of growing unemployment. The total number of unemployed rose to 1.3 million which represented an unemployment rate of 10.1 percent.

During 1980 the economic situation deteriorated further. High energy prices, the slow growth of world trade, domestic structural problems, and the government's inability to formulate and execute a broadly accepted plan of action led to continued stagflation with high unemployment. Despite a strong surge in agricultural production, real economic growth was less than 1 percent. During the third quarter, consumer prices increased an annual rate of 14.8 percent (International Financial Statistics, 1981, 45). In December 1980, consumer prices were 15.5 percent higher than they had been a year ago. During the year, hourly wages and benefits rose even faster than prices for those who were able to find work. In December, average earnings per hour worked were 20.7 percent higher than one year earlier. Many, however, could find no work. The number of registered unemployed at year's end stood at 1.4 million, 25.2 percent higher than the year before. Despite a decline in the size of the labor force, over 11 percent were unemployed (Banco de Bilbao, 1981).

These severe economic problems greatly increased the strain on Spain's still-recent democratic institutions. Together with the on-going tension between the central government and the periphery (especially the Basques), the political in-fighting within Suárez's UCD, and the discontent of important segments of the army, they led to two government reorganizations in 1980 and to Suárez's fall from power in early 1981.

At this time (February 1981), it is far from clear what the future holds for Spanish democracy. In my opinion, many observers have been too quick to write off the Spanish experiment in democratization. Undeniably, however, Spain does face severe problems, which could prove fatal to its new institutions.

If democracy fails in Spain, its demise will not be due exclusively to inflation and its associated economic problems. Hotly-debated political issues affecting the distribution of power between the central government and the regions and the relations between Church and State will also play a key role. Nonetheless, the relentless pressure of inflation has hindered the consolidation of democratic institutions in Spain and makes their future today much more somber than it would be in a more favorable economic climate.

NOTES

(1) The fullest treatment thus far of democratization in Spain is my own The Political Transformation of Spain after Franco, New York, 1979. Raymond Carr and Juan Pablo Fusi's Spain: Dictatorship to Democracy, (2nd ed, New York 1981) deals primarily with the Franco period although it contains a useful epilogue on post-Franco events. Juan Linz offers an illuminating comparative view "Spain and Portugal: Critical Choices" in David S. Landes (ed) Western Europe: The Trials of Partnership, Lexington Mass, 1977, pp. 237-296. See also his "Il sistema politico spagnolo" in Revista Italiana di Scienza Politica, 7, Dec. 78, 363-414. Other useful treatments may be found in Michael Roskin, "Spain tries Democracy Again," Political Science Quarterly 93, 4(winter 1978/79), p. 629-646; Jonathan Story, "Spanish Political Parties: Before and After the Election," Government and Opposition 12, 4 (1977) p. 474-495; Constantine Christopher Menges, Spain: The Struggle for Democracy Today, Beverly Hills, 1978; R. Alan, "All the Spains: A Survey" Economist, Nov. 3, 1979, p. 1-38; B. Pollack, "Spain: from Corporate State to Parliamentary Democracy," Parliamentary Affairs, 31, (winter 1978) p. 52-66; J.M. Maravall, "Political Cleavages in Spain and the 1979 General Election," Government and Opposition 14, (summer 1979) p. 229-317; Stanley G. Payne, "Terrorism and Democratic Stability in Spain," Current History 77, (Nov. 1979) p. 67 ss. A brief but interesting piece, "On Spain's Economy" by Charles McMillian appeared on the OP/ED page of the New York Times, Feb. 4, 1981.

REFERENCES

Banco de Bilbao, Renta nacional de España, serie homogenea, 1955-75, (Bilbao, n.d.)

______, Informe economico, 1978, Bilbao, 1979.

______, Situacion, 1981, n.2, February 1981.

Banco de Espana, Informe Anual, 1978.

Bustelo, Francisco and Gabriel Tortella Casares, "Monetary Inflation in Spain, 1800-1970," in Journal of European Economic History, 7 Spring 1976.

Cinco Dias, (Madrid), August 16, 17, 18, 1979.

El Pais, December 27, 1978.

______, October 27, 1979

Fundacion Foessa, Estudio sociologicos sobre le situacion social de Espana, 1975, Madrid, 1976.

______, Anuario estadistico de Espana, 1977.

Instituto Nacional de Estadistica (Spain), reported in ABC (Madrid), October 28, 1977.

International Financial Statistics, January, 1974.
______, January, 1976.
______, January, 1977.
______, January, 1979.
______, November, 1979.
______, January, 1981.
Menges, Spain: The Struggle for Democracy Today, (Beverly Hills, 1978).
Organization for Economic Cooperation and Development (OECD), Economic Survey: Spain 1976, (Paris 1976.)

Index

About the Contributors

JOHN F. COVERDALE is professor of political science at Northwestern University.

CATHARINE B. HILL is an international economist at the Congressional Budget Office.

JAMES R. KURTH is professor of political science at Swarthmore College.

LEON LINDBERG is professor of political science at the University of Wisconsin, Madison. His most recent book is The Energy Syndrome.

RICHARD MEDLEY, formerly an economist for the House Banking and Currency Committee, is currently with the Senate Democratic Policy Committee.

MICHAEL MUMPER is currently studying for his doctorate in political science at the University of Maryland.

JOHN D. POTHIER is assistant professor of political science at Yale University.

BARBARA STALLINGS is assistant professor of political science at the University of Wisconsin, Madison. She is currently writing a study of the International Monetary Fund.

SUSAN STRANGE is the chairperson of the Department of Political Science at the London School of Economics. She has published extensively on political economy issues.

ERIC M. USLANER is professor of political science at the University of Maryland.